T0203364

Digital Audiovisual Archives

Digital Audiovisual Archives

Edited by
Peter Stockinger

First published 2012 in Great Britain and the United States by ISTE Ltd and John Wiley & Sons, Inc.

ISTE Ltd
27-37 St George's Road
London SW19 4EU
UK

www.iste.co.uk

John Wiley & Sons, Inc.
111 River Street
Hoboken, NJ 07030
USA

www.wiley.com

© ISTE Ltd 2012

Library of Congress Cataloging-in-Publication Data

Digital audiovisual archives / edited by Peter Stockinger.
  pages cm
Includes bibliographical references and index.
  ISBN 978-1-84821-338-8
  1. Audio-visual archives--Case studies. I. Stockinger, Peter.
  CD973.2.D54 2011
  025.3'47--dc23
                                                                        2011042576

British Library Cataloguing-in-Publication Data
A CIP record for this book is available from the British Library
ISBN: 978-1-84821-338-8

Printed and bound in Great Britain by CPI Group (UK) Ltd., Croydon, Surrey CR0 4YY

Table of Contents

Introduction   xi

PART 1: ANALYSIS, REWRITINGS AND REPUBLICATIONS   1

**Chapter 1. Analyzing an Audiovisual Corpus
of *A Thousand and One Nights***   3
Muriel CHEMOUNY

   1.1. Introduction   3
   1.2. Creating a thematic educational dossier based
   on *A Thousand and One Nights*.   6
      1.2.1. Choosing an audiovisual corpus   6
      1.2.2. Text analysis   7
   1.3. Perspectives: ASWs and new forms of digital writing   18

Chapter 2. Analyzing a Corpus of Traditional Bread Making   21
Elisabeth DE PABLO

   2.1. Introduction   21
   2.2. Creating educational dossiers to raise public awareness   23
      2.2.1. Choosing a corpus   23
      2.2.2. Defining aims of the analysis   24
      2.2.3. Analysis   25
   2.3. Creating a communication dossier
   for improving cultural events   36
      2.3.1. Choosing a corpus   36
      2.3.2. Defining aims of the analysis   36
      2.3.3. Analysis   37

Chapter 3. Republishing Audiovisual Resources   41
Peter STOCKINGER and Elisabeth DE PABLO

3.1. Introduction   41
3.2. Breakdown of the (re)publication process
according to genre   44
3.3. "Rerecording" audiovisual texts   47
3.4. Interactive video books   50
3.5. Thematic folders   53
3.6. Educational folders   56
3.7. Narrative path   59

**PART 2: AUDIOVISUAL ARCHIVES, KNOWLEDGE
MANAGEMENT AND CULTURAL HERITAGE**   61

**Chapter 4. An Archive on the Intangible Cultural Heritage
of Andean Populations in Peru and Bolivia**   63
Valérie LEGRAND-GALARZA

4.1. Introduction   63
4.2. Scientific methodology and ethical
and participative approaches   65
    4.2.1. Scientific methodology for collecting
    and processing intangible cultural heritages   66
    4.2.2. An ethical and participative approach: recognizing
    and involving people and communities in collecting
    their heritage   70
4.3. The Andean intangible cultural heritage portal   75
    4.3.1. Why have a portal for Andean cultural heritage?   75
    4.3.2. Structure and themes of the portal   78
    4.3.3. The thematic description library   83
4.4. Interests and perspectives of the project   89
    4.4.1. Interests and objectives of the project   89
    4.4.2. Uses and perspectives   98
4.5. Conclusion   102

**Chapter 5. An Audiovisual Azerbaijani Cultural Heritage
Portal for Educational and Academic Use**   105
Aygun EYYUBOVA

5.1. Introduction   105
    5.1.1. Background to the creation
    of the AACH portal: context   106
    5.1.2. Research into teaching methodologies
    for Azerbaijani culture and language   106

5.2. Disseminating and transmitting cultural
heritages via the Internet   107
   5.2.1. Digitalizing and disseminating cultural
   archives via the Internet   107
   5.2.2. Issues in semiotic research for disseminating
   cultural heritages   109
5.3. Aims of creating an Azerbaijani cultural heritage
portal (AACHP) in the ASA-SHS project   110
5.4. Principal aspects of cultural heritage approach
in developing an Azerbaijani cultural heritage portal (AACH)   111
   5.4.1. Ethnical aspect of cultural heritage approach   112
   5.4.2. Communicative and informative aspects
   of cultural heritage approach   112
   5.4.3. Multi-source aspect of cultural heritage approach   114
   5.4.4. Legal aspects of cultural heritage approach   114
   5.4.5. Collaborative aspect of cultural heritage approach   115
   5.4.6. Valorizing aspect of cultural heritage approach   116
   5.4.7. Capitalizing on experience in cultural heritage
   approach: a development Log Book for the AACH
   and AICH portals   116
5.5. Analyzing audiovisual corpora for AACH in ASA   118
   5.5.1. Identifying areas of knowledge for the AACHP   118
   5.5.2. Library of thematic analysis schemes in AACH   122
   5.5.3. The AACH thesaurus   125
   5.5.4. Pragmatic analysis of semiotic descriptions
   of the AACH audiovisual corpus   127
5.6. Applications for the AACH portal
and the ASW environment   135
5.7. Conclusion: advantages, benefits and perspectives   137

PART 3: SOCIAL NETWORKS, WEB 2.0
AND MOBILE COMMUNICATION   139

Chapter 6. Academic Communication
via Facebook and Twitter   141
Jirasri DESLIS

6.1. Introduction   141
6.2. The ArkWork portal   142
   6.2.1. Nature of the resource   142
   6.2.2. Example of video analysis and adaptation   143
6.3. Facebook for sharing various types of information   145

6.3.1. Valorizing the ArkWork resources: sequences
and images taken from the video source 146
6.3.2. Type of information to be communicated
via profile "Walls" 150
6.3.3. From profile pages to professional (Fan) pages:
personalizing and adding other applications 152
6.4. Twitter as a means of publicizing short information 157
6.4.1. Twitter and sequential communication 158
6.4.2. Twitter and video extracts spread through
ArkWork video sharing platforms 164
6.4.3. Twitter and paper.li, an automatic publication platform 165
6.4.4. Communication between Twitter and Facebook 167

Chapter 7. Uses for Digital Content Sharing Platforms 169
Jirasri DESLIS

7.1. Introduction 169
7.2. Flickr 170
7.3. Twitpic 172
7.4. ArkWork on YouTube 173
7.4.1. Multilingual accessibility 173
7.4.2. Geographically contextualizing video content 176
7.4.3. An interactive video with annotation 177
7.4.4. YouTube and Apture videos 179
7.5. ArkWork on Dailymotion 181
7.6. ArkWork on Vimeo 183
7.7. Nomadic approaches: mobile communication
for sharing academic content 184

**Chapter 8. Uses for Content Aggregators
and Community Networks** 189
Jirasri DESLIS

8.1. Netvibes, a content aggregator 189
8.2. Pearltrees, a content curation platform 196
8.3. Sharing information on community portals:
the Louvre Community portal (communauté.louvre.fr) 199
8.3.1. Building a profile: using our resources
in cooperation with the Museum's collection 199
8.3.2. Marking our resources in relation to Museum events 201
8.3.3. Creating discussion groups 203
8.4. Conclusion 207

Chapter 9. Tracing Video Usage: The Potential of VDI 209
Francis LEMAITRE and Valérie LEGRAND-GALARZA

9.1. Introduction 209
9.2. Presentation of the scenario 211
9.2.1. Principles and objectives 211
9.2.2. Roles 213
9.2.3. Users 214
9.2.4. The technical environment 215
9.3. Walkthrough 227
9.3.1. User registration and authentication 228
9.3.2. Creating and publishing videos 229
9.3.3. Subscribing to videos 231
9.3.4. Removing videos 232
9.3.5. Downloading videos 234
9.3.6. Creating and publishing analyses 235
9.3.7. Subscribing to analyses 237
9.3.8. Removing analyses 238
9.3.9. Creating a channel 239
9.3.10. Posting an analysis onto a channel 240
9.3.11. Subscribing to posted analyses 242
9.3.12. Removing posts 243
9.3.13. Viewing analyses posted on channels 243
9.4. Conclusion 244

Glossary of Specialized Terms 247
Peter STOCKINGER

Glossary of the Acronyms and Names 271
Peter STOCKINGER

Bibliography 291

List of Authors 297

Index 299

Introduction

We discussed the issue of *analyzing* digital audiovisual corpora in [STO 11a] using a variety of concrete examples. We also examined in this book a working environment which enables us to analyze these corpora that are specifically adapted to their users' professional or personal needs.

Analyzing audiovisual corpora involves identifying the stages in work processes which define every digitizing project of knowledge heritages (i.e. scientific, cultural, etc.). This follows the (audiovisual) data collection stage which documents a "research terrain" and precedes the publication and dissemination of (analyzed, i.e. described, classified, annotated, interpreted etc.) data. Along with the technical processing ("cleaning", improving visual creation, etc.) and auctorial (i.e. mounting) stages of data collection and creation of field corpora, this is an unavoidable movement from transforming the status of virtually relevant digital data into a *potential resource* that is a potential *"advantage"* for the audience and its expectations, needs, and curiosities for various contexts of usage. In [STO 11a], various approaches are discussed which might define a concrete analysis and approaches such as:

– *stricto sensu* textual analysis, which consists of locating (identifying) only those passages in an audiovisual text that are genuinely relevant for an analysis project, presuming that for a given

Introduction written by Peter STOCKINGER.

analysis not the whole audiovisual text (no matter if it is a documentary or a simply "raw" recording of a cultural or scientific manifestation) is necessarily relevant. Once the passage(s) is/are identified, the *analyst* (a role given to an individual or group undertaking an analysis project) segments the audiovisual text, that is (virtually) extracts the identified passage(s), provides them with a provisory title, and records the temporal values corresponding to their beginning and end of the audiovisual text's linear progression. The analyst can always return to this analysis to modify, for example, the beginning and end of the segmented passage, to suppress segmented passages, or redefine identified passages, and so on;

– *meta-description* of which the object is not so much the audiovisual text or the analyzed passage of an audiovisual text. The aim of meta-description, rather, is to explain the aim of the analysis itself: its authors, aims, the *area of expertise* (i.e. the area of knowledge concerned) or even the *genre* that it represents (basic versus detailed analysis, an excerpt versus the whole audiovisual text, overall content versus visual and acoustic patterns, analysis as linguistic adaptation of the audiovisual text or part of it). Meta-description also defines its authors rights as well as the rights for its use and exploitation by an interested public (in a new analysis project, for example);

– *paratextual* description initially aims to specify the formal identity of the audiovisual text and/or each identified and virtually extracted excerpt. This involves identifying indicative information related to the author(s), directors, producers, and so on, of the audiovisual text (or an excerpt of it). This description enables us to identify the genre(s) which the audiovisual text represents and also identify the important times and places in the "life" of the text in question, for example the time and date of production, publication and dissemination, latest update, and so on. Another important point of the paratextual description is that of the explicit rights that govern ownership of the audiovisual text (or a particular passage) and of its various uses by the interested public;

– *audiovisual* description specifically focuses on analyzing the audiovisual patterns which are composed of the text (or a specific passage which was identified and virtually extracted). The focus of audiovisual description, for example, ranges from recording of different frames in a filmed event to the sounds accompanying it or synchronization between "acoustic" and "visual" patterns;

– *thematic* description involves explaining the content conveyed by an audiovisual text which is being analyzed (or an excerpt of this) including thematized events or situations (i.e. the domain to which the text refers), discursive thematization strategies (i.e. the perspective in which an event or situation is being examined, the progressive development of a theme in the text etc.);

– *pragmatic* description – in the wider sense, has three objectives: 1) highlighting the potential interest, the potential value of a text (or a specific passage) for an audience and a context of use, 2) enriching the text (or excerpt of it) (via commentaries, bibliographies (including Web) suggestions etc.) in order to adapt the text to the needs and interests of a targeted audience and the specific constraints of a specified context of use, 3) producing, if necessary, an appropriate linguistic version of the audiovisual text (or an excerpt of it) for an audience that cannot understand, or fully understand, the text's language of production (in general, this involves text translation (not necessarily a literal or "faithful" translation) or producing a *linguistic version* of the text which is better adapted to the sociolinguistic register of the audience's language. Note that the pragmatic description ends where technical and authorial processing of an audiovisual text or corpus begins: pragmatic description, specifically analysis in general, does not focus on the audiovisual text's "materiality". Modifying the audiovisual text's "materiality" involves processing audiovisual corpora from a purely technical perspective ("trimming" collected audiovisual data, cleaning files, improving acoustic or visual quality etc.) or from an authorial perspective (displaying audiovisual data according to a specific scenario, with additional music and voice overs (production technique where voice is not part of the narrative), post synchronization of visual and sound patterns etc.) .

To enable everyone to carry out "their" analysis projects with this variety and richness of approaches, a small group of researchers and engineers working at ESCoM (*Equipe Sémiotique Cognitive et Nouveaux Médias* [Cognitive Semiotics and New Medias Lab]) at

FMSH (Fondation Maison des Sciences de l'Homme)[1] in Paris have developed a sophisticated digital work environment called the *ASW Studio* in reference to the ASW-HSS (*Audiovisual Semiotics Workshop for analyzing corpora in Humanities and Social Sciences*)[2]. The ASW Studio is composed of several specialized workshops: the *Segmentation Workshop* (virtual) for audiovisual data, the *Description Workshop*, the *Publishing Workshop*, and the *Modeling Workshop* for the metalinguistic resources necessary for carrying out the analysis/description of the audiovisual data. The analysis of audiovisual corpora is carried out in the segmentation and description workshops presented in further detail in [STO 11a].

This book will develop the analysis of audiovisual corpora in further detail in terms of the *analysis projects*. Like any *project*, an analysis project of audiovisual corpora follows precise objectives, stages, and so on, (e.g. defining the project, analyzing the needs and project related audiovisual information that already exists, carrying out the project etc.) and is led by a person or team working in a given framework (social, community, institutional etc.).

We will examine the three types of analysis for audiovisual corpora which, in one way or another, explore new aspects and perspectives of production, dissemination, sharing, and enriching knowledge in an entirely digital context.

The first type of work relies on the creative reuse of audiovisual corpora which have often (but not necessarily always) been already analyzed and published (on a Web portal for example) to submit them to a new cycle of analysis and publication with a view to create new products or services from it (see [STO 99]) for specific audiences or fixed usage. This is carried out in what is presently known as

---

1 "House of the Sciences of Man", (http://www.msh-paris.fr/en/foundation/missions).
2 ASW-HSS (*Audiovisual Semiotics Workshop for analyzing corpora in Humanities and Social Sciences*) is a research project by ESCoM/FMSH financed by the ANR (Agence Nationale de la Recherche [National Research Agency]) in France. Its reference number is: *ANR-08-BLAN-0102-01*. ASW-HSS began in January 2009 and will officially end in December 2011. For further details, visit the official Website of the ASW-HSS project: http://www.ASW-HSS.fr/

repurposing or even *document reengineering*. Chapter 1 presents an analysis project focusing on a corpus which has already been published online based on *A Thousand and One Nights*[3]. Chapter 2 is dedicated to analyzing and re-analyzing corpora which have been partially published online focusing on the traditional production of bread in France and Portugal[4]. Chapter 3 examines different types of publications/republications which have proven particularly useful for experiments carried over a number of years at ESCoM in its Research and Development "Archives Audiovisuelles de Recherche" (Audiovisual Research Archives) program[5] (see [STO 11a] for further details), with support/help from a series of European and French research and development projects[6].

The second type of research focuses on using the *ASW Studio* for creation of digital audiovisual and specialized geographically thematized corpora, as well as for analyzing and publishing (or republishing) data composing these archives. Chapter 4 describes an area of experimentation based on constructing and using Andean Quechuaphone communities. This area of experimentation is part of the European research and development program *Convergence*[7]

---

3 The audiovisual corpora are sourced from the AAR program ("Archives Audiovisuelles de la Recherche") [Audiovisual Research Archives] from the ESCoM Research and Development program, presented in further detail in [STO 11a]; see also the program's official Website: http://www.archivesaudiovisuelles.fr/EN/

4 Parts of this corpus are also published on the AAR portal.

5 The official site can be found at: http://www.archivesaudiovisuelles.fr/EN/

6 This consists primarily of three projects; SAPHIR, LOGOS and DIVAS. SAPHIR ("Système d'Assistance à la Publication Hypermédia" [Assistance System for Hypermedia Publication]) is a French research project financed by the French ANR (Agence Nationale de la Recherche [National Research Agency]) and coordinated by the INA Recherche which began in 2006 and finished at the end of 2010. LOGOS is an acronym for *"Knowledge on demand for ubiquitous learning"*, a European research and development project financed in the 6th PCRD which began in January 2006 and finished in February 2009. DIVAS is an acronym for *"Direct Video & Audio Content Search Engine"* which is a European research and development project, which was also financed in the 6th PCRD beginning in January 2007 and ending in February 2009. For further details, see the glossary at the end of this book.

7 *Convergence* is a European research and development project which will run from June 2010 to February 2013. It is coordinated by the CNIT (Consorzio Interuniversitario per le Telecomunicazioni [Interuniversity Consortium for Telecommunication]) in Rome and financed by the 7th PCRD, No. FP7-257123). The aim of the *Convergence*

developing, among other things, technologies which enable us to trace all uses of digital data (such as a video) over the Internet. Chapter 5 describes an area of research in the ASW-HSS project based on creating an archive dedicated to cultural heritages (in this case, that of Azerbaijan).

The third type of research focuses on analyzing and publishing projects for audiovisual corpora using new possibilities presented by social networks, Web 2.0 or even mobile communications to better circulate, share and enrich previously analyzed and published audiovisual extracts. Chapter 6 examines case studies for publication and sharing of scientific information via *Facebook* and *Twitter*. Chapter 7 examines the importance of using dissemination platforms for digital data such as *YouTube, DailyMotion*, or *Vimeo*. Chapter 8 demonstrates how to use, in an analysis/publication project, "aggregators of Web 2.0 content" such as *Netvibes* or *scoop.it* or even research communities such as Louvre.fr. Finally, Chapter 9 explores the importance of "usage tracing" technology for digital data developed in the *Convergence* project by developing in a highly detailed and technical way, the area of experimentation examined in Chapter 4, including the diffusion of sensitive audiovisual content which documents the intangible heritage of Quechuaphone communities in Peru and Bolivia.

To conclude this examination, it should be emphasized that this book is the product of collective and interdisciplinary work converging "fundamental" and applied research, informatics, and human social sciences (specifically those of semiotics and linguistics). This has been led over a period of 10 years by a small team of researchers and

---

project is to enrich the Internet with a new *publication-subscription* service model focused around *content* and based on a shared container for each type of digital data, including people and real world objects (RWOs). This shared container, called a *Versatile Digital Item* (VDI) is a structured set of digital data and metainformation, identified in isolation (i.e. such as the URL on a Web page) and which includes the concept of a *Digital Item* defined by MPEG-21. The significance of ESCoM and the ANR program in this project relates to the fact that all uses of a video online can be traced via VDI technology. This opens up the possibility of circulating digital content and appropriating those that respect the rights of authors and owners. The official *Convergence* site can be found at: http://www.ict-convergence.eu/

engineers who have also written this book and [STO 11a]. I would like to formally acknowledge all of them and convey my regards to them.

Throughout the past 10 years of research and development, our team has benefited from the support of a number of friends and colleagues from France and elsewhere. In particular, we thank the following people: Patrick Courounet, Steffen Lalande, Abdelkrim Beloued, Bruno Bachimont (INA Recherche); Jocelyne and Marc Nanard (CNRS-Lirmm); Marie-Laure Mugnier, Michel Chein, Alain Gutierrez (CNRS-Lirmm); David Genest (University of Angers-Leria); Danail Dochev, Radoslav Pavlov (Académie des Sciences de Bulgarie); Stavros Christodoulakis, Nektarios Moumoutzis (Université technologique de la Canée);

Finally, we profusely thank Muriel Chemouny (FMSH-ESCoM) for having reviewed the contributions to this book and Elisabeth de Pablo (FMSH-ESCoM) for creating the manuscript.

PART 1

Analysis, Rewritings and Republications

Chapter 1

Analyzing an Audiovisual Corpus of *A Thousand and One Nights*

1.1. Introduction

The ALIA[1] Workshop (LHE - Literary Workshop of Here and Elsewhere) is one of the ASW-HSS projects, which include the Culture Crossroads Archives (CCA)[2] for cultural studies and the ADA[3] (ArkWork) for archeology. The aim of the ALIA (LHE) dossier is to communicate and improve the online literary heritage for various Internet audiences such as researchers, students, media professionals and so on.

The aim of the ALIA is to create an audiovisual corpus of French and world literature, analyze it using the ASW Studio and then publish it on a portal. The analyzed and published corpus on the ALIA (LHE) portal[4] (see Figure 1.1) can be accessed via several sections such as knowledge topics, thesauruses, collections of texts and so on.

Chapter written by Muriel CHEMOUNY.
1 Acronym of "Atelier Littéraire d'Ici et d'Ailleurs".
2 The CCA portal: http://semioweb.msh-paris.fr/corpus/ARC/FR/.
3 The ADA (Atelier des Arkéonautes, or ArkWork) portal: http://semioweb.msh-paris.fr/corpus/ADA/FR.
4 The ALIA portal: http://semioweb.msh-paris.fr/corpus/ALIA/FR/.

Figure 1.1. *First interface of the LHE portal*

The audiovisual LHE corpus is primarily composed of audiovisual texts from human and social science resources from the *Archives Audiovisuelles de la Recherche* [Audiovisual Research Archives - ARA] among others[5] following collaboration with researcher-academics (Jean-Yves Masson, professor of compared literature at University Paris IV Sorbonne; Jean Baumgarten, director of research at CNRS and specialist in Jewish cultural history; Frank Greiner, specialist in transmitting aesthetic and literary models at the University of Lille III), public figures (Jean Lacouture, journalist, reporter and author) or partner

---

5 For further details on the research and development dossier which was started by ESCoM in 2001, refer the foreword of this book. Further information can also be found on the AAR portal: http://www.archivesaudiovisuelles.fr/FR/about4.asp.

organizations[6], publishing houses[7] including interviews with authors, or video examples of literary expressions.

Another partnership, based on a rewarding collaboration was "A la rencontre d'écrivains". This association is directed by Francis Cransac, who had organized his first literary festival in 1994. Since then, this festival has been based on different themes for amateurs, academics, and professionals. The festival's content has also been recorded and published online on the ARA portal since 2006[8].

This highlights the importance of an active collaboration, not only with the LHE dossier management committee, responsible for verifying each stage of experimentation in the ASW-HSS project, but also with potential external users of publications from audiovisual corpus analysis, that is the management committee including researcher-academic, Jean-Yves Masson, responsible for verifying each stage of experimentation in the project, and eminent personalities from the literary establishment.

This framework was beneficial not only for systematically analyzing a large part of the LHE audiovisual corpus (accessible via the online portal) but also for leading a series of experiments such as those carried out in the *Décryptimages* project[9]. We will examine one of these experiments on audiovisual texts examining *A Thousand and One Nights*.

In order to do so, we will consider the different stages creating a thematic educational dossier through an example created on an

---

6 We should specifically highlight the partnership with "Décryptimages", a project initiated by Laurent Gervereau, historian and theoretician of political image, photography, and contemporary art, in cooperation with the Ligue de l'enseignement and the Institut des images, which specializes in image analysis and learning. Laurent Gervereau invited us to take part in this project to create educational dossiers about world folk tales and culture. For further information, see the Décryptimages website: http://www.decryptimages.net/.

7 Galaade publishers, set up in 2005 by Emmanuelle Collas, specialized in French and world fiction, literary essays and contemporary debate. See http://www.galaade.com for further details.

8 See, for example, the "Quatorzièmes Rencontres d'Aubrac" [Fourteenth Meetings of Aubrac] from 2009 based on the theme of a "Tour through the absurd": http://www.archivesaudiovisuelles.fr/1900/.

9 See footnote 5.

audiovisual corpus of *A Thousand and One Nights*. From this initial stage, which involves choosing texts from a vast collection of audiovisual literature, we will examine how their technical process depend on the type of initial sound document, that are segmented or non segmenting videos, extracting relevant parts for each specific theme, in order to adapt them to the demands of the thematic educational dossier. We will also consider the role of each of these texts in the overall structure of the learning dossier and reasons for these functions, primarily due to their semiotic features. Following this, we will focus on the process of analyzing these texts according to their individual characteristics that is semiotic in context, and final editorial choice. The aim, using this example, is to provide a critical overview both of the constraints imposed by the text and the ASW Studio, as well as the wide range of possibilities for detailed audiovisual semiotic analysis and publication for a predefined community of users.

We will conclude this chapter by examining some of the uses of the ASW studio in the context of developing digital records and sharing scientific and professional knowledge.

1.2. Creating a thematic educational dossier based on *A Thousand and One Nights*

1.2.1. *Choosing an audiovisual corpus*

The LHE workshop, like CCA or ArkWork, was principally based on audiovisual texts selected from the vast range of corpora in the *Archives Audiovisuelles de la Recherche* [Audiovisual Research Archives, ARA] and several theatrical productions carried out during the project. This includes interviews with academics on literature, literary production, experts on its relation with other disciplines such as human and social sciences, interviews with authors about their personal styles, as well as seminars and original stage productions and so on.

From this variety of material, there are several texts which can be selected for the theme of *A Thousand and One Nights*. There are three texts which are interesting for their variety in both genre and content because they provide three different perspectives on the subject:

– an interview with Joseph Sadan from Tel Aviv University (Israel) presenting *A Thousand and One Nights* within the general context of the "sociocultural aspects of classical Arabic literature"[10]. This interview was carried out during his visit to the *Fondation Maison des Sciences de l'Homme* (FMSH)[11], Paris, in 2007;

– a seminar by Aboubakr Chraïbi entitled "En dire plus ou en dire moins: traduire les *Mille et une nuits*" [Saying more or less: translating *A Thousand and One Nights*] examining eroticism in *A Thousand and One Nights*, comparing the original Arabic text with 19th Century translations by renowned authors;

– an original modern stage production, adapted from *A Thousand and One Nights* - "L'Amour impossible d'après les Mille et une nuits" [Impossible love according to *A Thousand and One Nights*] – performed by Bruno de La Salle, mixing narration with instrumental music and vocals[12].

1.2.2. *Text analysis*

Semiotic analysis of audiovisual texts is governed by original editorial choices: our selection is based on the type of publication which is a thematic educational dossier, where the dossier is aimed at an "absolute beginner" adult audience for life-long learning. Note, however, that even if these texts are compiled together, they can still be viewed separately and are reusable in other types of publications.

1.2.2.1. *Building the dossier: text structure*

In the learning dossier's thematic, we need to identify the role of each audiovisual text in our discourse on *A Thousand and One Nights*. This involves organizing them around a central axis. More generally, as shown through the interview that discusses sociocultural aspects of

---

10 The interview can be seen at the following address: http://semioweb.msh-paris.fr/corpus/ALIA/1972.
11 "House of the Human Sciences", (http://www.msh-paris.fr/en/foundation/missions).
12 The performance can be viewed on the ALIA website: http://semioweb.msh-paris.fr/corpus/ALIA/FR/_video.asp?id=1742&ress=5500&video=121341&format=9 1#22301.

classical Arabic literature, we will focus the discourse on a specific theme in *A Thousand and One Nights*, namely eroticism, as examined in Aboubakr Chraïbi's seminar[13] and exemplified in the contemporary theater adaptation. This articulation of the dossier, that is its "mode of use" is specified in the metadescription for each audiovisual text.

This organization is applicable thanks to our videos features. Other structures can also be used depending on the genre of the texts and the style of the discourse.

1.2.2.2. *Processing corpora: choice of analysis and segmentation*

Exploring this theme implies that we have undertaken a detailed analysis of a segmented video[14]. This approach is clearly expressed and described in the metadescription section in the analysis workshop[15].

However, we also need to account for the characteristics, and even constraints of each of these original texts. This is because their original form differs from each other. For example, the interview is already divided into audiovisual segments whilst the seminar and filmed stage production are not. In compliance with the analysis procedure we have opted for the segmented text, we will initially submit these last two texts to the segmentation workshop to create segments.

Segmentation of the seminar is carried out according to the speaker's discourse (see Figure 1.2) and, for the *Thousand and One Nights* production, in different threads of the narrative (see Figure 1.3). This segmentation process is carried out separately for each audiovisual document.

---

13 The seminar entitled "Saying more or less: translating A Thousand and One Nights" (translation) can be found online at the following address: http://semioweb.msh-paris.fr/corpus/ALIA/FR/video.asp?id=1670&ress=5259&video =8417&format=94.
14 The different types of analysis are examined in Chapter 3 [STO 11a].
15 On the function of metadescription, see Chapter 3 [STO 11a].

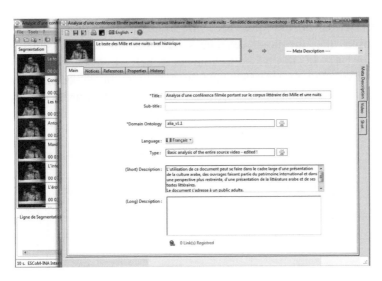

Figure 1.2. *Segmentation of Aboubakr Chraïbi's seminar on translations of A Thousand and One Nights and located in the section "Generalities" relating to each segment*

Title		Description	Durée
	« Once upon the ancient times… »	With his crystal instrument, Bruno de La Salle introduces us to the world of Arabian Nights. Two brothers, the first one, a king in Bukhara Shahryar - and the other one, king in Samarkand - Shah Zaman - are discovering the adulterous conduct of their respective wife… Revenge or love, which of the two sentiments will prevail?	00:03:25
	« The most miserable man of earth… »	Bruno de La Salle accelerates the tempo … Feeling of oppression, as if a disaster is imminent … King Shah Zaman, brother of the King Shahryar, deceived by his wife, feels that he is the most miserable man on Earth …	00:02:03
	« In the darkness of Shahryar's palace… »	Monotonous tinkling of some crystalline notes … Sensation of fate at work … Shahryar went out hunting, leaving his brother Shah Zaman, alone. This last one will discover some… unexpected things!	00:03:10
	« One more adultery and two more souls submitted to doubt, shame, and exile… »	Replay of the haunting crystallin tune, Shahryar comes back hunting… Shah Zaman, refusing to confess to his brother his discoveries, manages the situation so that he could see with his own eyes the misdeeds of his wife	00:02:57
	Exile … the great encounter that will " awake the beast in them" …	A feminine voice, on a crystalline sound background, punctuates the journey. During this journey, both kings meet a genius, who own a glass box, locked by four latches, from which escapes a beautiful vision … a young woman that will "awake the beast in them"	00:03:49
	Exile … The woman recites the list of her lovers by counting the wedding rings of her conquests, that she pulls out a small bag…	After having "awakened the beast in them," the young woman takes out a small bag containing a thousand rings, and spread them. Then she places them back, one by one in the bag, listing the characteristics of the owners of each ring, her lover, to the careless tone of a little nursery rythm, she sings an air of "One, two, three, going to the woods …"	00:02:45
	Revenge of King Shahryar against women …	Revenge of King Shahryar against women… Replay of the initial music rhythm … The revenge of King Shahryar against women is terrible. Hunted, trapped, veiled … He, then, slaughters all of them, every morning and every night …	00:02:37
	Scheherazade brings the King back to life	Scheherazade, the Prime Minister's daughter, goes to Shahryar, her secret childhood love, to start to sing a haunting song to pull him out of barbarism and bring him back to life…	00:02:21
	« Meddling in the affairs of others attracts a lot of trouble" »	Replay of the initial music rhythm… To make him change his mind, the vizier tells his daughter Scheherazade, a tale, like when she was small and he wanted her to eat her meals. So begins the tale of the donkey, the beef and the farmer …	00:03:32

Figure 1.3. *Segmentation of the video entitled "L'Amour impossible, d'après les mille et une nuits" [impossible love, according to A Thousand and One Nights, based on the story's narrative*

In terms of the interview, the segmentation process involves isolating the thematic sequences relevant to the dossier[16] (see Figure 1.4). In the video's hour and half duration, focus on *A Thousand and One Nights* is only for 20 minutes because Joseph Sadan discusses the history of classical Arabic literature with respect to its sociocultural aspects and only uses the example of this corpus to reinforce his main argument.

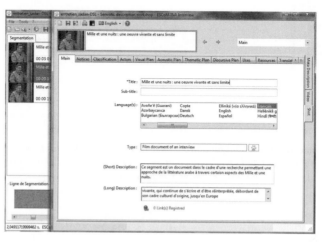

Figure 1.4. *Selection of segments about A Thousand One Nights in the interview listed in the section "generalities" relating to each segment*

Beyond these technical considerations, it is essential to consider semiotic specificities of each text. The importance of the interview and the seminar lies in the oral discourse's content whilst the stage production adds visual and acoustic content which provides an additional semiological approach.

1.2.2.3. *Analysis*

Once the text is "prepared", after segmentation and selection of one or more video segments, the task of analyzing, describing, and indexing can begin. The audiovisual text that we have chosen to analyze first is the interview which is the central axis on which the other two texts will depend.

---

16 See Chapter 2 in [STO 11a] regarding the segmentation workshop.

Joseph Sadan uses general scientific elements to contextualize the appearance and subsequent evolution of *A Thousand and One Nights'* corpus historically and geographically. In contrast, the seminar approaches the subject through specific perspectives, namely the theme of eroticism and translations of the text. Finally, the theater adaptation provides a modern representation of one of the stories from *A Thousand and One Nights*. Among the resources we have used, one of the most important was an archive on art in Arabic literature composed by the BnF (Bibliothèque Nationale de France [French National Library]), a broad overview of the history of *A Thousand and One Nights* corpus which highlights the multiple cultural layers composing it, from India, Persia and Egypt and its subsequent evolution through Western interpretations. The archive is illustrated with manuscripts from the BnF's art collection[17].

The importance of an interview conducted as a seminar, in reference to those created for the *Archives Audiovisuelles de la Recherche* [Audiovisual Research Archives], lies essentially in its content. There are few variations in the visual and acoustic patterns which can therefore be briefly and quickly described e.g. *wide shot, shot focused on the researcher, man or woman's voice and so on*. Indexing these scenes is a quick process. In contrast, emphasis is placed on themes with focus on oral discourse as we will see in the rest of this chapter.

1.2.2.3.1. The dossier's central axis: a scientific interview on classical Arabic literature

The indexing framework is provided by the vocabulary used by the researcher and the context of his discourse, which is also the case when approaching a written text. This method involves systematically identifying parts of his discourse that best contextualize the literary corpus by highlighting terms, expressions and concepts discussed by the researcher. In other words, this consists of answering the five classic "W"s and one "H" that is who, what, when, where, why, and how (see [LAS 48])[18].

---

17 The archive can be viewed at the following address: http://expositions.bnf.fr/liv rarab/gros_plan/mille.htm.

18 This model was proposed by Harold Dwight Lasswell (1902–1978), an American specialist in mass communication in his definition of communication: "Who says

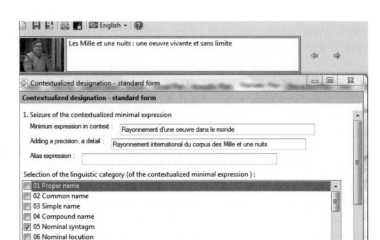

Figure 1.5. *Overview of contextualized classification*

In terms of indexation words, utterances and even set expressions are used to define each contextually. Several types of contextualizations are therefore included in the formula entitled "Contextualized classification" (see Figure 1.5).

The first feature to be mentioned is the minimum expression of the term with its linguistic category, with the possibility of adding a variant, even an alternative expression. Then it is provided with a discursive contextualization that is referential, spatial, temporal, historical, social, thematic, cognitive and so on, which is then accompanied by a synthetic presentation of the indexed piece.

In the interview there is an abundance of historical references to places, times, names of important figures, current researchers, texts, sometimes named in Arabic or Persian. Each concept, work, author, genre, character, literary theme, cultural feature, place, period and so

what to whom through which channel with what effect?" (See H.C. Lasswell in "The Structure and Function of Communication in Society", in The Communication of Idea, a collection of articles compiled by BRYSON, New York, Harper and Brothers, 1948, p. 37.

on can be indexed in various existing orthographic transcriptions using the corresponding description scheme.

Detailed description formulas are used for each field to identify the work, a specific excerpt in a complete text, the author, the literary genre accompanied by a synthetic description of the subject and so on using a glossary prepared by the LHE workshop. The original Arabic term is also included alongside each indexed word as well as its "aliases" that is various other orthographic transcriptions.

For example, in Figure 1.6 the name of the King, Shahrayar, one of the main characters in the narrative framework of *A Thousand and One Nights* in Scheherazade's story, is indexed under different Arabic transcriptions.

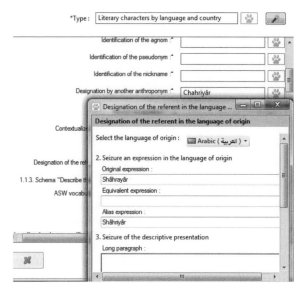

Figure 1.6. *Indexation formula of a character's name in the narrative framework of A Thousand and One Nights in the original Arabic (detail)*

This highlights the importance of contextualizing terms at the point of indexation, which is proven particularly in the title *A Thousand and One Nights* itself. A variety of versions from different periods and cultures (from both East and West) use the same title whether they are translations or adaptations. What could have been a real difficulty at the beginning is resolved by replacing the term precisely at each indexation in the different contexts that we have mentioned. The term is therefore systematically indexed multiple times under the same title but in separate description formulas. It is described and placed in its spatial, temporal, and discursive context.

Figure 1.7 provides an example of indexation for the title of the Persian work at the basis of *A Thousand and One Nights*. An initial indexation of the title is carried out in French and then a second in Persian.

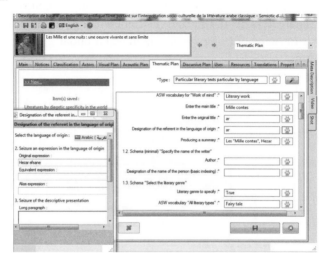

Figure 1.7. *Example indexation of the title "A Thousand and One Nights" corresponding to the original Persian text*

On the other hand, it was also essential with *A Thousand and One Nights*, created over centuries using multiple oral and written literary materials, to create in this narrative oral tradition a dynamic tradition which provides the essential style of the text. This was highlighted thanks to the description field of "Literary materials" (see Figure 1.8).

This description scheme enables us to identify various materials at the heart of a written text (i.e. oral stories, journey notes, diaries, historical events, various facts and drawings etc.) and account for the complexity of some texts' structures. Examples of this might be fairy tales, legends, mythology, and also journey accounts in travel guides.

The advantage of this systematic and extremely precise indexation is that Internet users can access video excerpts corresponding exactly to each area of research, thanks to various description schemes from literature and term contextualization.

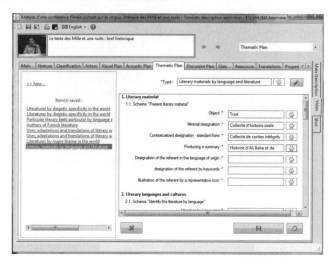

Figure 1.8. *Example of the description pattern for "Literary materials"*

1.2.2.3.2. A theater adaptation of a story from *A Thousand and One Nights*

Note that the original text had previously been segmented according to the various narrative threads of the story. Given the specificity of the audiovisual text, a semiotic approach took place which was slightly different from the two previous pieces. The visual (i.e. staging) and acoustic dimensions (i.e. instrumental music and singing) provide additional elements to describe the audiovisual text.

This adaptation of a story from *A Thousand and One Nights* is a narration of "L'Amour impossible, d'après les Mille et une nuits" [*Impossible love, according to A Thousand and One Nights*] by the musician, raconteur, and director, Bruno de La Salle. This is accompanied by the crystal *Baschet*[19], which was used by La Salle to

19 For informatiion on Baschet sound structures, see the site (in French): http://www.baschet.org/structures/lesfreresbaschet.php.

create crystalline sounds (see Figure 1.9), whilst another musician, Aimée Douce de La Salle[20], plays the tambura, a stringed Indian instrument (see Figure 1.10).

Figure 1.9. *Bruno de La Salle[21] (director and raconteur) playing the Baschet organ*

The structure of the analysis revolves around two axes; on the one hand the thematics involved, as with the two previous texts, examining themes, characters, places, literary references and so on, which are found in different sequences of the story's narration. Each protagonist, every town name, each significant object appearing throughout the narrative is carefully indexed, described and contextualized according to the process used for both the interview and the seminar.

The two additional axes, which show the importance of describing this kind of stage production, focus on visuals and acoustics. The first one, visual discourse, identifies and describes significant objects in the staging e.g. colors, decorations, costumes, changes in scene and so on. Even if there are not that many visual elements, they provide interesting indications, for example, the sari worn by the musician, the stringed instrument that she is playing, the tambura (a traditional classical Indian instrument, closely related to the sitar) (see Figure 1.10). These cultural indicators clearly refer to the Indian links of *A Thousand and One Nights*.

20 Aimée de La Salle's Website (in French only) can be found at: http:// aimeedelasalle.com/.
21 Bruno de La Salle is the artistic director of the CLiO – Conservatoire contemporain de Littérature Orale. For further details on the center, its news, training and events, see their Website (in French only): http://www.clio.org/.

Figure 1.10. *Aimée Douce de La Salle, singing and playing the tambura*

In contrast, acoustics focuses on the sounds, noises, voices, music, even audience applause, providing information on their type, characteristics and intensity (identifying the technique of the sound) and so on.

In the framework of this thematic dossier, we have clearly chosen to emphasize the relationship between the narration and the music (both instrumental and vocal). A brief consideration of the story's content itself is also very important. "Impossible love" focuses on the last of the stories in *A Thousand and One Nights* which Scheherazade tells to the Sultan Shahrayar to try and persuade him not to kill her. It tells the story in which the Vizier is pleading for love.

The story relates the chance meeting between a Persian prince, Ali Ben Bekar, and a princess, Shams al Naar, the favorite mistress of the Caliph Harun-al-Rashid, and their subsequent falling in love. It tells the story of an impossible and pure love, describing three meetings which lead inevitably to their demise. The atmosphere is tense and tragic with the piercing, almost oppressive rhythm of the crystal organ accompanying their unavoidable doom, and indicating the fatal outcome of the story. The instrumental partnership also expresses the love of the two characters for each other. Similarly, the singing during Scheherazade's enchanting pleading to Shahrayar, conveys her love for him.

To return to indexing terms in acoustics, therefore, when we index the name of the instrument, we also indicate its expressive function in relation to the various passages in the narration.

1.3. Perspectives: ASWs and new forms of digital writing

Just as *A Thousand and One Nights* was composed orally which was then written, rewritten, translated, altered and interpreted in a multitude of ways encouraging human thought and producing more western and eastern versions, each audiovisual text can emerge as material for encouraging thought or generating reflection in a community of users, whether they are individuals or communities of individuals from research, media, the art world or the world of publishing and so on.

This example of use of audiovisual texts in the strict framework of a thematic dossier demonstrates the wide range of possibilities offered by the ASW-HSS environment, not only in terms of analysis but also for releasing videos and, more generally, with regard to experimenting with multimedia writing.

The analysis and video publication tools provided by the ASW Studio and its hypertextual nature (see [STO 07][22]) can help users to publish their thoughts on a text's semiotic content and therefore provide a wider interaction than those of existing electronic reviewers[23]. The same text can therefore be the subject of multiple approaches and analyses and can be included in multiple specialist publications, measured in relation to each other using this hypertextual function. Therefore, video analyses can be used as a point of departure for other analyses as many times as the video makes individuals or communities of individuals reflect on issues from various areas of

---

22 According to P. Stockinger, this function allows us to put into context, according to a chosen production framework or scenario, the textual elements involved so that each aim of the communication has a "good" chance of being achieved. See "La place de l'hypertextualité dans le traitement de corpus audiovisuels et/ou multimédias numériques" [The place of hypertextuality in Processing audiovisual corpora and/ or digital media]: http://www.semionet.fr/ressources_enligne/Enseignement/06_07/tim/fascicule_1.pdf.
23 For example, revue.org.

study. In addition, collaboration between several individuals or groups of individuals working in the same field or even different disciplines can decipher and analyze the same audiovisual corpus according to a previously defined scenario.

The project set up by Laurent Gervereau, historian, art historian and president of the *Institut des images*, is a good example of collaboration in terms of deciphering images. Established in partnership with the *Ligue de l'enseignement* and the *Institut des images*, his project focuses on analyzing the semiotics of images, whether drawn, filmed, photographed and so on to propose modules for thematic and age analysis (this can be viewed online on the *Décryptimages* Website or the *"Portail d'éducation aux images"*). This project has benefited from the support and participation of organizations such as the CNC (*Centre national du cinéma et de l'image animée* [National center for cinema and animated images][24]), the *Societé française de la photographie*, the *Maison européene de la photographie*, universities and well known figures from film and the media[25]. The aim of the ASW-HSS project, which follows the development work started by the *Archives Audiovisuelles de la Recherche* (Audiovisual Research Archives, AFA) lies in part in visual semiotics, as studied by the *Décrytimages* work group. Methodological reflection in meetings between Laurent Gervereau, members from the *Ligue de l'enseignement*, the CNC and the ESCoM team has resulted in the production of a semiotic analysis of a small corpus of thematically defined and selected videos from the CCA[26] and LHE[27] dossiers, of which *A Thousand and One Nights* was one, to make them available to Internet users on the *Décrytimages* portal.

---

24 CNC Website: http://www.cnc.fr/Web/fr.

25 The Décryptimages portal can be found at the following address: http://www.decryptimages.net/index.php.

26 These texts are mainly interviews with ethnologists, for example, Roberte Hamayon examining shamanism (http://semioweb.msh-paris.fr/corpus/arc/2004/home.asp) and Rina Sherman and her experiences living among the Ovahimba people (Namibia) (http://semioweb.msh-paris.fr/corpus/arc/1873/home.asp).

27 Travel literature is one of the chosen themes alongside that of folk takes (see, for example, the interview with François Moureau "La littérature des voyages" [Travel literature]: http://semioweb.msh-paris.fr/corpus/ALIA/1817, and the seminar

However, an interesting approach, in which research led in the ASW framework has in fact found its place, was that developed by the *Pôle ImageSon*[28] in the *Mediterranean House of Human Sciences* (MHHS). The site, run by research groups from various parts of the MMSH laboratories, aims to be a "place of experimentation, discussion and publication links for the various multiple links between text and images in scientific writing and communicating knowledge in human and social sciences"[29].

The innovative forms of analysis and publication produced in the ASW project aid general reflection about new approaches for electronic writing, not only for freedom of use or even appropriation on the part of the user, but also for recommunicating knowledge thanks to the ASA framework's nuanced editing system which can be adapted to users' needs.

The *Mediterranean House of Human Sciences* (MHHS) has therefore expressed interest in the ASW project and has participated in our research during a conference organized in 2010 by the head of sound archives at the MHHS, Véronique Ginouvès, in collaboration with Florence Descamps, researcher at the *Ecole Pratique des Hautes Etudes* entitled "Le chercheur et ses sources sonores et audiovisuelles. Comment les partager? Comment les diffuser? Besoins, risques, contraintes, atouts et benefices" [The researcher and sound and audiovisual resources. How to share and publish them? Needs, risks, constraints, assets, and benefits][30]. The LHE presentation created a large amount of interest with the help of researchers and archivists with respect to ways of improving and disseminating knowledge.

"Etude du conte populaire des XIXe et XXe siècles" [Studying folk tales of the 19th and 20th Centuries]: http://semioweb.msh-paris.fr/corpus/ALIA/1968.

28 The Pôle ImagesSons site can be found through the Mediterranean House of Human Sciences (MHHS) site: http://www.imageson.org.

29 ImageSon can be found at the following address: http://www.imageson.org/document499.html.

30 For the complete schedule of the seminar, see: http://imageson.hypotheses.org/17.

Chapter 2

Analyzing a Corpus of Traditional Bread Making

2.1. Introduction

Continuing on from Chapter 1 which focused on a concrete use of the ASW studio in creating a thematic educational dossier for *A Thousand and One Nights*, we will examine in this chapter the processes used to develop the two dossiers based on a series of situations developed through ASW-HSS project. These two dossiers focus on artisan bread making.

Our choice of subject will obviously be based on a subject that is an integral part of food culture in a number of countries and of which we have a representative body of data. There are a number of ways of studying this, both scientifically (i.e. anthropology, ethnology, sociology, etc.), professionally and technically (i.e. relating to the food industry, professional and commercial methods).

This choice is also justified by current events since "the gastronomic meal of the French" has been classified as part of the

Chapter written by Elisabeth DE PABLO.

Intangible Cultural Heritage of Humanity by UNESCO[1], and bread is considered as a basic source of food in Western civilization since the world is witnessing food crises and the challenges due to these crises. The aim is therefore to create:

– an educational dossier to educate people about a culture and tradition, which face extinction if the cultural and family traditions that have so far kept it alive begin to disappear;

– a communicative dossier to valorize the cultural events.

Importance of these evaluative and educational online dossiers lies in the fact that they invite reflection, increase awareness and, above all, become places of exchange, due to the possibilities offered by Web 2.0. They also provide scientific and professional domains where anyone can express and compare his/her opinions, thereby enriching these dossiers in turn.

It should be noted here that the dossier in the ASW-HSS project was created by defining and identifying its potential uses, as well as its educational and valorizing themes (for example, allow the use of scenarios in the classroom or in the establishment of the communication of a temporary exhibition on a cultural event), based on the stages identified during the ASW project[2]. The usage scenarios are used as input when defining the models for republication and create a "usage" service. The themes of education and valorization enable us to develop an indexing style which accounts for a corpora specificity in relation to its relevance to a specific context.

This chapter is divided into two parts, the first part focusing on the construction of an *educational dossier*, and the second on creating a *valorization* dossier. These two sections are further divided according to the choice of audiovisual objects and the processes of analysis, annotation, and description, depending on the dossiers' objectives and target audience.

---

1 See the complete article on the UNESCO Website: http://www.unesco.org/culture/ich/en/RL/00437.
2 For further information on this subject, see the technical reports of task 1 of the ASW-HSS project: the project's specification and operational context can be found at the following Web address: http://semioweb.msh-paris.fr:8080/site/projets/asa/spip.php?article52.

2.2. Creating educational dossiers to raise public awareness

2.2.1. *Choosing a corpus*

The audiovisual corpus used for the dossier was selected from the Culture Crossroads Archive (CCA)[3], which is one of the pilot sites of the ASW-HSS project. The resources from this site are organized around overall themes focusing on paradigms, methods, and research in cultural studies (in the sense of *"Kulturwissenschaften"*[4] which seeks to deconstruct the culture and multidisciplinary research).

As mentioned earlier, we have selected a sizeable corpus of audiovisual texts focusing on bread, including seminar recordings and reports and interviews with researchers and professionals in France and Portugal, which was released as an online audiovisual document. On the basis of these online documents, we then need to choose an editorial objective.

Figure 2.1. *Picture representation of the selected corpus*

3 Website is available at the following URL: http://semioweb.msh-paris.fr/corpus/ Arc/FR/Default.asp.
4 For a more general overview of this discipline, see: http://de.wikipedia.org/wiki/ Kulturwissenschaft. See also, the thematic workshops on *Kulturwissenschaften* proposed by the *Centre Interdisciplinaire d'Etudes et de Recherche sur l'Allemagne*: http:// www.ciera.fr/ciera/spip.php?article1594.

For the first dossier, we have therefore selected the following texts:

– extracts from the seminar "Le pain dans tous ses états" [Bread in all its forms][5], organized by Mouette Barboff (ethnologist and president of the *Europe, Civilisation du pain* [Europe: civilization of bread]) association at the Gulbenkian cultural center in Paris in 2008;

– extracts from the audiovisual text *La fabrication du pain domestique au Portugal* [Making domestic bread in Portugal][6] created with the help of Mouette Barboff in Portugal in 2008;

– excerpts from the audiovisual text *Du grain au pain aux moulins Bourgeois* [Grain and bread in Bourgeois mills][7], created with the help of Mouette Barboff in Verdelot in 2008;

– extracts from a report *Rencontre avec Jacques Mahou, artisan-boulanger* [Meeting Jacques Mahou, artisan baker][8] created with the help of Mouette Barboff in Tours in 2008.

As stated, the corpus created in 2008 which combines highly varied film genres, was headed by Mouette Barboff who conducted research on bread in France and Portugal for a number of years, enabling us to follow this subject and create a highly scientifically and culturally rich corpus.

2.2.2. *Defining aims of the analysis*

Before proceeding to the segmentation and description phases for the selected audiovisual data, we need to formally identify the objectives of creating the dossier. This involves describing its context and use as well as its potential applications.

Our choice is based on the concept of creating an educational dossier designed to inform the wider public (either with some or no knowledge)

---

5 The seminar can be viewed online at: http://semioweb.msh-paris.fr/corpus/ Arc/1869/.

6 The text can be viewed at the following address: http://semioweb.msh-paris.fr/ corpus/Arc/1970/.

7 To see the text, refer to: http://semioweb.msh-paris.fr/ corpus/Arc/1999/.

8 The report can be viewed at the following Web address: http://semioweb.msh-paris.fr/corpus/ Arc/1767/.

about the family and cultural traditions of making leavened bread in France and Portugal. We will attempt to describe the traditional production process for leavened bread, followed by the stages involved in bread making (kneading, shaping and baking) in two cultural contexts, namely French artisan bread and domestic Portuguese bread, to allow the dossier's users to:

– be able to compare the two cultural processes;

– gain know-how they can use and put into practice;

– view scenarios of everyday European life which are not so different from their own;

– gain awareness of the importance of traditions and preserving cultural heritage.

As such, the dossier provides several visual and acoustic perspectives on the topic which come from the diversity of genres being analyzed and which enable us to examine different kinds of discourse that is both scientific and that of the "concerned" actors, both professional and domestic.

2.2.3. *Analysis*

Once the corpus was chosen and its aims and objectives were identified, we need to identify the analysis process which will be used to create the dossier. Even if each analysis, depending on its objectives, is based on a model that is specific to it, we can still use the articulation axis from a general model, which we will now attempt to schematize.

As Figure 2.2 shows, a central utterance can be constructed around segmented reference discourse (S1, S2, S3, S4, S5) onto which related segments can be grafted (SL1, SL2, SL3, SL4). The analyst can then organize the new narrative axis of his/her dossier.

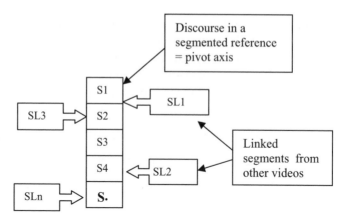

Figure 2.2. *Schematization of the dossier creation process*

2.2.3.1. *What is the role of each text in the dossier's structure?*

On the basis of Mouette Barboff's involvement, through the seminar *"Le pain dans tous ses états"*, which explains her methods and research in domestic and artisan bread making in Portugal and France, respectively, we want to provide examples of these subjects and production methods by leaving the participants' (named in the presentation) speech in the recorded reports *in situ*, for example, that of artisan baker, Jacques Mahou, master patissier, baker, ice cream producer, and chocolatier. He has also won the *Médaille d'argent des meilleurs ouvriers de France* and is a member of the *Institut français du goût*. He has also worked with Celeste Correia Carvalho Sousa, a former employee of the Estrela Vermelha cooperative (*Etoile Rouge*) in Ermidas do Sado, Alentejo, Portugal. As mentioned in Chapter 3 [STO11a], these priorities are set out in each indexed texts' meta-description. The researcher's discourse provides our central axis. Each created video (audiovisual texts from which excerpts are taken), is indexed on a general (i.e. basic) level. Each retained (i.e. participating) segment in the dossier is then subject to detailed (see *following section*) indexation.

2.2.3.2. *What are the features that are linked to video processing and analysis in this structure on the basis of this assertion?*

It soon becomes obvious that we are leaning toward a partial segmentation of the chosen genres and a detailed analysis of the selected segments. So far, this was done using an extract from a seminar and various other excerpts from a report and other audiovisual texts. The passages that we have selected are not necessarily individual segments in the original texts.

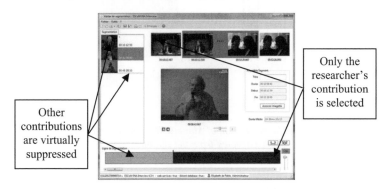

Figure 2.3. *Example extraction of Mouette Barboff's contribution*

We begin our central axis with the personal message of researcher and anthropologist, Mouette Barboff. In the original video, the seminar is segmented only according to their different contributions when it is put online. Therefore, it is first necessary to extract Mouette Barboff's contribution from the original film. An initial segmentation is carried out as follows: the complete film is taken into the Segmentation Workshop and the applicable parts are retained and segmented to produce a relevant analysis.

As we can see in Figure 2.4, the analyzed segments from this extract correspond to segments S1, S2, S3, S4, and S5 in our model. The analysis that follows this extraction will be detailed and justified in the metadescription section of the Description Workshop. This is achieved by using the "*themes*" and "*discussion*" tabs proposed in the video sections and the segments from the Description Workshop whose main points are indexed. In this case, we will not ignore the visuals and acoustics which are not immediately relevant to our dossier.

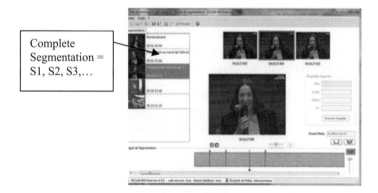

Figure 2.4. *Segmentation of Mouette Barboff's contribution,*
extracted from the seminar

The researcher's universe of discourse (or domain of discourse) enables us to select and index scientific references, possible examples, places and research methods, thus essentially summarizing all the elements necessary for detailed indexation and contextualization of our subject.

The themes section provides us with a choice of adapted formulas in a library of subjects focusing on "cultural studies". These description models have been created for our Culture Crossroads Archive (CCA) Workshop Website. The subjects proposed here are not exhaustive as they have been developed as a reference corpus[9].

As we have seen in the previous chapters, the Description Workshop segments the overall video and indexes the segments themselves. It is the analyst who has to make a choice about what level of indexation to choose in view of these objectives.

Creating awareness among Internet users (i.e. the public) about bread and artisan bread making involves a shared choice that is applicable to all the selected segments, about a description theme for the library. Our choice is therefore naturally based on the description model "foods of the world" enabling us to focus on "bread" alone. This description model will therefore be completed, for the videos, for

_____

9 See section 5.7 of 5 [STO11a].

all of the chosen texts. Here, the conceptual term [bread] is a common denominator to which other explanatory or illustrating terms from detailed indexations can be added.

Figure 2.5. *Extract of the subject library which can be seen on the ARC Workshop Website*

We have initially decided to index [bread] in "Mouette Barboff's contribution" to the seminar. This was the central axis for our dossier and the indexation of the topic of food [bread] (i.e. in videos) uses description formulas for each of these segments. We therefore have parallel indexations for:

– a sub-segment, S1, corresponding to the subject "introduction of the authors";

– a sub-segment, S2, corresponding to the subject "technical and artisan know-how";

– a sub-segment, S3, corresponding to the subject of "cultural transmission";

– a sub-segment, S4, corresponding to "food production techniques";

– a sub-segment, S5, corresponding to the subjects "production and baking techniques" and "tools, instruments, and utensils".

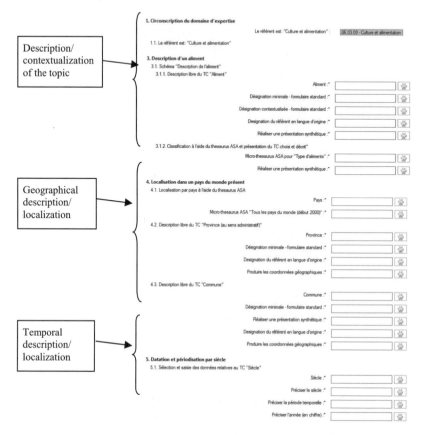

Figure 2.6. *Visualization of the three levels of description formulas on the subject "foods of the world"*

We note that these varied subjects cover a rich indexation focusing on words, utterances, and concepts mentioned by the researcher. It is precisely these elements with which we will "enter" into the formula's fields.

These fields provide indexation at three distinct levels: topic, space (i.e. place, geographical location), and time (temporal location). We will now examine these three levels in further detail.

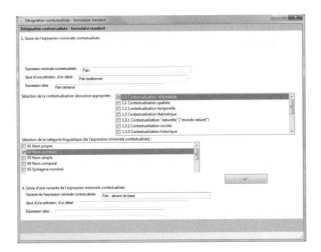

Figure 2.7. *Contextualized classification viewed in the formula for describing the subject "foods of the world"*

1. Topic (or theme)

This is the primary level, defining the area of expertise, includes several schemes and formulas which enable:

– free or standard indexing (with the help of minimal or contextualized classification, which can be done using free synthetic example – textual instruction);

– controlled indexing (i.e. classification using micro-thesauri which may be accompanied by free synthetic example – textual instruction);

– composite indexing (including elements of both free and composed indexation).

In our example, we have favored (still for transversal indexation[10]) the composite indexation proposed in the "food description" scheme. The choice is governed by our analysis and the collected data.

As such, the "contextualized design" enables us to index the minimum term [bread] and qualify this with [traditional bread] and

---

10 I.e. shared by all the videos in the dossier.

add an alternative name [artisan bread] while being able to select an appropriate discursive context [referential, thematic, cultural], indicating the linguistic category of the minimal expression [noun], to use a variant of the contextualized minimal expression [bread – basic food source]. We then use the micro-thesaurus, developed in the ASW-HSS project for "types of food" which refers us to the nouns [bread], [wheat], and [corn] in the category [cereal derived products].

We then index the topics as segments S1, S2, S3, S4, and S5 in the same way by selecting the formulas related to our chosen subject.

For example, the indexation of the sub-segment S2 corresponding to the subject "technical and artisan expertise" enables us to provide information on the following topics:

– "technical and artisan expertise" using the "simple classification" formula with [family knowledge];

– "describing practices in artisan bread making" using the "contextualized classification" formula for [baker], [artisan baker], [family bakery], and by using the micro-thesaurus "artisan" [artisan food sector].

These systematic contextualized indexations enable the Internet user to search for a word or precise phrase and therefore access one or several parts (i.e. passages) of the videos corresponding to their search.

In our dossier creation example, these example indexations (of both the video and its segments) and the central video (the central axis on which the dossier is based) will be accompanied by detailed indexations (of the whole video and segments) from the segments of other selected videos designed to illustrate the researcher's discourse.

2. Geographical location

This kind of information enables us to provide the location of the subject, as well as the place(s) featured in the video. Indexation is done in a controlled way using micro-thesaurus classification of "all the countries in the world (as of 2000)" either freely or by using minimum classification, with which an additional indexation of the referent in the original language can be included, along with the precise geographic coordinates of the place in question that is state, county, and so on, for placing on an interactive map.

In our example, we have again decided to classify using the thesaurus and free description of the area by entering references to the place of recording and the subject which, in this case, are identical, namely [Paris].

We continue to provide this level of information in detailed indexations of segments from the overall selected video.

3. Temporal location

Providing information on this level enables us to locate the video or segment temporally either by date or by period. Again, there are a number of choices available to us: free, where we can specify a time period and/or year, or controlled where we use classification referring to the specific century. These indexations enable us to carry out the research throughout different timelines. In our example, we have chosen to use both century [21st Century] and year [2008].

We will do the same for the detailed indexations for all the segments in the selected videos.

2.2.3.3. *Features added through indexing segments linked to other videos*

As shown in Figure 2.2, segments from other videos (SL1, SL2, SL3, and SL4) must illustrate the researcher's linear discourse. These segments are indexed according to the theme as we have just seen. To these themes, for each segment we also add indexation of visuals and sound recordings which are designed to extract the excerpts' sounds, key moments, and images to illustrate the discourse.

For example, in the segment of the report "*Rencontre avec Jacques Mahou, artisan-boulanger*" [Meeting Jacques Mahou, artisan baker] [11], entitled "*le pétrissage*" [kneading], Jacques Mahou explains 'orally'

---

11 The report can be viewed online at: http://semioweb.msh-paris.fr/corpus/ Arc/1767/.

the different stages of altering the dough after kneading. His explanations are split into sections that examine the dough during kneading. This segment is full of different themes enabling us to identify an indispensable tool in baking [dough], an essential action in this industry [kneading] and see the actor [baker] in action. These three terms are indexed as themes via the subjects "tools, instruments, and utensils", "preparation techniques", and "trade".

Figure 2.8. *Visualization of indexing visuals*

We will now analyze the visual objects represented in this segment and how they are used in the scene by analyzing its visuals. These visuals enable us to identify two types of objects: visual theme objects and functional visual objects[12]. We will focus on these visual theme objects by choosing the "produced visual object" to represent the [dough], the "visual activity object" for the action of [kneading], and finally the "visual actor object" for the [baker] himself. To each of these objects, we attach an image of the process technique: [wide shot], [close up], [tight angle], and [high angle shot].

There is also a sound element in the report. Apart from the mere "voice" of the actor, there are also ambient sounds (*soundscape*) created by background noise that is the sound of flames in the oven,

12 See Chapter 4 "*L'analyse de l'expression audiovisuelle*" [Analyzing audiovisual expression] (section 4.2) in [STO11a] for further details on visuals.

and the sound of various machines and tools being used. Acoustics enable us to index these elements. Like visuals, acoustics enable us to identify two types of objects: theme sound objects and functional sound objects[13]. We can focus on theme sound objects such as "sound effects of a technical environment" indicating the sound universe of the object [dough] by intensifying its visual representation and the "speech sound object" which indexes the "voice" of the [baker] as he explains what he is doing. Again, for each of these objects, there is a recording technique, for example, [medium sound level], [high sound level], as well as its duration [sound level lasting between 41 and 60 seconds].

As we have seen, examination of visuals and acoustics provides an added value to our thematic indexation in that it identifies the representations of sound and visual objects which will be easily retrievable during Internet searches. As we will see in section 2.2.3.4, these indexations are essential.

2.2.3.4. *Finalizing the dossier*

As previously mentioned, we now need to bring the different analyzed segments together to construct our dossier in an educational setting. To do so, we need to re-examine our initial schema and link each segment. Each segment's place has been annotated in terms of their metadescription. The Publication Workshop of the ASW studio will be used to combine them, thereby enabling us to republish our corpus in the form of a dossier. The *Semiosphere* application (operating the ASW's Publication Workshop) proposes a library of different models for publishing dossiers. We choose one and ensure that the four parts of our authoring scenario have been fully satisfied, including:

– the section "identifying information" relating to the scene's author, its title, copyright information, and so on;

– the section "content of use" where we specify the use proposed in the dossier;

– the section "resources" where we will indicate which segments have been chosen and how they will be presented;

---

13 Again, refer to "*L'analyse de l'expression audiovisuelle*" (section 4.3), for further details on acoustics [STO 11a].

– the section "context of use" detailing the institutional framework in which the dossier will be used.

2.3. Creating a communication dossier for improving cultural events

Working around the same theme, we will now examine another type of analysis which enables us to create an information dossier designed to valorize a corpus of a cultural event. More precisely, we will create a dossier that will be presented in an exhibition on regional bread in Portugal.

2.3.1. *Choosing a corpus*

We will segment and analyze all the videos from the online audiovisual document "Domestic bread making in Portugal"[14] to create the dossier. This text is made up of a series of videos describing and presenting the domestic bread making by using corn and wheat in two highly contrasting regions of Portugal, the Northern Minho region and Alentejo in the South.

Our choice is based on three specific extracts from the corpus:

– making traditional domestic bread from corn baked in a wood oven;

– making stone-baked bread, a domestic bread produced from corn cooked on hot stone;

– producing traditional wheat bread cooked in a wooden oven.

In contrast to the previous dossier, all these videos are reports.

2.3.2. *Defining aims of the analysis*

The aim of this dossier is to "valorize a cultural heritage", namely the production of domestic bread in the previously mentioned regions

---

14 The text can be viewed online at the following address: http://semioweb.msh-paris.fr/ corpus/Arc/1970/.

of Portugal by "presenting a cultural event" at an exhibition on regional Portuguese breads. The target audience is therefore visitors to the exhibition who may have some or no knowledge of the subject.

We will provide the extracts from the selected videos in the form of "trailers" (lasting less than 5 minutes) where the images are favored over textual content. The aim of these trailers is to encourage the visitors to watch these videos on computers provided for this purpose.

2.3.3. *Analysis*

Our analysis will involve highlighting the videos' content and valorizing the exhibition's theme using a series of images. In this case, there is no pivotal axis but a series of images which highlight the visual theme objects: actors, objects, gestures, places, and so on, in the form of visual representations which are intensified using techniques such as very wide angles, wide angles, panoramas, high angle shots, and low angle shots. Here, sounds are of secondary importance since these extracts in the trailer will be accompanied by a voice-over adapted to this visual form of rewriting. Themes are important in this sense as they help us to describe the segments that we have chosen in our dossier.

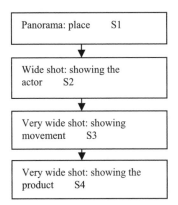

Figure 2.9. *Schematization of the indexation of the first few minutes of the valorization dossier*

As this chart shows, the dossier's rhythm is based around segments from each video ranging from the general to the specific, for example:

– S1 represents the place of action;

– S2 represents the actor carrying out the action;

– S3 represents the action itself;

– S4 represents the object created by the action and so on.

2.3.3.1. *What is the role of each text in the dossier's structure?*

In this case, every text has the same role since four major scenes must be selected from the three videos to create the montage. Only one choice should be made when creating the dossier to determine whether the "trailer" shows the corn or wheat bread first. This choice will also determine the recording of the commentator in the accompanying voice over.

It therefore seems to be obvious that we need to proceed in two stages. First, we carry out a complete segmentation followed by a global analysis of each video to identify the segments. Once we have extracted these video segments, we can analyze them in detail.

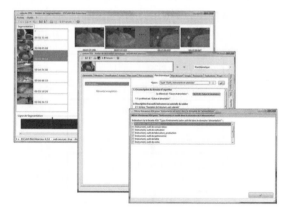

Figure 2.10. *Visualization of the themes in a selected segment*

Analyzing the themes in each segment enables us to contextualize them according to our parameters, that is place, actor, process, and production. Analyzing the visuals enables us to visualize and name these parameters, and account for their technical production procedures. This process is then repeated for the three chosen extracts.

2.3.3.2. *Finalizing the dossier*

The Publication Workshop in the ASW Workshop is again used to put our publications together. After having chosen the model we want to use from the library, we select the segments and combine them to create a new publication.

As we can see from these various examples, an audiovisual corpus can be analyzed for a multitude of reasons. Indexation can be carried out to execute and facilitate searches of archives or bring these archives to life by proposing new forms of rewriting and republication to accompany or illustrate lessons, technical explanations, or even create new products to promote cultural or scientific events.

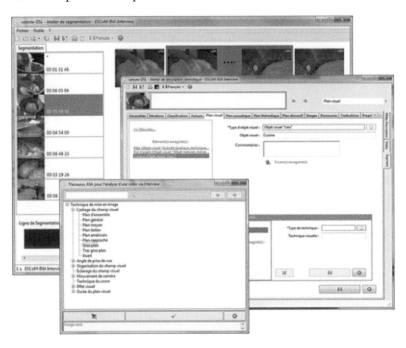

Figure 2.11. *Visualization of a selected segments visuals*

Chapter 3

Republishing Audiovisual Resources

3.1. Introduction

One of the main challenges of the ASW-HSS project is to link the online audiovisual texts to specific contexts of usage such as training, teaching, research, or even valorizing scientific (or, more widely, cultural) heritage.

As we know, an online audiovisual text does not, in general, necessarily fulfill a particular purpose *in its present state*. In other words, it is only a *potential resource* for specific purposes such as educational, scientific, or "communication". To become a truly relevant resource, it must be subject to a series of procedures for processing and analysis, such as the ones that we have examined in the previous chapters of this book (also see [STO 11a] for further details). These procedures include, for example:

– identifying and (virtually) extracting the segments which are more relevant than others;

– describing and indexing using description models which are closer to the needs and expectations of the target audience;

Chapter written by Peter STOCKINGER and Elisabeth DE PABLO.

– annotating (i.e. producing comments of various kinds) and re-contextualizing it in an intellectual reference field of production;

– partially translating it in a "target" language;

– publishing it as a text adapted to its target use.

These different procedures are also used for initial publications, that is, publishing a *lato sensu* corpus (see [STO 11a]) as well as for different updates, adaptations, "versions", and other republications. From a purely analytical perspective, we should distinguish between "publication" and "republication".

With the term *publication*, we mean an initial publication of a *lato sensu corpus* or selecting a field corpus. Under the term "republication", we will include any form of repeating an audiovisual text or a corpus of previously published texts.

Let us consider the simple but highly common example of recorded interviews. Publishing this kind of interview normally involves creating a "field" corpus (i.e. rushes or other texts), building a processing and analysis corpus, analyzing the corpus, and then publishing it on a site specifically for interviews or in another form (see [STO 11a] which describes the work process adapted to the ARA program in detail). We note that the publication process is, to a certain extent, punctuated by reference milestones which represent the creation of different types of audiovisual corpora (which may have a more of less brief material existence):

– a *field corpus* (*lato sensu*) is used to produce/collect the audiovisual data;

– an *analysis corpus* is the result of initial work by the analyst consisting of selecting audiovisual data relevant to its analysis;

– the *processed and analyzed corpus* which is the result of processing (techniques, montages, post-synchronization) and analysis;

– the *corpus published* based on a text genre.

Here, the *republication* process indicates the repetition either of the *published interview* (e.g. on a Website) or of one or several corpora used to publish the interview to create a new publication from it.

As such, republishing an interview can only involve changing, for example, a Website specifically for an interview with the researcher X in a thematic or educational folder. Here, we are speaking about republishing by genre (see below).

However, the republication process can also include re-examining a previously analyzed and processes corpus. Such a repetition can, for example, focus on the same previously analyzed audiovisual data but which is re-described, re-interpreted, and re-commented. The republication process can also focus on the audiovisual data which had not been considered during the initial analysis. In concrete terms, while republishing an interview with researcher X, some of the rushes (passages) which are not considered during the original publication may be reconsidered. Finally, the republication process could even involve returning to the original field corpus and adding to it (in the form of a new interview, for example).

The republication process therefore includes fairly complex but essential dynamics for "bringing to life" the audiovisual resources and adapting them to the needs and requirements of the target audience and developments in the areas of related knowledge.

In this chapter, we will limit ourselves to *publication and/or republication by type of publication*. We can recall that a published audiovisual corpus is accessible and can be explored and appropriated by an audience due to and via publication models or genres.

A main type of publication, that of *access* (which is thematic by type of audiovisual text, geographical or temporal location, specialized thesaurus, etc.), is described in detail in [STO 11a]. These publication models form the main part of the Web portal from which the audiovisual resources can be explored and used by the public.

A second type of publication is *event sites* which are central to the AAR program (see also [STO 11a]). The term "event" should be understood here in its broadest sense that is any occasion for which a field corpus has been collected and produced. For lack of a better term, "event" has the advantage, as we have seen in Chapter 1, of highlighting the reasons for which an audiovisual text has been created.

A third type of publication is composed of a series of *specialized genres* such as thematic, bilingual, and educational folders, or even narratives in the form of links between segments or passages which are part of several videos, Web documentaries, SMOs ("small multimedia objects"), and so on.

On the basis of the experiments on content carried out over several years[1], this chapter will develop in more detail several specialized genres of publications/republications which form the basis of the library of publication models in the *ASW Studio* work environment and, more specifically, its *Publication Workshop*.

Section 3.2 will briefly examine some of the issues involved in best situating the republication process in work with and around the audiovisual corpora. Sections 3.3–3.6 present the different types of publication which are part of the ASW Studio's library of publications in more detail.

3.2. Breakdown of the (re)publication process according to genre

There are a few online texts which can realistically serve as a resource for teaching, research, or even for communication valorization campaigns for scientific heritages or scientific work, and so on, are few and far between. In general, the "user" (teacher, student, trainer, researcher, editor, "communicator", etc.) of an online audiovisual text can provide more or less important additions and modifications to it in order to adapt it to his/her own intentions of use.

In other words, the user of an online audiovisual text D1 *becomes in turn the author* of a new text, D2, which has already been created from the text D1. The text, D2, can be a more or less faithful version of the text D1, a significant alteration, a more or less free version, a completely new creation, and so on. The text, D1 can be an "input" among others sources for the new text, D2 (see also Chapters 1 and 2). Between text D1 and new text, D2, we can identify relatively complex

---

1 Initial republication experiments have been carried out in two R&D projects, the French SAPHIR project (financed by the ANR): http://www.semionet.fr/FR/recherché/projets_recherche/06_09_saphir/saphir.htm, and the European LOGOS project (financed under the 6th EU PCRD).

intertextual relations which express, for example, a relationship of refutation (i.e. D2 refutes D1); spoof or parody (D2 as a parody of D1), a relationship of consensus; and epistemic reinforcement (D2 reinforces a vision or aim of D1), a relationship of causality (D2 is a consequence of D1); and so on.

These few examples of relationships between one or more texts open up a new field of exploration and experimentation around the production, dissemination, and sharing process as well as for the evolution of knowledge, a natural, social, historical, and cognitive process.

In all these cases, we are confronted with the question that was also discussed in the context of the knowledge industry, of *auctorial function* (see [STO 02]) and the profound consequences (intellectual, legal, economic, etc.) of questioning (more or less definitively) its traditional definition (i.e. in the sense of the author as a person or group of easily identifiable individuals). A very new, but already widespread example is that of *"rerecording" parts of audiovisual productions* (for example, reports from traditional television channels) by Internet users and Internet communities and republishing these segments on private, personal, or community based Web TV, made possible due to sites such as YouTube or Dailymotion.

In the original publication image, republishing an audiovisual text is, as we have already seen, a complex process which automatically takes place in an *intercultural* context defined on the one hand by the cultural profile of the potential addressee of the "new" text, D2. Note that the writing/rewriting process for an audiovisual corpus or part of it are cognitive processes of "communicating a message" and adapting it to the profile and cultural identity of the target audience. These cognitive processes are therefore (more or less successful or effective) "solutions" faced with large questions about any kind of communication.

Figure 3.1 shows an existing audiovisual text (e.g. an hour of video in a fixed framework recording a seminar from Master 2 in anthropology in the Quechua speaking world) can be published or republished as:

1. a recording of an audiovisual text, published in different contexts for different purposes;

2. an interactive video book (organized according to the traditional book format with its "formal devices" i.e. cover page, introduction, synopsis, bibliography, index of themes and places etc. and, of course, chapters and sections composed of a selection of segments from the source text etc.);

3. a thematic folder (split into several larger subjects, "isotopes" in semiotic terminology, around which a number of segments are arranged developing and discussing them, etc.);

4. a video-glossary (organized as a classical dictionary in a series of "key words" defined or commented on in chosen audiovisual segments);

5. an educational folder (organized as a traditional lesson with linear learning path providing little or no freedom to the user);

6. one or more narrative paths offering the user specific paths of exploration in the content in the original audiovisual text (these paths are organized according to the principles or "maxims" which are initially simple and become progressively more difficult or present general context followed by details etc.).

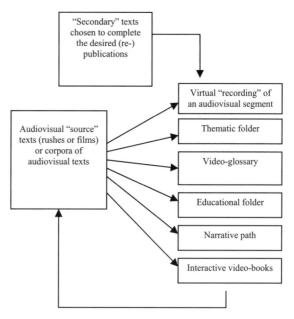

Figure 3.1. *Types of (re-)publication and relationship to an existing text*

There are many other types of republication (for example, "bilingual folders" which are extremely important in the multilingual context of the worldwide Web), however, the ASW-HSS project has focused on the six genres identified above.

3.3. "Rerecording" audiovisual texts

This is perhaps the simplest type of publication but it can be sufficient for a specific type of use. For example, an audiovisual segment (at most a whole text in total) interests a specific group of users (i.e. teacher or researcher) with the condition that this new segment may be published on a new Web page while being accompanied by explanations, comments, and potential links to other online resources. For example, a passage of 10 minutes as part of a seminar recording (of Master 2 level) which focuses on globalization for 80 minutes could be used by a teacher in a class on intercultural communication. However, to do so, he/she needs the ability to:

– "pick out" the passage (i.e. isolate and extract it virtually from the original recording);

– integrate it into an html page on the desired Website on intercultural communication;

– provide comments relating to the video's content;

– add helpful information for the students.

The result of this kind of usage is shown in Figure 3.2 This is an extract of a Master 2 level seminar in sociology given by Michel Wieviorka at the *Ecole des Hautes Etudes en Sciences Sociales* (EHESS) in Paris and which has been reused in a class on intercultural communication[2] at the *Institut National des Langues et Civilisations Orientales* (INaLCO), also in Paris.

The functional model underlying this example is shown in Figure 3.3 (for a theoretical and methodological explanation of the specifications of Web publications, see [STO 05, BEC 10]).

---

2 http://www.semionet.fr/FR/enseignement/annees/08_09/0809Cilm/Wieworka Globalisation 09.htm.

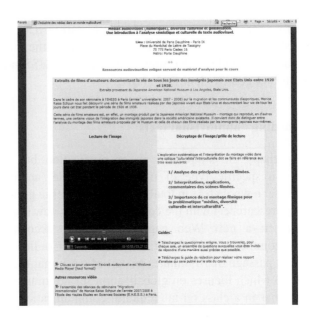

Figure 3.2. *Example of republication picking out a segment and its publication in a new context*

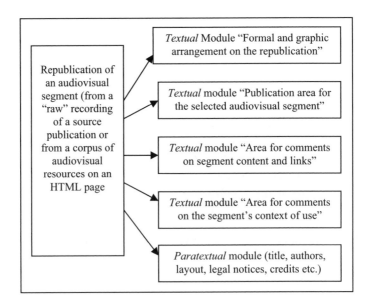

Figure 3.3. *Functional scheme specifying the main elements of the "Republication" publication model*

Five factors should be considered when generating a computer "re-recording" model for an audiovisual text on an HTML page in order to enable its "use" for adaptation to a specific context of use and social practice (teaching, research etc.):

– the HTML page itself must be able to perform both as a platform and resource for the publication (defining the formal and physical layout of the information, videos, graphic charts, etc.);

– the textual region where we will find the previously selected (and described, indexed, annotated, etc.) segment;

– three types of functionally specialized areas: first one is reserved for adding comments, links, and so on, relating to the audiovisual segment and/or its use, the second area is reserved for describing the context of use (teaching, research etc.). A third area is used for different *paratextual* elements such as the author, copyright, latest updates, and so on.

It goes without saying that an area type can be physically located in one or more "places" on an HTML page, depending on the author's editorial choice.

Figure 3.4 shows a typical framework for a publication model called "re-recording of a segment/audiovisual text" (implied – in a new context of dissemination/sharing).

Figure 3.4. *Model of the publication type "re-recording an audiovisual segment"*

3.4. Interactive video books

The (re-)publication genre "interactive video-book" refers to and relies on the traditional format of the "classic" book and its formal apparatus which have been developed during the course of its existence. Recording a conference of a specific length can be changed, if desired, into an online video book presented as a traditional book with a cover, title page, introduction, series of chapters (and segments) composed of audiovisual segments from the original recording, bibliographies, annexes, a back cover, and so on.

Figure 3.5. *Example of an interactive video-book published on the AAR program portal*

However, interactive videos can also be presented as a kind of "collective work" or "anthology". In this case, the segments composing the video-book's chapters come from different audiovisual resources such as, for example, a corpus of recordings of several interviews, conferences, seminars, and so on.

The interactive video-book is one of the publication models used in the *Archives Audiovisuelles de la Recherche* (ARA) program. Figure 3.5 provides a concrete example of this in the form of an interview with a researcher[3] in the form of a text which is divided into chapters and are freely searchable ("browsable") by the visitor/reader.

In the ASW-HSS project, this model had several important modifications to make it more flexible and more easily adaptable to specific and varied uses. For example:

– each chapter can be split into sections;

– a chapter will propose a series of information (comments etc.) on the content of a segment and/or its use (in a similar way to that used for "re-recording an audiovisual segment");

– the sequence of chapters will be semantically motivated (in a similar way to that for "narrative path" which we will examine shortly);

– audio-visual segments not only come from a single text source (as is the case for publications on the AAR portal) but also from a corpus of audiovisual texts (similar to an anthology or a collective work, in the classical sense of the term).

Figure 3.6 shows the functional layout which defines all the necessary elements for developing the computer model for the "interactive video-book" genre. Figure 3.7 shows this kind of concrete model which will be used in the ASW-HSS project.

The models represented in Figures 3.6 and 3.7 can be chosen beforehand to adapt them to both the editorial line of audiovisual library's site (in the case of the ASW-HSS project, this includes the CCA, LHE, ArkWork, PCIA libraries, etc.) and the expectations and interests of the community of users.

---

3 An interview with Jean-Yves Masson of University Paris IV Sorbonne by Muriel Chemouny, 23rd January as part of the AAR program and published on both the ARA and LHE portals, which is one of the ASW-HSS project's areas of interest: http://semioweb.msh-paris.fr/corpus/ALIA/1677/introduction.asp.

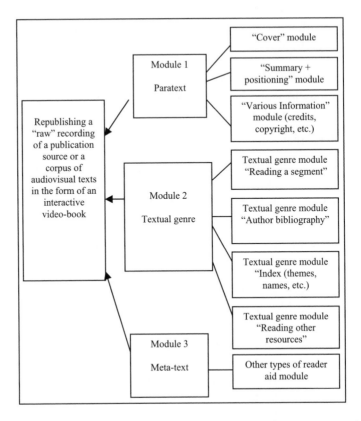

Figure 3.6. *Functional plan detailing the main elements of an interactive video*

Figure 3.7. *Model of the "interactive video-book" genre*

3.5. Thematic folders

The term "thematic folder" implies a type of publication (or republication) of audiovisual data on a chosen subject, that is a theme, issue, event, situation, personality, period, place, and so on.

An initial version of this type of (re)publication has already been defined and experimented with in the European LOGOS R&D project[4] with participation from ESCoM in their ARA program. Figure 3.8 provides a concrete example of a thematic folder. This is a republication of an interview with the Argentinean journalist Gregorio Manzur about the last descendents of the Huarpe[5] Indians living in extreme isolation in the Mendoza region of Argentina. As Figure 3.8 shows, the folder is composed of:

– a section entitled "Passages" which combines all the segments of the interview used to create the folder. This is a selection of "the most relevant moments" of the interview carried out by Gregorio Manzur given the subject of the thematic folder;

– a section "themes" classifying the folder's segments according to the themes covered (for example, some of the segments examine the natural environment where the last descendents of the Huarpe lived, whereas others consider the cruel history of colonization and the exploitation of the Huarps, others focusing on their popular beliefs etc. Of course, if relevant, a segment can be classified into two, even several themes);

– a section entitled "vocabulary" which lists alphabetically all the terms that are sufficiently and semantically rich to make them key words required for a better understanding of the subject in question (each selected term is a reference point in the segment(s) where it is defined and/or explained);

– finally, a section called "reading/using video content", proposed in the chosen segment (a segment is composed of a textual area

---

4 For more information, refer to the ESCoM Website under the section "Recherche" [research]: http://www.semionet.fr.

5 See the online version of this folder at the following address: http://www.culturalheritage.fr/803/introduction.asp.

reserved for the clip itself, textual areas proposing information complimenting the content developed in a chosen segment i.e. comments, links to other electronic resources, etc.).

Figure 3.8. *Example of a thematic folder focusing on the last descendants of the Huarpe living in the Mendoza region of Argentina*

However, the model for a thematic folder developed and tested in the LOGOS European research project has several major limitations, specifically the following two:

1) The selection of relevant segments is limited to a source recording (i.e. it does not cover a sample from a corpus of different audiovisual resources or different recording sources).

2) The selection of relevant segments is difficult to update (i.e. the addition and/or removal of segments is difficult to carry out once the folder has been published, limiting the usefulness of the thematic folder as a dynamic publication enabling us to account for the evolution of knowledge around a given subject).

In the ASW-HSS project, these two limitations are eliminated. The thematic folder dedicated to a knowledge subject (i.e. area, issue, period, etc.) is composed of a selection of segments from a corpus of different audiovisual texts (therefore produced previously by a community of authors) and can be easily updated by adding new segments or deleting/modifying already existent segments.

Figure 3.9 shows the functional scenario for this type of publication. Figure 3.10 shows the typical model used in the ASW-HSS project to create a "thematic folder" type publication/republication.

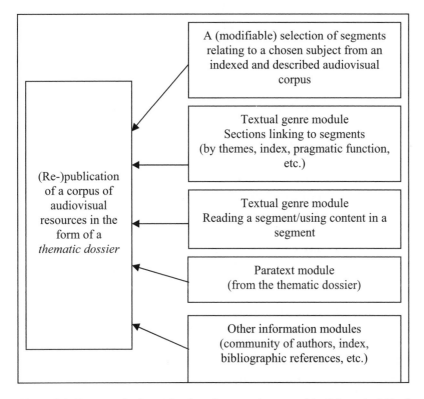

Figure 3.9. *Functional scheme detailing the main elements of the "thematic folder" publication model*

Figure 3.10. *Model of the "thematic folder" genre*

3.6. Educational folders

One of the most important uses of corpora of audiovisual texts focusing on scientific or cultural heritage is that of *education*, whether formal, non-formal, or informal. We know that life-long training (learning) is one of the key sectors of research and development in an information society based on an "intangible" economy or knowledge. Archives and audiovisual libraries are undoubtedly an indispensable and essential potential resource for this kind of project.

Thus, a quasi "natural" field of application and experimentation of all R&D activities dedicated to (re)publication of digital resources are constituted by teaching and learning in its broader sense. The publication/republication models presented in this report are essentially communication "strategies" aiming to improve the usage of (scientific) content by an audience engaged in a *lato sensu* learning/training process (i.e. not restricted to formal learning). However, among these models, it is educational folders which aim to optimize the use of new knowledge *step–by-step* following explicit validation *methods for acquired information*.

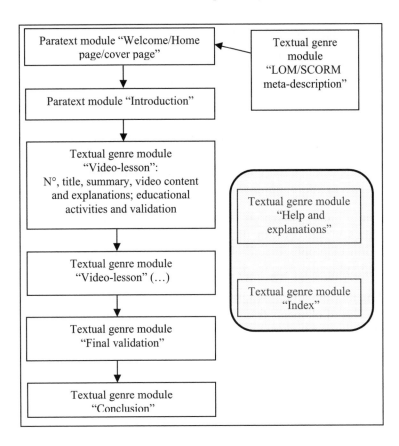

Figure 3.11. *Functional plan detailing the main elements
of an "educational folder"*

Figure 3.11 shows the main components of the context requiring this type of publication in the ASW-HSS project. It should be noted that an educational folder is mainly constructed based on a series of *video-lessons*. A video lesson is followed by another in a predefined learning path. A video lesson is typically structured as follows:

1) The title plus number of the lesson.

2) Summary of the lesson and its aims.

3) Reminders of previous lessons.

4) The textual area containing the video segment.

5) Explanations of the segment's content.

6) Explanations about using the content.

7) Proposed exercises, tests, research, and so on.

8) Checking answers.

The *paratextual* module "Introduction" should be fairly brief and propose an overall picture of the folder, its content and objectives, as well as its authors and contributors. It should also position the folder in relation to a formal/informal educational framework.

The "Final validation" model proposes exercises and other activities which contextualize and/or expand acquired knowledge in the form of proposed rereading of some segments, tests covering all the video lessons, new work, further reading, and so on.

Finally, the "LOM/SCORM metadescription" module is composed of a series of elements from the LOM.fr standard in order to make the ASW-HSS educational folder compatible with this standard's requirements.

Figure 3.12. *Publication module for an "educational folder"*

Figure 3.12 shows the model that will be used in the ASW-HSS project to publish and disseminate the educational folders created for the three pilot sites such as ARC, ALIA, and ADA.

3.7. Narrative path

Narrative path is a "syntagmatic" form of publication which enables the users of a library and/or an audiovisual archive to explore, in a progressive and structured way, an area of knowledge texted by an audiovisual corpus. Figure 3.13 demonstrates a typical case of linear exploration of an area or a subject using a range of relevant segments.

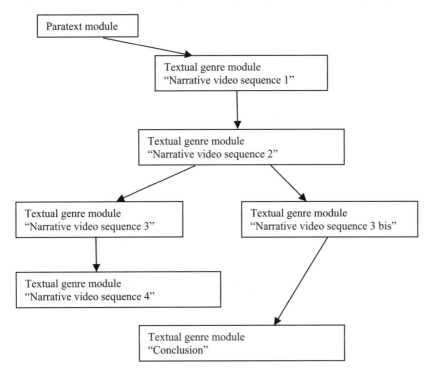

Figure 3.13. *Functional plan specifying the main elements of the "narrative path" publication model*

On the one hand, the arrangement of the segments presupposes that there is a selection of segments which are available (obtained thanks to the description and indexation of an audiovisual corpus) and, on the other hand, the choice of a specific type of path (see also [STO 99]). One type or genre of path is constructed based on *maxims*, or rules, such as:

– "from the most general to the most specialized" (i.e. initially, the audio-visual segments proposing easily understandable content, then only the segments with more specialized, less accessible content);

– "first examples then more theoretical developments" (i.e. first, the audiovisual segments providing concrete examples of a subject or topic, followed by the explanations and other more theoretical developments;

– "first, contributions from author(s), followed by the contributions of (an)other author(s) and so on".

There is, of course, a wide diversity in the type of syntagmatic construction *maxims* used to develop explorations of audiovisual corpora adapted to the profile and expectations of a targeted audience. The arrangement where a construction maxim is made between *video links* is called as a *video sequence*. Each video sequence is typically constructed as follows:

– title (of the segment);

– a brief summary (if available) of the segment;

– textual area containing the audiovisual segment;

– area containing various information relating to the segment (provided by the previous description/indexation of the segment);

– area proposing a more systematic exploration of the cognitive space belonging to the audiovisual segment (via key words, subjects, etc.).

In the ASW-HSS project, narrative paths have been developed and tested experimentally, but this type of publication has not been developed to a great extent. However, this will be approached in another research and development project dedicated solely to this topic.

PART 2

Audiovisual Archives, Knowledge Management and Cultural Heritage

Chapter 4

An Archive on the Intangible Cultural Heritage of Andean Populations in Peru and Bolivia

4.1. Introduction

As an innovative concept and object of large international consensus, Intangible Cultural Heritage (ICH) has generated a great amount of interest in both academic circles and the general public. Conducting our doctoral research on Peruvian sung poetry in Quechua[1], we have attempted to better understand how this oral tradition which is locally viewed as a living heritage could also be recognized internationally due to the ICH[2] concept. This perspective is of particular interest because, far from being a mere simple theoretical object, ICH is a new type of categorization which plays an active role in revalorizing traditions that have long been ignored or neglected.

Chapter written by Valérie LEGRAND-GALARZA.

1 A PhD thesis in anthropology entitled "Les chants *"wayno"* en langue Quechua: un patrimoine immatériel andin (région de Cuzco, Pérou)" ["Wayno" songs in Quechua: an Andean intangible cultural heritage], CERLOM (*Centre d'Etudes et de Recherche sur les Littératures et les Oralités du Monde*), INaLCO (*Institut National des Langues et Civilisations Orientales*).

2 See the 2003 UNESCO Convention for the Safeguarding of the Intangible Cultural Heritage (17th Oct 2003, in force with effect from 20th April 2006).

Recognizing orality in native languages through actions of promotion has proved to be of increasing importance in Peru and Bolivia where the Quechua language remains strongly undervalued in comparison to Spanish.

As such, we have dedicated a large part of our research to cooperating with cultural and scientific institutions[3] working on living heritages to reflect on different ways of treating and promoting them. In this purpose, we have therefore collaborated in two projects, the French ASW-HSS project[4] and the European Convergence project[5], in which we are developing an audiovisual archive on intangible heritages of Andean populations in Peru and Bolivia[6] (see Figure 4.1). The ASW-HSS and Convergence projects provide researchers with a completely new possibility to preserve, archive, describe, and publicize living traditions using pioneering and attractive multimedia platforms which enable interactive reproductions of these traditions and encourage their revitalization. In the era of new technologies, it is increasingly important to consider their appeal to new generations and the potential of multimedia platforms for revalorizing threatened cultural heritages.

In this chapter, we will introduce our audiovisual portal "Intangible Cultural Heritage of Andean populations" (ICHA) which is one of the ASW-HSS's areas of study. We will initially examine the scientific methodology used in the project and our ethical and participative approach. We will then develop the structure of the personal description

---

3 ARA (Audiovisual Research Archives) at ESCOM-FMSH (www.archives audiovisuelles.fr), the Intangible Cultural Heritage sector on the UNESCO (www.unesco.org/culture/ich/) and the IREPI Program (*Inventaire des Ressources Ethnologiques du Patrimoine Immatériel* [Inventory of Ethnological Resources for Intangible Heritage]) at Lavel University of Quebec, Canada (www.irepi.ulaval.ca/).
4 See the project's official site: http://www.asa-shs.fr/
5 See the project's official site: http://www.ict-convergence.eu/
6 "Andean populations" refers to the populations living in the Andes in Peru and Bolivia in South America, at altitudes ranging between 1,500 and 5,000 m. My project focuses specifically on Andean populations in Southern Peru, particularly the Cuzco region, where I am conducting my doctoral research and the Cochabamba region in Bolivia. Among these populations, there are both urban and rural areas where there are two types of communities: *"centros poblados"* (small populated centers) and rural communities called *"comunidades campesinas"*, agricultural administrative district's based on collective land ownership.

library, while focusing on the Intangible Cultural Heritage (ICH) model. Finally, we will consider the main aims, objectives, and future perspectives of the project in research, teaching, and field of culture.

Figure 4.1. *Map showing the different dialects of Quechuan,*
C. Itier, J. Robert, IFEA 2010

4.2. Scientific methodology and ethical and participative approaches

Our aim to develop an audiovisual portal on the living cultural heritages of Andean populations is motivated by the following two main objectives:

– archiving and publishing our research on a scientific, interactive, and globally accessible platform which allows a better reproduction than the traditional written format;

– promoting and valorizing the living traditions of Andean populations via an attractive media for new generations and which may help to revitalize these traditions.

In the context of creating an archive on the ICH of Andean populations, we have developed a range of ethical and scientific procedures in order to respect the people involved and ensure the longevity of collected materials. In the first section, we will therefore examine our methodology used to collect and publish the living cultural heritages as well as our ethical and participative approach.

4.2.1. *Scientific methodology for collecting and processing intangible cultural heritages*

Our scientific methodology relies, on the one hand, on an anthropological approach based on the field ethnographic investigation using description, participative observation, interviews, and audio and video recordings of everyday activities, and celebrations. This approach has enabled us to identify the main subjects for our portal, which we will examine in section 4.2.1.1. On the other hand, we were also inspired by other cultural institutions working on ICH[7] to adjust our processing procedures to account for current legislation and new technologies. In the rest of this chapter, we will therefore examine the different methodological stages of collecting and processing the living cultural heritages published on the AICH portal.

4.2.1.1. *Preliminary information and informed consent*

When publishing or using ICH data, we initially need to ask for "informed consent", either orally or in writing, from the people or communities concerned. *Informed consent*[8] is a request for agreement, accompanied by prior information about those leading the project, the investigation's purposes and objectives, the type of activities carried out (recordings, transcriptions, translations, etc.), and the future treatment of the collected data (archiving, publishing, online publication, etc.). Information and requests for consent should obviously be adapted to the aims of the investigation, the information being collected, data and the people involved, accounting specifically for their language and mode of communication (i.e. whether Quechua or Spanish, oral or written), and their mode of social organization (i.e. individual or collective)[9].

---

7 In July 2008, we participated in the IREPI program (Inventory of Ethnological Resources for Intangible Heritage) at Laval University in Quebec, Canada (www.irepi.ulaval.ca/) and also spent five months working in the UNESCO Intangible Cultural Heritage sector in Paris (www.unesco.org/ culture/ich/).
8 See [BAU 06].
9 The consent form should be adapted to the type of community where it is being used. It would, for example, be difficult to ask for individual consent for an oral culture where individual rights have no meaning.

We created an ASW (Audiovisual Semiotics Workshop) attestation in Spanish[10], specifying our aims and the main information about the project. In order to work in a formal framework, we decided to develop a written consent model in the form of various alternatives, creating real choices for people involved who can freely accept or refuse certain modes of publication for data (i.e. an agreement to put it online but not to describe the video)[11]. This contract model and its signature have also been adapted for collective usage, thereby enabling the people involved to sign collectively via a representative or a series of individual signatures. When a signed written contract is not possible, the agreement is made orally in the language of the speakers and according to the same terms as the written model. This oral agreement is also recorded digitally to preserve it to the same extent as a paper document.

When recording a carnival in a bilingual community (Quechua and Spanish speaking), we obtained "collective" authorization from a rural community by presenting our intentions orally in both Quechua and Spanish in front of the community authorities present at the celebration who, after having questioned certain points, conferred and finally accepted the collective request on the condition that we provide them with a DVD copy of the collected material and it would not be used for commercial purposes. Information and consent are therefore an essential stage when carrying out research because, beyond merely being a question of ethics, they allow us to build confidence and generate interest among the people who are involved in the research.

4.2.1.2. *Audiovisual filming and recording*

4.2.1.2.1. Interviews

We conducted a number of interviews in both Quechua and Spanish with different persons in towns and rural communities: individuals, authorities, musicians, craftspeople, dancers, specialists, and anthropologists, both as individuals or in a collective way. Our interview method relied on creating an open interview guide either in Spanish or in Quechua which was adapted thematically to the person

---

10 See "Attestation_ASA_Valerie_fr "and "Attestation_ASA_Valerie_es" at the following address: semioweb.msh-paris.fr:8080/site/projets/logasa/spip.php?rubrique33
11 See: "Form_ASA_Valerie_fr" and "Form_ASA_Valerie_es" at the following address: semioweb.msh-paris.fr:8080/site/projets/logasa/spip.php?rubrique29

being interviewed. The interview was carried out in the form of a conversation recorded on audio and/or an audiovisual medium without any limit on its length or number of subjects, so as to give free reign to everyone's comments and opinions.

4.2.1.2.2. Cultural events

With respect to oral traditions or celebrations, most often we recorded songs and folk tales in context, but we also asked people to undertake performances out of context. In these cases, we also carried out parallel interviews which we integrated into the montage to provide comments and interpretations of the performance.

4.2.1.2.3. Recording material

To collect our field data, we used both audio and audiovisual digital recording equipment as well as a camera to construct our corpus of data and conveyed the results of our research in the final publication as faithfully and as extensively as possible. Our choice of material was guided by our research objectives and field conditions. We therefore decided to use an AVCHD (a new format) digital camera with an internal 120 GB memory disk and additional memory cards providing a large degree of freedom while filming, thus using a large memory capacity which requires less memory space on the computer, enabling us to record in new formats (HD, Blu Ray).

4.2.1.3. *Saving, indexing, and archiving collected data*

Having completed our filming and recording, the next step consists of saving and indexing the collected data on perennial bases and in a logical archiving system.

4.2.1.3.1. Saving video files

Copying digital video files is both simple and fast without the need to encode analog signals as in the case of mini-DV cameras. With the aim of ensuring the longevity of our data, we have backed up our video files in computers as well as in different external disks stored in different locations, as normally recommended[12]. Following this, the

---

12 See the recommendations of the *Bibliothèque nationale de France* in their guide: "Écrire un cahier des charges de numérisation de collections sonores, audiovisuelles

same files are also backed up on to the FMSH servers and then – as registration of copyright – in the *Bibliothèque nationale de France* (BnF).

4.2.1.3.2. Indexing and archiving systems

When copying the digital files, we also transfer all the metadata, or contextual information, regarding the recording, such as:

– date (day, month, year, potentially the exact time as well, if relevant);

– the exact location (village, region, province, etc.);

– duration/length;

– name of people/communities being recorded;

– language;

– type (e.g. story, song, interview, ritual);

– themes involved (e.g. an interview on making a charango).

This information is essential both for scientifically archiving the collected data and completing the different fields in the ASW's Description Workshop. With the aim of giving our research data longevity, we have also attempted to create a logical and durable archive structure adapted to our data and able to evolve with their accumulation. We have therefore created a digital inventory video file[13] which enables their classification and indexing.

4.2.1.4. *Treating and analyzing data*

4.2.1.4.1. Editing the audiovisual material

The first stage in processing our audiovisual data consists of editing the collected raw material. This involves creating simple video montages containing the main information related to the filmed event

---

et filmiques" [Writing a specification for digitalizing audio, audiovisual and film collections], Ministry of Culture and Communication, Digital Management Committee, Mission de la Recherche et de la Technologie, August 2009.

13 Digital references are recommended for archiving files. See the BnF's recommendations on this subject: [BNF 09].

(titles, sequences, chapters, copyright, etc.) which, if necessary, also includes audio or video extracts of interviews relating to the event and providing further comments on it. Following the editing stage, we export the finished montage into two current widely used publication formats, MPEG 2 DVD and MPEG 4. We then carried out the different conversions into the publication formats used by the ASW-HSS and Convergence projects.

4.2.1.4.2. Analyzing and interpreting the data

Once the audiovisual materials had been edited and converted, we then analyzed them using the ASW Description Workshop (see Chapters 3 and 5 and also [STO 11a]) and created multimedia folders on the themes found in our portal. We also produced textual transcriptions and translations of the videos in Quechua to create a corpus of texts within the framework of our doctoral research.

4.2.1.4.3. Publication and uploading the files online

Finally, we published our videos on two types of platforms:

– DVD: we locally released our videos on DVD by providing the videos to the people involved and those who participated in local research and promotion projects on oral traditions.

– Internet portal: we placed the commented videos online using the ASW studio's Publication Workshop (see Chapters 8, 9, and 10 and also [STO 11a]).

4.2.2. *An ethical and participative approach: recognizing and involving people and communities in collecting their heritage*

Beyond being a simple archiving platform, the ICH portal on Andean populations is also designed to be a means of expression for local populations, thereby conveying their knowledge, products, and performances providing a voice to the holders of these traditions and the populations involved. This approach becomes even more important with Quechua speaking populations where written practice is still under developed and whose main expectations involve revalorizing their language, speech, and heritage.

We have therefore decided to develop this portal in close cooperation with the populations involved to allow them to actively participate in the project and reflect on the different ethical and legal considerations involved in research about cultural heritages. One of the key issues raised by the UNESCO Convention for the Safeguarding of the Intangible Cultural Heritage (ICH) is the involvement of peoples and communities in identifying and managing their heritages. Involving communities introduces a range of legal issues with respect to their rights over collected materials and the obligations of researchers and institutions toward them[14], notably regarding cooperation and returning data. These demands also conform to the recommendations of the 2003 UNESCO convention for the safeguarding of the ICH which places great emphasis on recognizing the role of communities and individuals in cultural heritage intervention programs and enables them to be active in making decisions about their ICH[15].

4.2.2.1. *The rights of peoples and communities over content*

The creation of a Web portal which publishes living cultural heritages in the public domain raises legal questions, notably about

---

14 Since the 1989 recommendation about protecting traditional culture and folklore, the international scientific community has been encouraged to "adopt an appropriate ethics for approach and respect for traditional cultures". The Washington Conference on global evaluation following a recommendation in 1989 requested UNESCO (in its 5th recommendation) to "encourage international groups (researchers, cultural experts etc.) to create and adopt ethics codes which ensure that appropriate and respectful procedures are followed toward the traditional culture and folklore" [BAU 06].

15 "*Recognizing that communities, in particular indigenous communities, groups and, in some cases, individuals, play an important role in the production, safeguarding, maintenance and recreation of the intangible cultural heritage, thus helping to enrich cultural diversity and human creativity*" (2003 UNESCO Convention for the Safeguarding of the Intangible Cultural Heritage: Introduction). From this approach, communities, groups or individuals are encouraged to actively participate in implementing the convention: "*Within the framework of safeguarding activities of the intangible cultural heritage, each State Party shall endeavor to ensure the widest possible participation of communities, groups and, where appropriate, individuals that create, maintain and transmit such heritage, and to involve them actively in its management*". (Article 15: Participation of communities, groups and individuals).

rights over content and publication rights concerning data collection practices and using oral data[16] (see Chapter 9).

In the case of ICH the issue of authorship rights often appears to be problematic because the concepts of "author" or "knowledge ownership" are not transcultural. With regards to the rights of the author[17], the law currently recognizes three categories of author:

– *single author*: the person or entity provided with legal status;

– *collective works*: the person or entity having created the work has authorship rights;

– *collaborative works*: each author has the same entitlements.

These norms and type of classification come from the European system which does not always correspond to local realities. Our anthropological experience in Peru demonstrated the need to adapt our approach to the kind of currently existing local notions about intellectual property and link up European law with that of rural communities which are based on collective organization, where individual property is not relevant concerning oral tradition. The majority of oral products are not considered as the "property" of an individual author, rather as a particular interpretation of collective traditions. These traditions should be recognized both by the person interpreting it and the community as a whole. As Jocelyne Pierre and Sylvie Grenet (see [GRE 08]) have suggested, it may be wiser to add categories such as *author* and *collectives of creators*, "such as '*living communities*' (country, ethnicity, village etc.) seeking to be recognized as holders of an intangible asset".

The collaborative work conducted with these communities has enabled us to reflect not only on the adaptation of "official" legal

---

16 About these issues, see [BAU 06] which offers both extensive reflection and useful methodologies for approaching legal problems relating to ICH. See also Marie Cornu [COR 03]: "*Droits des biens culturels et des archives*" [Rights over cultural goods and archives], 2003, at the following link: www.educnet.education.fr/chrgt/ biensculturels. pdf

17 The author's rights is an "exclusive intangible property right, enforceable against all, which includes all moral prerogatives (right to disclosure, authorship, right to the work's integrity, right of withdrawal) enjoyed by the author over his/her work by the mere fact of its creation" [BAU 06].

norms, but also on different aspects of the project requiring revision from the community view point and according to a precise socio-cultural reality. After investigation, the ASW Studio has therefore been adapted to account for such cultural specifics. A category "Collective entity" has been added to describe the video's actors, thereby allowing us to account for all types of groups or collective grouping, such as an institution or even a cultural community. The ability to select multiple languages in the videos has also been added to the "generalities" tab of the video which enable us to describe bilingual or multilingual situations. These two modifications represent a genuine improvement to our portal which includes various videos filmed in rural bilingual (Quechua/Spanish) communities. In this context, it is essential to be able to identify the social community involved and indicate the two languages in the description of these videos.

4.2.2.2. Returning data to peoples and communities

Throughout our research in Peru and our work experiences with institutions focusing on living cultural heritages, the issue of returning information to people and communities has always been a crucial ethical issue. Being present on the ground often involves long-term expectations and it is therefore reasonable that researchers listen to the expectations of communities and reflect on means of restitution to them, ranging from returning data, to creating community projects.

Within a reciprocal research project, we were fully committed to returning the collected data to the people or communities involved in the form of an edited DVD or raw video files. This also allows the populations to use the data concerning them and reuse it in the future, that is to create new DVDs, promote their heritage, or even build new local archives. Giving material data is also part of the consent application, thereby requiring the researcher to contribute to the local patrimonialization of knowledge.

4.2.2.3. Cooperation and action research

Currently, many communities have precise claims over the research concerning them. In Peru, we have been widely solicited to contribute to implementing local cultural revalorizing initiatives. One of the most successful solutions for responding to these expectations consists of involving communities or their members in research through effective and reciprocal cooperation between the researchers and holders of traditions. It is for this reason that in the ASW-HSS and Convergence projects, we have created a partnership convention[18], in both French and Spanish, aimed at establishing formal cooperation between ESCoM-FMSH (the main partner in the ASW-HSS project and in the European Convergence consortium) and all local collective organizations whether cultural centers, official institutions, or rural communities. The main axes of cooperation of this convention concern both cooperation with regard to research materials (research aids i.e. access to archives, borrowing materials or premises, exchanging data, researching financing in implementing the community projects and creating networks of researchers, teachers, and specialists) and collaborating in using scientific data (publication, communication, Internet publications, multimedia productions, and educational tools). Through this, we established several partnerships with organizations such as the Centro Bartolomé de las Casas (CBC)[19] research center in Cuzco, the "Qhapaqñan" heritage program[20] at the National Institute of Culture of Peru and several rural communities in the Cuzco area.

Beyond this simple collaboration, we can also develop community projects through action research[21], by actively involving communities

---

18 See "Convention_partenariat_ASA_Valerie_fr" and "Convention_ partenariat_ ASA_ Valerie_es" at the following address: semioweb.msh-paris.fr:8080/ site/projets/ logasa/ spip.php?rubrique30.

19 CBC: Regional Studies Center Bartolomé de las Casas (Cuzco, Peru): NGO, research center and guest house for people coming from Cuzco's provinces. We have been associated with this center since 2008.

20 The "Qhapaqñan" program is designed to collect, restore and valorize various surviving Inca paths in Peru so that they are recognized as "World Heritage of Humanity" by UNESCO. We have therefore collaborated with them in collecting and valorizing Quechua oral traditions alongside archeological works on these paths.

21 According to Hugon and Seibel (Hugon, M.A. & Seibel, C. eds (1988), *Recherches impliquées. Recherches action: Le cas de l'éducation* [Involved research. Research action: the case of education], Brussels, De Boeck: 13) the concept of action-research refers to "research where there is a deliberate action to change reality; research has a dual objective: to transform reality and raise awareness about these changes" (Hugon and Seibel, 1988: 13). For more than 50 years, a scientific approach in social sciences called action-research has emerged and has been developed globally, notably in the U.S. and Canada. This methodology in social sciences involves both the researcher

and encouraging the exchange of knowledge and skills, creating a new kind of interactivity between researchers, communities, and the public. Research-action therefore aims to provide the results of the investigation in different media which are hopefully more often than not accessible to all. Depending on the context and preferences of those involved, this can include specialized training for learning technical skills, creating a Web portal or building a local cultural center, organizing cultural events or even getting populations to take part in education programs. We will focus on this kind of activity in more detail when we examine the aims and objectives of the ICH portal[22].

4.3. The Andean intangible cultural heritage portal

In this section, we will examine the ICH portal itself. We will begin by taking into account the reasons for creating an audiovisual archive on intangible heritage. Following this, we will look at the structure and description library of the ICH portal, focusing on the four main description models developed.

4.3.1. *Why have a portal for Andean cultural heritage?*

Conducting our research in Peru for more than 8 years on forms of a sung oral tradition in Quechua, *waynos*, we became aware of the risk of extinction of this musical art and the importance of recognizing it to ensure its continuation. In this purpose, we collaborated with cultural institutions working on collecting and disseminating oral traditions to acquire scientific knowledge and technical skills which we could then use to process, disseminate, and valorize the living heritage in question. These experiences introduced us to the concept of "intangible cultural heritage" which appear to be not only relevant as a conceptual category for our research but also useful for revalorizing. According to the UNESCO definition in the Convention for the Safeguarding of the Intangible Cultural Heritage (published on 17th October 2003, and which came into force with effect from 20th April 2006), intangible

---

and those involved in the investigations in the research process through participative action such as involving local populations and spreading knowledge about them.
22 See section 4.4 "Interests and perspectives of the project".

heritage includes "practices, representations, expressions, knowledge, skills – as well as the instruments, objects, artifacts, and cultural spaces associated therewith – that communities, groups and, in some cases, individuals recognize as part of their cultural heritage. This intangible cultural heritage, transmitted from generation to generation, is constantly recreated by the communities and groups in response to their environment, their interaction with nature and their history, and provides them with a sense of identity and continuity, thereby promoting respect for cultural diversity and human creativity".

This is therefore the main motivation for designing a portal on the intangible heritage of Andean populations which we will now define more precisely.

4.3.1.1. *The intangible: an innovative concept introducing new perspectives*

Used for the first time during the 1982 "World Conference on Cultural Policies"[23], the expression "intangible heritage" relates to the phenomena that have always existed and coexisted with "material heritage", recognized more than 30 years previously[24]. The discrepancy between these two conventions is significant, not only of the hierarchy between the two types of heritage but of the Western conceptualization of the notion of heritage. For example, in France, the term *Intangible Cultural Heritage* can appear contradictory because the majority of conceptions on heritage relate to the "material". Recognizing an "intangible" property of heritage therefore involves deconstructing our perceptions of heritage and viewing it from a new perspective.

This dynamic perspective, while new to France, is however not new in many countries where oral traditions have always played a decisive part in the definition of the cultural identity. In the Andes, speaking about the heritage or oral tradition is not considered as an innovation. It is for this reason that in 1973 Bolivia was the first to draft a proposal to

---

23 A conference organized by UNESCO lasting from the 26th July to the 6th August 1982 in Mexico. The transcript of this conference "Mexico City Declaration" can be found on the UNESCO Website.
24 "Convention Concerning The Protection of World Cultural and Natural Heritage" (Paris, 16th November 1972).

UNESCO regarding the protection and promotion of folklore. Thirty years before the 2003 Convention on the Safeguarding of the Intangible Heritage, this Andean country had already raised the question of broadening the scope of cultural protection beyond the material heritage (see [LES 04]). The term "intangible" was therefore introduced by UNESCO, guided by a general desire to fill the gap left by the 1972 Convention which had created a disproportion in the distribution of material heritage between the Northern and Southern hemispheres; with Europe having more than 50% of sites registered on the list of cultural heritage sites, while those in Sub-Saharan Africa account for less than 15% (see [SME 04]). This new designation was therefore a more ideological than explicative move, aiming both to recognize forgotten sides, of heritages and to break the use of former terminology such as "folklore"[25], which can often have negative connotations.

The fundamental factor largely encouraging the use of the term "ICH" is therefore the differentiation it creates with other pre-existing categories, therefore allowing us to institute the necessary reassessment of our considerations. This concept therefore provides a new perspective on continually evolving living and creative cultural processes, encouraging us to focus our attention on dynamic elements and the holders of these human heritages.

4.3.1.2. The issue of a new conceptual category

The ICH term has also introduced a new concept reuniting a range of practices which had previously been relegated to various areas of research such as oral literature, traditional music, or even arts and crafts. This term therefore creates a new category of identification which allows us to consider the practices as part of the same area of study and to think of them in relation to one another.

By including a range of undervalued practices in the "prestigious" term "heritage", this also creates a new patrimonial dynamic

---

25 Designing at the beginning the people's knowledge (Folk: people, Lore: knowledge), the term "folklore" included the range of a people's collective output passed down from one generation to another orally or, through the current example of ICH. However, since the 1960s, folklore has developed in French negative connotations, referring to superficial manifestations which imitate, deform and fossilize "tradition".

encouraging the recognition of these practices. The ICH term is in fact very popular in countries that saw an opportunity to promote the value and visibility of their traditions which until now had not been recognized internationally. Precisely with this aim in view, we have chosen to name our portal "The Andean intangible cultural heritage" in order to valorize the existing knowledge, tradition, and crafts of this culture at an international level.

4.3.2. Structure and themes of the portal

To create our portal, it was necessary to reflect on local representations of heritage to identify the subjects of the portal and construct relevant and representative classification and description categories (see Table 16.2).

4.3.2.1. Identifying subjects

To select the subjects in our portal, we undertook ethnographic investigations among the local populations. By carrying out our field research on oral traditions in the Cuzco region for more than 8 years, we became familiar with the various expressions of celebration and cultural events characteristic of the region. To build our portal, we have therefore chosen the heritages which are most representative of the regions studied and which are most relevant from a local perspective. We have therefore drawn up an inventory of the main subjects through interviews with local populations to identify those elements which were recognized locally as having both an identity and patrimonial value. This was based on the statements citing the importance of these subjects for the region or community in question and the significance of handing this information down to future generations, so that these elements do not disappear.

There are therefore four main local principles identifying a subject as patrimonial:

– local significance and recognition of the subject;

– pride in representing an identity through practices or knowledge;

– the issue of protecting these traditions for future generations faced with the risk of disappearing;

– transmitting and diffusing knowledge and cultural ideologies through these practices.

In order to determine the value and importance of these traditions, we have also considered their functions in the concerned local populations, knowing that these diverse roles may be combined in the same heritage:

– *social functions*: establishing or reinforcing social links between groups or individuals through links of kinship, affinity, or even power. For example, the ritual of cutting hair for the first time creates a spiritual relationship of kinship during the child's christening;

– *identity functions*: reinforcing and valorizing the identity of a specific group internally and externally. For example, weaving or cooking are the activities that denote a specific local identity;

– *educational functions*: passing on knowledge and fundamental cultural elements to new generations. For example, oral traditions often fulfill educational functions such as stories about choosing a spouse, or riddles teaching about local flora and fauna;

– *spiritual functions*: establishing, reinforcing, or even articulating the relationship between man, nature, and deities. For example, ritual offerings to *pachamama* (mother earth) and *apus* (mountain gods) forge spiritual links to request harmony and fertility in the forthcoming year.

An event, practice, or even words can constitute intangible heritage when considered as a medium for local knowledge and a specific cosmovision. Intangible heritages are in effect human representations and vectors of identifying values, expressing an ethic and particular vision of the natural and social environment through specific symbols in each culture.

4.3.2.2. *Classification and nomenclature*

Our classification and nomenclatures originate from both native categories and UNESCO's official categorization with respect to the ICH. We have therefore attempted to define the description categories which are as close as possible to social reality and are justified from a local perspective and are relevant in the framework of international research.

In this framework, we followed the pattern of the five categories of ICH expression defined by UNESCO[26]:

– oral expressions and traditions, including language as a vector of the ICH;

– performing arts;

– social practices, rituals, and celebratory events;

– knowledge and practices on nature and the universe;

– knowledge about traditional arts and crafts.

From the UNESCO model and the listed subjects, we have identified 11 primary categories enabling us to logically regroup and classify the different subjects (see Table 4.1):

1. *The Quechua language*: the language is both considered as a vector of ICH and as an ICH in its own right. We have chosen to focus on the Quechua language spoken in the two regions little studied because this language is still documented and is threatened by Spanish. This section includes interviews with researchers and academics about the structure and use of Quechua, video extracts of oral varieties of Quechua in different regions, language registers, and videos about teaching the Quechua language.

2. *Oral expressions and traditions*: transferred via speech, oral traditions and expressions are used to transmit the knowledge, collective memory, and cultural and identifying values. These expressions are a combination, – variable according to genre, context and artist – of imitations, improvisation, and creation. This category resembles oral performances by classifying them according to the mode of enunciation in different forms, whether narrative, sung, poetic, short and stereotypical or incantatory.

3. *Music*: musical arts are presented in more diverse ways, whether religious or secular, classical or popular, related to work or entertainment or with a political or economic dimension. The occasions where music is used can also be varied: weddings, funerals, rituals and rites of passage, festivities, entertainment, as well as other social contexts.

---

26 See the introduction of the 2003 UNESCO Convention for the Safeguarding of the Intangible Cultural Heritage.

Music is therefore often an integral part of other forms of performing arts and other areas of intangible cultural heritage such as rituals, festive events, or oral traditions. This category also includes interviews with musicians and musical practices, whether free performances, concerts, or musical performances accompanying a ritual or celebration.

4. *Living arts*: the area of "living arts" includes different types of art performances such as body art (coordinated significant body movements conveying a symbolic message) and theatrical or stage arts. This category also includes physical arts such as dance and theater.

5. *Rituals and celebrations*: rituals and celebrations are customary activities structuring the lives of people and communities by reaffirming the identity and cultural values of those participating in it. These practices remind a community of certain aspects of their conception of the world, their history and memories on the occasion of important events taking place in specific times and places outside of daily occurrence. These practices also contribute to marking extraordinary occasions in both individual and collective life, such as the passing of seasons, times in the agricultural calendar, the human lifecycle, or even periods in history. This section includes two types of practices, rituals and celebratory occasions.

6. *Knowledge and practices on nature and the universe*: knowledge and practices concerning the nature and the universe include a wide range of information, expertise, practices, and detailed representations developed by communities in their interactions with their social, natural, and supernatural environment which constitute their identity. This area includes numerous elements such as traditional knowledge about the environment, indigenous knowledge, knowledge relating to flora and fauna, traditional medicines, cosmology, shamanism, or even social structure. This domain can be further subdivided into three main categories: knowledge and practice about nature (e.g. indigenous classifications, climatic predictions, farming livestock, agricultural expertise, and practices), knowledge and practices concerning human beings (i.e. healing methods and practices, notions about the body and soul), and knowledge and practices regarding the universe and the supernatural (e.g. cosmovision, astronomical concepts, and classification of supernatural beings).

Categories	Types of subjects	Examples
Quechua language	Interviews about Quechua	*Interview with C. Itier (linguist)*
	Varieties of Quechua	*Samples of different regional varieties of Quechua*
	Teaching Quechua	*Lessons in Quechua at the INaLCO*
Oral expressions and traditions	Narrative forms	*Stories, historical narratives*
	Sung forms	*Sung genres: waynos, carnivals*
	Poetic forms	*Harawis (Andean poems), waynos*
	Short, stereotypical forms	*Riddles*
	Incantatory forms	*Ritual prayers*
Music	Interviews with musicians	*Interview on the use of instruments*
	Musical practices	*Concerts, musical performances*
Living arts	Dances	*Indigenous carnival dances*
	Performances	*Inti Raymi (ancient Inca festival of the sun)*
Rituals and celebrations	Rituals	*Fertility rituals, first haircut*
	Celebrations and festivals	*Festival of Q'eswa Chaka (Inca bridge)*
Knowledge and practices on nature and the universe	Knowledge and practices on nature	*Classifications of flora and fauna, agricultural and pastoral knowledge and practices*
	Knowledge and practices about human beings	*Healing Practices, notions of the body and soul*
	Knowledge and practices about the universe and supernatural	*Knowledge of astronomy, climactic predictions*
Arts and crafts	Weaving	*Weaving methods, meaning of motifs*
	Ceramics	*Pottery making techniques*
	Musical Instrument making	*Making Andean instruments*
Culinary traditions	Traditional dishes	*Silpancho (Bolivia), Chiri Uchhu (Peru)*
	Traditional drinks	*Chicha (maize beer), Guarapo (grapes)*
	Culinary techniques	*Drying methods (corn, meat)*
Politics	Representations of power	*Presidential elections 2011 (Peru)*
	Political structures	*Community political structures*
Research and teaching about the Andes	Researchers and teachers	*Interview with G. Urton (historian)*
	Lessons and seminars	*Seminar by G. Rivière (anthropologist)*
	Academic events	*Martes campesinos local debates*

Table 4.1. *Structure and subjects of the portal on Andean intangible cultural heritage*

7. *Arts and crafts*: The area of expertise related to arts and crafts includes the entirety of processes, knowledge, and expertise necessary for artisan production. Emphasis is placed on "immaterial" elements accompanying material production. There are a number of arts and crafts expressions, among which we will focus on three of the most representatives: textile crafts, musical instrument making, and ceramics.

8. *Culinary traditions*: culinary traditions include traditional dishes and drinks (e.g. maize beer), food knowledge, culinary practices (the method of cooking underground), and ways of preserving food (e.g. drying potatoes).

9. *Politics*: this area includes representations of power and indigenous political structures. We will focus on the local concepts of power and heritage of specific political systems (e.g. Andean responsibilities system) which are part of Andean intangible heritage.

10. *Research and teaching about the Andes*: this section includes interviews with researchers, teachers, and specialists; recordings of classes, seminars, and talks; as well as academic events. These different videos allow us to document and comment on the main cultural events covered, thereby providing different types of analysis and interpretations.

It is important to emphasize that these categories are not exclusive and the same subject can be classified into different domains if necessary. For example, *wayno* songs can appear in the category of "sung oral traditions", "music", and "living arts".

4.3.3. *The thematic description library*

To create our portal, we also developed new models for our library as well as using the description models used in the creation of the "Culture Crossroads Archive" (CCA) video library which is one of the areas of experimentation of the ASW-HSS project[27]. We have reused the main structure of these models by replacing the ASW micro-thesaurus with an Andean micro-thesaurus. For example, we

---

27 See the CCA site directly: semioweb.msh-paris.fr/corpus/Arc/FR/

created geographical micro-thesauri for the specific regions in Peru and Bolivia or even Andean musical genres. The following areas of information have also been adapted:

– "cultures, peoples, and civilizations" adapted to "civilizations and peoples in the Andes";

– "languages, language families, and proto-languages" adapted to "languages of the Andean world";

– "music of the world" adapted to "Andean music and dance";

– "culture, food, and cuisine" changed to "Andean culinary traditions";

– "knowledge of cultures" adapted to "research and teaching on the Andes".

We have also created four new description models:

– intangible cultural heritage;

– cultural transmission;

– memories, stories, and identities;

– politics.

4.3.3.1. *Description model: "Intangible cultural heritage"*

With regard to the main theme of our portal, we have begun by creating a new description model specifically for ICH (see Figure 4.2). We have defined the five sub-categories using the 2003 UNESCO Convention concerning the five areas of expression which we examined previously[28]. UNESCO, the renowned international cultural organization, after extensive reflection and deliberation has established a convention which has since been recognized and signed by a number of countries. It therefore seemed appropriate to reuse the models and categories used within this convention. Moreover, our experience in section of the ICH for processing and archiving videos accompanying

28 Oral traditions and expressions, including language as a vector of ICH, performing arts, social practices, celebratory rituals and events, knowledge and practices around nature and the universe and expertise linked to traditional arts and crafts.

folders for listing intangible heritage has enabled us to understand the usefulness of these categories and understand their relevance.

We have therefore decided to use the following five conceptual categories in the ICH model, closely following those recognized by UNESCO:

– oral traditions and expressions;

– performing arts;

– festive rituals and events;

– expertise linked to the techniques for arts and crafts;

– knowledge and practices concerning nature and the universe.

Intangible cultural heritage

1. Choice of sub-category:

EXAMPLE: *"Oral expressions and traditions" formula*

2. Name of the element in its different forms (free field) + **Choice of language by name if necessary**

EXAMPLE: *"waynu/ wayñu" in Quechua*

"Huayno" in Spanish

"Wayno" in bilingual version Quechua and Spanish

3. Choice of one or more sub-categories if necessary (optional choice from a micro-thesaurus of sub-categories)

EXAMPLE: *sung form + poetic form*

4. Description of the element (free field) + **Language of the performance**

EXAMPLE: *Originating from Andean traditional poetry and Music, wayno in Quechua is considered in oral literature, as a genre of popular song in the Peruvian Andes. These songs, danced*

Figure 4.2. *Description of the "Intangible cultural heritage" model*

in couples are performed in different celebratory events marking both the earth cycle (sowing, harvest, fertility rites) and the lifecycle (baptisms, marriages, funerals).

EXAMPLE: *Quechua language*

5. Contexts of transmission/ performance (free field)

EXAMPLE: *the wayno song recorded was performed during the Q'eswa Chaka festival of dance, accompanying the ritual construction of the Q'eswa Chaka woven grass bridge which takes place on the second Sunday of June in the Huinchiri community in the Canas area of the Cusco region.*

6. Justification for heritage status: function, value, heritage status in the group concerned

EXAMPLE: *Recognized as a strong identifying element, waynos accompany key moments in people's lives both in rural communities and urban areas. Beyond a simple "means of entertainment", this performing art is also a conveyor of poetic resources and complex symbolic messages along with fundamental issues such as choice of partner, growing up or boundaries between the human and natural world literature.*

Figure 4.2. *(continued) Description of the "Intangible cultural heritage" model*

4.3.3.2. *Description model "Cultural transmission"*

We have created the "Cultural transmission" model (see Figure 4.3) to describe the phenomena for transmitting, publishing, and teaching and especially individuals' statements explaining their teaching activity or their motivations for transmitting a particular art or expertise. This model is further sub-divided into two categories:

– transmission via institutional teaching;

– transmission by traditional teaching.

Transmission by institutional teaching/traditional teaching

1. Language of transmission (language/s in which the message is conveyed)

2. Sender (person producing the message)

3. Receiver (person receiving the message or at whom the message is aimed)

4. Mode of transmission (means of transmission)

5. Content of the transmitted message

6. Context of transmission (place, time, event)

Figure 4.3. *Description model for "Cultural transmission"*

4.3.3.3. Description model "Memories, stories, identities"

Memorial/historical/identity discourse and practices

1. Name of discourse/practice (if applicable)

EXAMPLE: *Inti Raymi, ancient Inca festival of the sun*

2. Type of discourse/practice (individual, collective, official, public, private)

EXAMPLE: *Public and official collective practice*

3. Characteristics of the discourse/practice (description)

EXAMPLE: *Inti Raymi commemorates the ancient Inca winter solstice festival*

4. Context of the discourse/practices (place, time, context of transmission)

EXAMPLE: *24th June at Sacsayhuaman (Ancient Incan citadel in Cuzco)*

Figure 4.4. *Description model for "Memories, stories, identities"*

We have defined a new category called "Memories, stories, identities" (see Figure 4.4) to classify and comment on the different memorial, historical and identity discourses and practices such as claims of identity or expressions of the importance of knowledge for future generations. This model is also divided into three sub-categories:

– memorial discourse and practice;

– historical discourse and practices;

– identity discourse and practices.

4.3.3.4. Description model "Politics"

We have also created a new model for classifying and commenting on the different types of discourse and practices concerning politics (see Figure 4.5) such as a representation of power, political organization, power structures, political discourse, political opinions, and so on. This description model is even more relevant this year with the 2011 Peruvian Presidential Elections.

Politics

1. Name of discourse/practice

EXAMPLE: *View of community X on the 2011 presidential elections*

2. Type of discourse/practice (individual, collective, official, private)

EXAMPLE: *Collective*

3. Characteristic of the discourse/practice (description)

EXAMPLE: *This discourse expressed the opinions of community X on the candidates*

4. Context of the discourse/practice (place, time, context of transmission)

EXAMPLE: *Eve of the second round of the presidential elections, community X.*

Figure 4.5. *Description model for "Politics"*

4.4. Interests and perspectives of the project

4.4.1. *Interests and objectives of the project*

The creation of an audiovisual portal dedicated to the intangible heritage of Andean populations in the ASW-HSS project provides a number of new advantages. There are three, in particular, that represent real scientific contributions in relation to our research expectations. Initially, the ASW environment enables us to protect and preserve the research data and heritages without freezing them, due to an evolving and interactive archiving system. This platform of publication and exchange also helps to valorize and revitalize threatened traditions through media which will attract new generations. Finally, it is also a research tool which enables us to describe and scientifically index audiovisual texts legally and according to a variety of approaches.

4.4.1.1. Safeguarding and preserving living heritages: a dynamic and interactive archive

Protecting our field data has always been one of the main objectives of our research. We work mainly on living heritages, and our corpus of data primarily includes sound and audiovisual recordings. There are currently archiving programs for archiving sound data[29] but there is not such a program for archiving, publishing and indexing audiovisual data. Moreover, more than just preserving our data, it was also essential to think about the protection of the heritages we are studying, specifically those that are threatened by extinction, the Quechua language being a case in point.

4.4.1.1.1. The challenge of preserving a continually evolving cultural heritage

One of the recurring problems with ICH involves its evolving and dynamic "nature" which is difficult to combine with protecting and safeguarding objectives. The 2003 Convention underlines the dynamic nature of ICH: "*This intangible cultural heritage, transmitted from*

---

29 See the LACITO research labs (Laboratoire de Langues et Civilisations à Tradition Orale [Laboratory for Oral Languages and Civilizations]: lacito.vjf.cnrs.fr) and the CREM labs (Centre de Recherche en Ethnomusicologie [Ethnomusical Research Center]: www.crem-cnrs.fr).

generation to generation, is constantly recreated by the communities and groups in response to their environment, their interaction with nature and history, and provides them with a sense of identity and continuity, thus promoting respect for cultural diversity and human creativity" (Article 2). This definition therefore highlights the three main elements of ICH: human transmission, creativity, and identity.

The principle of human transmission defining ICH involves continual processes of recreation and updating in relation to new social contexts to which the heritage must adapt. A good example of this might be the sung form we have examined, *waynos*, where new forms appear in the context of the migration of Andean populations to the large cities on the Peruvian coastline. This has given way to *waynos* mainly in Spanish with themes based on the new urban social environment (e.g. references to trucks rather than rivers). However, this is not an issue of seeing one as better or worse than one another or to reify them as a model, but to view them within their sociocultural context to identify their meaning and function. The current and contemporary aspects of ICH are in direct relation with its relevance in its culture of reference. In this context, it is essential to account for their active reappropriation by peoples faced with changes and globalization. Far from being passive subjects losing their heritage, these are living actors, redefining their heritage in relation to their new value systems. In this context, accounting for the contributions of new generations reinterpreting their heritage and mixing cultures, is therefore necessary, if not essential.

We therefore need to understand how, in light of this "dynamic" quality, safeguarding the culture is possible without freezing cultural practices or even curbing the process of their transmission. Similarly, it also necessary to examine the different means of managing, accounting for and ensuring the evolution of these heritages. The models for approaching heritages created for static data should be questioned while attempting to preserve the living heritages. The ASA-HSS project, through using new technologies and implementing an interactive and dynamic archiving system, enables us to reflect on these different issues.

4.4.1.1.2. Modes of reproduction and interactive platforms: online multimedia archives

The advantage of new technologies is undeniable and, indoubtedly they provide the necessary conditions for processing intangible material. As Laurent Aubert states in his article on "*nouvelles voies de la tradition*" [new ways of tradition], preserving ICH "*nécessite donc le développement de supports technologiques adaptés à sa nature propre. Les ressources de l'informatique ont ainsi multiplié les possibilités de stockage de données de façon considerable* [therefore requires the development of technological platforms adapted to it's [the ICH's] nature. In this way, the computer resources have considerably increased storage possibilities] (see [AUB 04, p. 117]). One of the many challenges of disseminating ICH is valorizing and conveying its "living" quality. From this perspective, it seems to be important to reflect on new forms of interactively presenting and displaying information where new technologies play a fundamental role. Lists of living practices should also be continually evolving, that is continually updated so that the studied heritages do not become fixed models which might inhibit any creativity and to which future artists might turn to obtain a certain degree of legitimacy.

The classical approach for archiving used by the heritage professionals had to adapt to the fluidic forms constituting ICHs and move toward much more interactive platforms and processing methods. ESCoM, through its various online audiovisual archiving programs, has ensured the important protection and wide dissemination of intangible heritages whether through interviews with specialists, seminars, or even cultural events. The creation of thematic folders and networks of links between different recordings of videos enables the conception of a dynamic approach to living heritages. Digitalized online multimedia archives can also be used as a means of communication, and not only for the conservation purposes, allowing us to effectively account for the living nature of ICH, but also to promote it in the wide area of exchange that is the Internet. Ever since the 1980s, the Internet revolution has been highly beneficial for publishing audiovisual data which had previously not been, or at least under represented institutionally. Currently, the Internet is an unavoidable resource with rich potential. Exploitation of such a rich potential which begins to be exploited only now in the ICH domain. Its interactivity, coupled with its ease of access and exchange between the far corners of the world makes this media a vector for publishing and promoting global ICHs, thereby enabling all the users to view hitherto unpublished and inaccessible cultural phenomena.

4.4.1.2. *Valorizing and revitalizing threatened practices using attractive media: creating a platform of expression for oral cultures*

Beyond merely being a simple archiving and publishing platform, an audiovisual portal on living heritage has a genuine attractive potential for new generations as well as valorizing and revitalizing these heritages.

4.4.1.2.1. Attractive cultural expression platforms for new generations

New means of disseminating audiovisual resources via the Internet have also created a new dynamic for sharing heritage and revalorizing it by updating it (see Chapters 6, 7, and 8). In fact, there is no better means than the Internet for promoting and providing access to endangered heritages in attractive domains and as carriers of modernity. This media can evoke renewed interest in younger generations who are often disinterested in the traditions of their elders. We have therefore used a statement from a young inhabitant of Cuzco who had moved to Lima and who, due to the Internet, had watched chants from his region on YouTube. Due to the Internet, the nostalgia of migration, coupled with the possibility of access to the sounds and scenes of childhood have helped to develop this young person's interest in the cultural traditions with which he had not previously been concerned. Dissemination via a new media filter can prove to be beneficial for heritages which are judged to be "traditional".

YouTube is a good example of this phenomenon. There are numerous videos concerning rituals or indigenous Andean traditions uploaded by the populations themselves. These videos are also often accompanied by numerous comments by the people from all over the globe, showing the attractive power of this mode of communication, not only locally with young people but also for the worldwide diaspora. These different elements are therefore indicative of a turning point in interest for living traditions, both intergenerationally and internationally by reuniting a dispersed community on its identifying references.

In addition, the multilingual aspect of the comments, both in Spanish and in Quechua as well as other global languages demonstrates how, far from inhibiting linguistic revalorization, new technologies become a platform that enable the free expression of often locally undervalued languages. Disseminating oral heritages through interactive multimedia therefore helps us to revalorize these oral productions and their language of production. As a dynamic platform for conserving and disseminating language and knowledge, audiovisual portals in the ASW-HSS research project are not a simple static and closed place for archiving, but are increasingly a platform for interactive and dynamic exchanges. Beyond this, they are also a means of expression for local populations, who can use indigenous languages to communicate their knowledge and traditions. It is all the more significant in the Andes, where Quechua is in a diglossic relationship with Spanish and remains a largely oral[30] language. In this context, which mode other than the audiovisual, a can convey the speech of holders of tradition and communicate this to Quechuaphone speakers in the same way? An article written in Spanish, with testimonies in Quechua would be far too biased to express the viewpoint and expectations of these populations in relation to their heritages. By creating an audiovisual portal, we hope to be able to meet the expectations of the populations we are working with by contributing to promote their traditions and the Quechua language.

4.4.1.2.2. Reviving and revitalizing the transmission and creative process

As Aubert highlights about human memory *"La mémoire électronique et la mémoire humaine ne sont pas de même nature: la première est passive, cumulative et neutre, alors que la seconde est active, sélective et créative. A cet égard les progrès de l'une ne*

---

30 The use of Quechua in its written form remains limited in Peru. Whilst bilingual teaching was introduced in Peru in the 1970s, the primary aim remains to teach in Spanish while Quechua is used as a vehicular language for younger children. In addition, there is also no definitive written standard for Quechua which stops the formal production and dissemination of it in its written form. The situation is a little better in Bolivia although Quechua still has inferior status to Spanish. For further information on this topic, see the literature review "Cronicas Urbanas", *Año* 13 (14), 2009, which dedicates a large section to the "Quechua world" analyzing Quechua from various perspectives.

remplacera jamais les ressources de l'autre; l'archivage conserve un corpus, il protège une tradition de l'oubli; mais il ne garantit pas pour autant la persistance de cette tradition". [Electronic and human memories are not the same: the first is passive, cumulative, and neutral; whereas the second is active, selective, and creative. For this reason, the development of one will never replace the resources of the other; the archiving of a corpus protects a tradition from being forgotten but it does not guarantee the persistence of this tradition] [AUB 04]. As such, the practice of human transmission remains to be one of the main elements involved in safeguarding and revitalizing, although new technologies can also play a role in this process.

Beyond merely "preserving" or "conserving", the aim of safeguarding also involves reactivating the oral method of passing on knowledge by supporting innovations in tradition. This "revitalization" involves promoting and revalorizing practices which have often been discredited or under recognized by a dominant culture, while such practices are recognized in their own community and risk being depreciated by future generations. This is therefore not a question of forcibly conserving obsolete traditions but making people locally and internationally aware of the value of this heritage and, as such, bringing it to life. It is *"la présence inspirante d'une telle vitalité qui nous poussera et nous donnera l'énergie nécessaire à la création de nouvelles formes qui augmenteront la pertinence des anciennes"* [the presence of such an inspiring vitality which moves us and provides us with the energy required to create new forms that will increase the relevance of the old ones] ([NAI 04]). From this perspective, various interventions can be useful, for example helping practitioners to carry out their art, not so much supporting the created forms, but the social act of creation on their production. From this same viewpoint, it also seems necessary to create access to traditional knowledge for new platforms and media, so that they persist and are attractive for younger generations. As Pais de Brito, director of the National Museum of Ethnology in Lisbon, has suggested, we can also invent new functions and purposes for artisan skills by *"ouvrant le champ à l'innovation et à un processus créatif, par lequel ce savoir-faire tient un rôle actif dans de nouvelles formes d'imagination sociale"* [opening up the field to innovation and a creative process by which this knowledge has an active role in new forms of social imagination] (see [PAI 04]).

Finally, one of the key points in the revitalization process is combining the safeguarding of ICH with education[31], by encouraging learning and teaching of ICH knowledge in schools using holders of these traditions. As we will examine in more detail, one of the possible uses for this portal specifically concerns education.

4.4.1.3. *Scientifically describing and indexing audiovisual data*

Finally, one of the main objectives of the ASW-HSS project is not merely to be a simple traditional archiving project but to be a scientific conservation program, analyzing, and indexing as well as disseminating audiovisual data and knowledge (see Chapter 1 [STO 11a]).

4.4.1.3.1. An ethical, legal and scientific framework

This project provides a new scientific and legal framework for uploading and describing videos. Developed by the ESCoM, a French research laboratory, this project offers the principal advantage of being a scientific guarantee for the published data, in contrast with other more informal Internet portals. The different agreements made between ESCoM and renowned cultural and scientific institutions also ensures the long-term durability of this research data since the videos are archived on servers and on FMSH premises initially, as well as those of the Bibliothèque nationale de France (BnF) for legal deposit.

On the other hand, in order to account for the specificities of the make up of intangible cultural heritages in so-called native communities, the ASW-HSS project has also developed a series of ethical standards which provide an extra value to this program. Each

---

31 See Article 14 of the 2003 Convention: Education, awareness raising and capacity-building. Each State Party shall endeavour, by all appropriate means, to:
(a) ensure recognition of, respect for, and enhancement of the intangible cultural heritage in society, in particular through:
(i) educational, awareness-raising and information programmes, aimed at the general public, in particular young people;
(ii) specific educational and training programmes within the communities and groups concerned;
(iii) capacity-building activities for the safeguarding of the intangible cultural heritage, in particular management and scientific research;
(iv) non-formal means of transmitting knowledge.

video recording is subject to informed consent and is often accompanied by written consent. Each description systematically cites the different rights associated with each video, that is image rights, authorship rights, and copyright. Each video is therefore "legally" indexed and annotated, the names of different people involved are included, whether the director or the speaker, and references and locations are provided enabling a greater transparency and better communication on the project.

Finally, since the issue of collective rights was cited earlier, the ASW-HSS project is also open to any improvement or modification to its legal framework from an ethical scientific research perspective. Several members of the project were therefore responsible for testing the tools and categories developed by the ESCoM in different cultural contexts, ranging from the Andes to Azerbaijan (see Chapter 5). The aim of ESCoM and the ASW-HSS project is to not only be relevant in a Western context but also to be useful and applicable in a variety of cultural situations, one of the objectives which sets it aside from other existent projects.

4.4.1.3.2. Multilingualism

The ASW environment also offers a number of possibilities for multilingualism, from describing the video to online publications (see Chapter 6 [STO 11a]).

When we write the basic description of a video in the "Generalities" tab of the ASW Description Workshop (see Chapter 3 [STO 11a]), we can choose the language(s) of the video from a wide range of sample languages from all around the world, with the multiple selection of languages being a major advantage for multilingual videos. Our description itself can also be written in the language of our choice and we can also create translations of our comments and video extracts. Finally, when uploading our portal and publishing our videos, we can choose to do this in different languages by translating our description models. We eventually hope to translate our portal into Spanish and Quechua and even English to adapt it to potential future users.

Multilingualism is therefore both an advantage for the researchers working on languages and for all cultural communities globally capable of having access to these videos, so that they can use and appropriate the ESCoM tools to develop their own portals. This is important in that it does not limit the future users of ESCoM tools but denotes a great cultural opening up of the project and its international ethical nature.

4.4.1.3.3. Indexing, describing, and meta-describing videos

One of the principal innovations of the tools developed in the ASA-HSS project is multiple semiotic descriptions for audiovisual resources (see Chapter 3). This tool offers the possibility of not only being able to describe a simple video but also to be able to comment on the different segments from the same video and from several different angles.

A good example in this case is that of the carnival ritual dedicated to ensuring the fertility of Andean camel herds (Lamas and Alpacas). This ritual features a number of identifying cultural elements; the ritual stages themselves, ritual chants in Quechua, accompanying music and dance, specific clothes for the event and statements from participants about their customs. All these different levels of analysis can appear separately in a video segment which we have to define but are often mixed in the same segment. The possibility of commenting on one segment from different approaches is therefore highly relevant.

Segmenting a video into different extracts is the first stage in video analysis which enables us to use the video resource from a chosen description perspective (see Chapter 2 [STO 11a]). For example, in the case of the carnival ritual, we can choose to specifically describe the musical sequences in the ritual and segment the video according to the different musical changes involved in the ritual, making segmentation significant from musical perspective. We can then reedit our original video from a different approach, for example, the gestures used in the ritual. For each type of approach chosen, the ESCoM tools offer us a series of description models to comment in detail our video on the thematical, discursive, visual, and acoustic level (see Chapters 4 and 5 [STO 11a]). The fact that the project aims to develop the personal description models adapted to each portal's specific purpose is of even greater interest (see Chapters 1–5).

These possibilities for multiple descriptions of a single video are therefore a real advance in research, specifically for linguist anthropologists and ethnomusicologists working on living heritages. For the case of a detailed linguistic or musicological analysis, these tools enable us to segment the video sequence precisely as the best sound analysis software would. Moreover, they also provide a range of description and indexing resources, going far beyond the simple analysis, enabling us to establish links between videos and/or video segments and observe relevant patterns which may have otherwise been missed. In the case of musical analysis of Quechua songs, if we decide to report a geographically relevant pace information such as levels of ecology or even the administrative district, we can, for example, potentially see what types of instruments or even what themes are used according to different regions and altitude levels. Beyond being a mere archiving portal, the ASA-HSS project therefore provides communities of researchers with innovative new analysis tools in line with the evolution of current research which is more and more based on the usage of new technologies.

4.4.2. *Uses and perspectives*

The AICH portal has multiple uses and perspectives, but we will mention a few here, specifically in the fields of research, education, and culture, both in a local and in an international context. The different fields of application for a video can be specified in the ASW Description Workshop in the "Uses" tab which directs the analysis and facilitates the recovery of videos by target audiences (see Chapter 6 [STO 11a]). In this sense, we will benefit from the technological contributions of the European Convergence research project (see Chapter 9).

4.4.2.1. *Uses in research*

We have developed our portal in the context of our anthropological doctoral research, so its main aim lies in the field of scientific research in human sciences. As previously mentioned, the tools developed in the ASW-HSS framework are not only a means of safeguarding research data but also enabling them to be indexed, described, and analyzed. The AICH portal therefore provides us not only with an archive for our corpus of data but also a platform for publicizing our research for free internationally.

4.4.2.1.1. Research on culture

Our specialization being anthropology, the chosen area of research for the AICH portal therefore involves the culture and different human sciences related to it. Every researcher, student, specialist, or amateur can access raw data as well as specialized studies on different aspects of living Andean culture, whether history, music, beliefs, knowledge, or expertise.

4.4.2.1.2. Research on languages

Our other specialization concerns the Quechua language and we have also decided to focus on part of our research on linguistics, in particular, pragmatics. We aim to provide an analysis of various dialects of Quechua and different language registers depending on the social backgrounds and contexts of interaction to produce an archive on pronunciations of Quechua depending on region and dialect. This also provides access to a corpus of oral texts in Quechua, thereby facilitating future research in this area.

4.4.2.2. *Uses in education*

The audiovisual resources of the AICH portal can also have interesting applications in education, both in an international context for teaching programs on Andean languages and cultures, and locally for intercultural bilingual education programs.

4.4.2.2.1. Teaching about Quechua and Andean culture

As a part of our series of lessons on Quechua and Andean anthropology at the INaLCO (National Institute for Oriental Languages and Civilizations), we have held different classes focusing on Andean oral traditions, the one concerning Quechua texts in new media. We have also tried to develop our portal with the aim of improving this teaching, both in terms of the expectations of teachers and students. The AICH portal can therefore serve as a support for teaching oral Quechua and can provide teaching material for studying and understanding Andean beliefs, classifications, and categories using observations and analyses of different collected facts and statements.

4.4.2.2.2. Bilingual intercultural education programs in Quechua and Spanish

As we have already mentioned before, the material concerning ICH can also play a major role in education programs and it is therefore to be expected that researchers reflect on the significance of their research in this area and how they can respond to the expectations of local populations. Since a school is an archetypal place for transmitting and acquiring knowledge, introducing ICH into this context seems to be the best way for ensuring its survival and revitalization. In Andean countries (notably, Ecuador, Peru, and Bolivia), oral Quechua tradition is an essential resource which should be accounted for while designing the new intercultural bilingual education programs.

We will dedicate part of our doctoral research toward the possibility of combining ICH inventory with bilingual Quechua/Spanish education programs[32]. Our postdoctoral research also aims to create a program for collecting oral data made by children with their families which would then be updated throughout their school careers. This would consist of not only collecting this literature, but also understanding through what kind of practices they express themselves and which interpretations they elicit. This project therefore requires the active participation of members of the community in teaching their children at school because parents can transmit speech that will be reused at school and thereby contributing to revalorizing the oral heritage of which they are holders. Lastly, our portal could therefore be used in the development of educational material for bilingual schools.

---

32 In Peru, Quechua language and oral literature still remain undervalued in comparison with Spanish. In terms of education, Quechuaphone children also experience a number of difficulties notably in reading and writing because for a long time (and still often today) they have been taught directly in Spanish, a language that many do not understand. For 30 years, Andean states have aimed to totally rethink children's education in rural areas by developing Intercultural Bilingual Education (IBE). IBE is increasingly focused on integrating Quechua orality into new educational programs.

4.4.2.3. *Local cultural uses and perspectives: creating an ICH cultural centre in Cuzco*

Returning the collected materials when creating the video library, mainly through creation of copies of audiovisual documents, can also be accompanied by the creation of local cultural centers aimed at conserving and presenting the collected heritages. With the aim of contributing to a better dissemination and understanding of oral literature in Quechua language and participating in returning our data to the communities with whom we have worked, we would like to create a cultural center dedicated to the ICH in Cuzco[33], as well as in the communities where we have led our research. This center could not only be used as a place of conservation but also as a space for highlighting the value and reflecting on the local heritage. Beyond this, it could also be a creative center where activities can develop on the protected materials by establishing creative and learning workshops. The portal will therefore serve as platform for this data and a means of promoting the cultural center.

4.4.2.3.1. A center for archives on living heritage

This center would primarily enables us to preserve an heritage and a threatened language by preserving different expressions and demonstrating its diversity. It could also be used as a center for documentary resources, giving unprecedented access to oral texts for all those who are interested by the subject, whether researchers, students, or even bilingual education teachers.

The creation of an archive center also involves prior reflection on ethical questions surrounding the rights of the author and collecting oral texts and on inventory and archiving systems which should give way to updating evolving oralities.

---

33 This cultural center will be opened in 2012. The choice of the town of Cuzco is strategic because it is a town attracting significant cultural tourism and where there is real demand for learning by visiting outsiders or volunteers. In addition, this town is highly cosmopolitan since it attracts people from all around the local rural area and tourists from all over the world. It can therefore potentially serve as platform for exchanging Andean knowledge and heritage.

4.4.2.3.2. A training center for populations on collecting ICH and using new technologies

Transferring skills by creating and training workshops on collecting ICH and using new technologies for local populations is also one of the objectives of this cultural center. It is therefore designed to offer specialized training in teaching, for example, recording, processing, and data analysis methods as well as teaching local populations how to use new technologies which could also follow the collecting project. Training in the use of ESCoM tools is also a way for the communities involved to appropriate the different processes involved in managing ICH thereby allowing them to create their own archives.

4.4.2.3.3. A teaching center for Quechua language and Andean culture

We would also like to make this center a place for teaching Quechua language and Andean culture by creating classes in language, civilization, music, cuisine, and arts and crafts such as weaving and pottery. These classes will be aimed at not only the local people wanting to learn or improve on the subject but also for the foreigners hoping to acquire knowledge in this field.

4.4.2.3.4. A center for promoting ICH through cultural activities

Finally, this center will also include interactive cultural activities aiming to spread and promote ICH. This could also take the form of live concerts, debates on a given theme or skills demonstrations, encouraging exchange between the practitioners of these skills and the public.

4.5. Conclusion

As a medium for cultural identity, world Intangible Cultural Heritage has emerged as a real international issue, not only out of fear that these traditions will disappear but also because they represent the active and current face of the cultures. In the context of recognizing cultural diversity and respecting human rights, we could also consider that the recognition of ICH in native languages is a geopolitical issue which is even more important in a number of countries where these languages remain undervalued in comparison with dominant or official languages. Therefore it is essential then to account for the concerns and expectations of the populations involved in our research with regards to the linguistic, cultural, and educational problems which they currently face. With the new enthusiasm for preserving and valuing cultural diversity, new initiatives accounting for Intangible Cultural Heritage can therefore play an essential role in tolerance by contributing to creating dialog between "us" and other cultures by sharing living art.

Participation in the two projects, the French ASW-HSS project and the European Convergence project, has provided us with a means of responding to these different issues and expectations by creating a portal on the intangible cultural heritage of Andean populations. The opportunity to work on these projects has provided a great contribution both for reflecting on our topic of study as well as for acquiring innovative technological skills for publishing our research globally and according to scientific ethics. We therefore hope that the significance and potential of this new technology will also be recognized and used by the international research community and far beyond.

Chapter 5

An Audiovisual Azerbaijani Cultural Heritage Portal for Educational and Academic Use

5.1. Introduction

The Audiovisual Azerbaijani Cultural Heritage Portal (AACH)[1], one of the main pilot portals of the ASW-HSS project, is created using the tools and knowledge of semiotic description developed by ESCoM. The creation of the AACH portal is rooted in concrete requirements and is based on long-lasting academic research and investigation. As such, the parallelism between the field and theoretical research which has benefited the development of the AACH portal has been one of the major factors of its success.

Initially, a historical view of the AACH project is necessary to understand the motivations and objectives of our research. It will also enable us to trace the evolution of our reflection on how to

Chapter written by Aygun EYYUBOVA.
1 The Azerbaijan Democratic Republic is a country located in the Caucasus region on the Western side of the Caspian sea. For further information, see EYYUBOVA, A., *Présentation générale de l'Azerbaïdjan et de son patrimoine culturel* [General introduction to Azerbaijan and its cultural heritage]: http://semioweb.msh-paris.fr/corpus/azeributa/FR/.

disseminate and teach the cultural heritage, by using traditional methods as well as new technologies.

5.1.1. *Background to the creation of the AACH portal: context*

In March 1999, Azerbaijani[2] was first taught in France at INaLCO[3] in Paris. Having taught this language for 10 years, from the beginning we found that there was a distinct lack of methodology for teaching Azerbaijani to Francophones and a lack of materials for teaching about Azerbaijani culture. In fact, without direct links to France during its 70 years as part of the USSR and because there was not a significant Azerbaijani diaspora in France[4], few resources on Azerbaijan, little was known about this country in France. In order to respond to the requirements of our investigation, we have decided to create our own methodological aids and teaching materials. In addition, we have also begun to investigate other means of filling these gaps.

5.1.2. *Research into teaching methodologies for Azerbaijani culture and language*

Real and imperative professional needs have instigated our research into teaching the Azerbaijani language and culture. In our MA[5] research work and doctoral thesis[6], we have examined historical, linguistic and methodological issues of teaching Azerbaijani. We have also focused

---

2 Also known as Azeri.

3 Institut National des Langues et Civilisations Orientales (National Institute for Oriental Languages and Civilizations), Paris.

4 Historical note: Founded on 28th May 1918, the Azerbaijan Democratic Republic (ADR) was the first Eastern democratic state. However, the ADR only existed for 23 months before it was invaded by the Red Army on the 28th April 1920 and incorporated into the USSR as the Azerbaijan Soviet Socialist Republic. It was only in 1991 following the collapse of the USSR that Azerbaijan regained its independence.

5 EYYUBOVA, A., Enseignement de l'azéri aux francophones et turcophones: problèmes et propositions pédagogiques [Teaching Azerbaijani to Francophones and Turkophones: Educational issues and suggestions], M.A.S. research work, 2000, INaLCO, Paris.

6 EYYUBOVA, A., Méthodologie de l'enseignement de l'azéri langue étrangère: approche comparative (français, turc) et application à Internet [Methodology for teaching Azerbaijani as a foreign language: a comparative approach (French, Turkish) and application to Internet], doctoral thesis, 2006, Paris.

on how to improve access to resources on Azerbaijani culture. Given the growth in the significance of new technologies, we were attracted by the potential applications of the Internet. We therefore studied the potential advantages of this medium for teaching language and culture and have proposed a program for teaching Azerbaijani language and culture via the Internet as an alternative or complimentary method to traditional techniques.

Gradually our research turned to wider questions such as the potential of the Internet for teaching and research in human and social sciences and its role in disseminating knowledge, specifically on cultural heritages.

5.2. Disseminating and transmitting cultural heritages via the Internet

5.2.1. *Digitalizing and disseminating cultural archives via the Internet*

With the growth in the significance of heritage in cultural identity and technological progress, digitalization seems to be a means of protecting and preserving archives of both material and intangible heritages against physical and temporal restriction.

The primary advantages of the Internet (storage, large databases, universal accessibility, and virtual cross-border communication) have made it a highly attractive mode for sharing, transmitting, and diffusing cultural and academic knowledge. From this perspective, the Internet has a major role in an information society and an unprecedented period of globalization.

In parallel with private practice, official institutions have seized the opportunity provided by the Internet for cultural heritage and have progressively built online archives. Initiators of such archives are often governemental organizations in culture, research, and education as well as national and international organizations, museums, and libraries, such as the UNESCO, the *Bibliothèque Nationale de France* (BnF), the British Library, the European portal Europeana[7], or again the Louvre.

---

7 http://www.europeana.eu/portal/.

As such, the UNESCO "World Digital Library" portal[8] aims to collect essential knowledge on humanity and civilization from the Internet in the form of digitalized heritage from national libraries of United Nations party states.

The online catalog "Digital heritage", initiated under the guidance of the French Ministry for Culture and Communication, is responsible for "valorizing digitalized collections in France and enabling access to digital resources"[9].

"Gallica"[10], the digital library of the BnF (Bibliothèque nationale de France), provides free Internet access to a collection of more than a million books, maps, images, sound recordings, scores, and digital journals. The "Europeana" portal[11], enables us to explore digital resources from museums, libraries, archives, and European audiovisual collections. With its 15 million digital items, "Europeana" is a real treasure trove of European cultural and academic heritage. One thousand five hundred institutions such as the British Library, the Rijksmuseum, and the Louvre, as well as smaller institutions have contributed to the project.

Disseminating cultural archives via the Internet is best achieved through audiovisual media. With the development of new technologies, the arrival of audiovisual data on the Web marks a new stage in the dissemination of cultural heritages online. YouTube, a megaspace for uploading videos that are accessible to all, is certainly the most obvious example of sharing and disseminating audiovisual archives online. On the basis of this success, official portals and traditional brands often use the visual components as in the case of, for example, HarmattanTV[12]. *Web TV*, focused on cultural themes, for example Web TV Culture[13], also uses this method.

---

8 UNESCO, *World Digital Library (WDL)*: http://www.wdl.org [Last accessed 17/06/2011].
9 Ministry for Culture and Communication, *Digital heritage*. http://www.numerique. culture.fr/mpf/pub-fr/a_propos.html [Last accessed 17/06/ 2011].
10 Bibliothèque nationale de France. *Gallica*: http://gallica.bnf.fr/ [Last accessed 17/06/2011].
11 *Europeana*. http://europeana.eu/ [Last accessed 22/06/2011].
12 Harmattan *Films, DVD, VOD Dvx, on Harmattan TV*: http://www. harmattantv.com/ [Last accessed 25/06/2011].
13 Web TV Culture: http://www.web-tv-culture.com/ [Last accessed 26/06/2011].

However, spaces for open audiovisual sharing such as YouTube are generally characterized by the diversity of their content and a lack of multiterm or systematized search systems often based on the key words or themes. Spaces that are more specialized are normally not open to public contributions and their audiovisual archives are more restricted.

5.2.2. *Issues in semiotic research for disseminating cultural heritages*

Digitalizing and disseminating audiovisual cultural heritages online are part of the cultural policies of official institutions for preserving and transmitting cultural heritages for future generations and developing intercultural dialog.

However, faced with the variety and proliferation of information on the Web, simply uploading/storing of digitalized archives is inadequate. To survive, and be accessed and used, an archive of digital information should correspond to the potential needs of its users and be able to respond precisely to their demands.

This factor supposes that the content of a Web portal must be carefully selected, presented in an organized, systematic, and ergonomic way, and also be described and indexed to enable us to find quickly the information corresponding to their search criteria.

In addition, official institutions are also involved in developing new, creative uses for cultural heritages online. This issue is clearly formulated by Christine Albanel, the former French Minister for Culture and Communication, in the report "Numérisation du patrimoine culturel" [Digitalizing cultural heritage]: *"Trois pistes semblent particulièrement prometteuses: la transmission des savoirs et les usages éducatifs, l'offre culturelle numérique des institutions pour leurs visiteurs; les usages du Web 2.0 qui démultiplient la réutilisation des contenus patrimoniaux et favorisent la participation des publics et la création de nouvelles ressources"*. [There are three methodologies which seems to be particularly promising: transmission of knowledge and educational applications, institutions offering digital culture to their visitors, the usage of Web 2.0 to multiply the reuse of heritage contents and to favor public participation and creation of new resources.][14] [DES 09].

This indicates that online cultural heritages should be adapted to educational and academic applications and that archives' structures should offer the users means of using and appropriating content accordingly.

The developing of cultural archives online represents a complex procedure. This involves multidimensional analytic reflection, identifying the objects to be included, understanding the users' requirements, designing the interface' structure, and identifying the function of the portal. This procedure also involves developing description models for indexing content and building new personalized folders adapted to different types of users. The procedure also includes developing tools for use of archives and ensuring the compatibility of the portal with new technologies.

Investment by official institutions in semiotic and computer research projects for disseminating, managing, and using cultural and academic heritages online demonstrates the growing importance of this knowledge in an information society. The ARA program and ASW-HSS project[15] created by ESCoM are good examples of this generation of projects.

5.3. Aims of creating an Azerbaijani cultural heritage portal (AACHP) in the ASA-SHS project

The Audiovisual Azerbaijani cultural heritage portal which we have created in the ASW-HSS project is designed, like the other four pilot portals of the project, to test and enhance the semiotic and technological environment developed through the project as well as improving its adaptability to the specificities of an audiovisual archive of the concrete cultural heritage.

---

14 DESSAUX, C., ZILLHARDT, S. (led by) "Numérisation du patrimoine culturel" [Digitalizing cultural heritage], Culture and research report, no. 118, Département de la recherche, de l'enseignement supérieur et de la technologie du ministère de la Culture et de la Communication, Paris, 2008-2009.
15 See a detailed overview of these projects in Chapter 1 [STO 11a].

This environment has enabled us to create an audiovisual portal for Azerbaijani culture adapted for academic and educational uses. We have created, based on the general semiotic description environment designed by the ASW-HSS project, the theoretic, semiotic, and technical framework of the AACH portal.

Another aspect of our theoretical contribution to the ASW-HSS project was the creation, with the example of the Azerbaijani cultural heritage Portal, of a methodology including different stages and procedures in creating an audiovisual cultural heritage portal. The term *démarche patrimoniale culturelle* [cultural heritage approach], introduced by Peter Stockinger characterizes the best, records the nature of our approach and we have therefore adopted it as a part of our working vocabulary.

Initially, we have identified three action areas in the cultural heritage approach. The first area focuses on the development of a cultural heritage portal including the acquisition (collecting or recording) of audiovisual resources and their processing. The second area focuses on the conception of the portal and the processes of publishing, indexing and republishing contents online. The third incorporates the two previous fields and relates to the logistics of developing an online portal, specifically defining its objectives, identifying its main themes, and creating an action plan. Strategies for constructing audiovisual collections, creating the technical framework, considering legal issues, communicating and promoting the online portal, as well as examining work management and managing collected resources, are also important.

5.4. Principal aspects of cultural heritage approach in developing an Azerbaijani cultural heritage portal (AACH)

The study of Azerbaijani cultural heritage and creating the AACH portal's corpus was achieved through field research in Azerbaijan. This work was also part of our cultural heritage approach. The skills we developed previously through ESCoM, our analytic reflection on the subject and our empirical field experience enabled us to identify the main aspects of this approach.

5.4.1. *Ethnical aspect of cultural heritage approach*

Our research on the cultural heritage of Azerbaijan and the creation of an audiovisual portal dedicated to this heritage are based on the normative principles of the UNESCO "Declaration on Cultural Diversity" and the "Convention for the Safeguarding of the Intangible Cultural Heritage". The respect for Azerbaijani cultural heritage and human rights[16] [UNE 01] has become the essential principle of our project.

In addition, one of the articles of the UNESCO Convention for the Safeguarding of the Intangible Cultural Heritage recommends that *"Within the framework of its safeguarding activities of the intangible cultural heritage, each State Party shall endeavor to ensure the widest possible participation of communities, groups and, where appropriate, individuals that create, maintain and transmit such heritage and to involve them actively in its management..."*[17] [UNE 03]. In addition, the study and creation of the AACH portal's corpus were carried out with direct participation of individuals, carrier institutions and important figures in Azerbaijani cultural heritage. Their involvement in the study, safeguarding and diffusion processes for Azerbaijani cultural heritage through the AACH portal goes hand in hand with respect for their rights and contributions to our project.

5.4.2. *Communicative and informative aspects of cultural heritage approach*

Communication is a key element while creating a cultural heritage portal, not only at the corpus building stage but also in valorizing and promoting the portal. If communication aids the creation of an adequate corpus of cultural heritage, then it is also indispensible for the portal's usage and dissemination.

Communication during our work in Azerbaijan fulfilled first and foremost an informative function. Our presentations of the ASW-HSS

---

16 UNESCO, 2001 *Declaration on Cultural Diversity*: http://unesdoc.unesco.org/images/0012/001271/127160m.pdf.
17 UNESCO *Convention for the Safeguarding of the Intangible Cultural Heritage*, 2003: http://unesdoc.unesco.org/images/0013/001325/132540f.pdf.

project and the AACH portal led us to use two types of discourses depending on whether the audience was French or Azerbaijani. The semiotic and computing infrastructure and the terminology developed during the ASW-HSS project were complex and specialized. We therefore had to adopt a simplified meta-language to explain to the audience the nature of the project, the publication and description processes, as well as the know-how of the semiotic ASW Description Workshop functions. However, with the help of computer specialists or those who were at least familiar with indexing techniques, we were able to use academic terminology.

Information on the ASW-HSS project and the AACH portal is presented orally as well as in the written form, in the form of a working document containing a brief description of the project and portal's purpose, a statement by the project's director, Peter Stockinger, recorded consent forms, and online partner contracts[18].

The ASW-HSS project and AACH portal have highlighted their importance in preserving and valorizing Azerbaijani cultural heritage internationally. They have also proved to be very significant for intercultural education and dialog as well as enabling us to explain the principles of collaboration for potential contributors. The creation of the AACH portal in French has enabled Azerbaijani culture to be recognized on a francophone Web space and has provided resources for teaching Azerbaijani culture and civilization. The portal also makes francophone audiences aware of the practices and activities of carriers of the culture as well as those in Azerbaijani research and education. A copy of the documents on the AACH portal will also be stored in the servers/storage systems of the highly prestigious *Bibliothèque nationale de France* (BnF). This opens up new perspectives for establishing internationally cooperative projects. In addition, the ASW project offers the individuals and institutions the possibility of creating their own corpora online due to the ASW semiotic description and publication platform. These numerous advantages and perspectives provided by the AACH portal are decisive

---

18 See the statements for the AACH portal: http://semioweb.msh-paris.fr:8080/site/projets/logasa/spip.php?rubrique33. See the consent forms and online contracts for the PACA portal: http://semioweb.msh-paris.fr:8080/site/projets/logasa/spip.php?rubrique29. See the partner contracts for the AACH portal: http://semioweb.msh-paris.fr:8080/site/projets/logasa/spip.php?rubrique30.

for motivating people who are interested in Azerbaijani culture to contribute to the development of the portal themselves.

5.4.3. *Multi-source aspect of cultural heritage approach*

The audiovisual corpus of the AACH portal is composed of recordings of interviews, academic events, seminars, lessons, practical cultural events, as well as different comments, reports of cultural events (exhibitions, concerts, museum galleries), televised programs, and documentaries.

Our co-contributors have added to the AACH portal corpus not only through their own additions and making their own available texts (audio and video recordings, photos, newspapers, books, articles), but also suggested other sources and means of obtaining new corpora by placing us in contact with people and institutions who might also contribute to our project.

The resources in the AACH portal have been selected initially according to the criteria of thematic relevance, intellectual and cultural value, and guarantees of authorship rights.

5.4.4. *Legal aspects of cultural heritage approach*

We respect authorship rights which is reflected and confirmed in a series of consent forms and contracts for putting material online which are adapted to different purposes (consent forms for taking, disseminating and republishing images of individuals and institutions, uploading contracts, and making information freely available) and video recordings by both individuals and institutions in French and Azerbaijani[19]. Even if the models for the contracts have been created previously[20] they are all subjected to modifications on the ground according to their actual requirements. The shared features of all the legal documentation in the ASW-HSS project include the right to

---

19 The consent forms and online consent forms for the AACH portal can be viewed at: http://semioweb.msh-paris.fr:8080/site/projets/logasa/spip.php?rubrique29.
20 The ethical and legal documentation was written with the help of Valérie Legrand, head of the Andean Cultural Heritage Portal project. See Chapter 4 for further details.

retract, listing possible uses for the videos, the responsibilities of leaders of the ASW project toward publications, commitment to non-commercial usage of recordings and respect for the authorship rights of the contributors.

It should be noted that, given the non-lucrative and non-commercial nature of the AACH portal, voluntary contributions by our individual and institutional partners are even more precious. For our part, we are required to submit a prepublication of each event for the approval of its contributor before final publication. We also need to guarantee the preservation of the authenticity of the agreed contributions in our publications.

5.4.5. *Collaborative aspect of cultural heritage approach*

Exchanges with researchers, teachers and representatives of Azerbaijani culture during our collecting of corpora of Azerbaijani cultural heritage have also led to sustainable collaborations and partnerships. These partnerships are defined through partnership contracts[21] signed by the Azerbaijan University of Languages (AUL)[22] as well as the "Simurg" Association of Azerbaijan Culture[23].

The Azerbaijan University of Languages has provided us with material, IT, and textual support in creating the AACH portal. Due to the initiatives and progressive ideas of the dean of AUL, Samed Seyidov, the university has a highly developed IT infrastructure and is particularly interested in integrating computer applications into the teaching process for languages and civilizations. The university has also expressed interest in testing the ASW publication and indexing platform for creating its own online audiovisual resources.

"Simurg" has a significant educational and academic social function through its seminars and publications. It aims to contribute to intellectual progress and development of cultural research and education by studying the wealth of world culture under the assumption that disseminating the

---

21 The partnership contracts for the AACH portal can be viewed at the following address: http://semioweb.msh-paris.fr:8080/site/projets/logasa/spip.php?rubrique30.
22 Azerbaijan University of Languages: http://www.adu.edu.az.
23 "Simurg" Association of Azerbaijan Culture: http://www.simurq-az.org.

principles of dialog and intercultural cooperation will generate interest and knowledge about Azerbaijani culture in other countries. "Simurg" has contributed to the ASW project and the creation of the AACH portal by making available video recordings of seminars as well as providing us information about Azerbaijan culturology.

5.4.6. *Valorizing aspect of cultural heritage approach*

Communication while implementing a cultural heritage portal helps us not only to create a human network facilitating the creation of a working corpus, but also helps in publicizing the portal and encouraging people to use and test it. As such, communication on the project and the portal can encourage new projects, partnerships and give new impetus to the original project and ensure the portal's maintenance. In summary, communication enables the portal to live and evolve[24].

In addition to individual communication, we have also used communication to disseminate and valorize the ASW-HSS project and the AACH portal through a variety of different publications, presentations of doctoral or post-doctoral thesis in seminars in Paris in 2011, and even a round table meeting on cultural relations between France and Azerbaijan which has been recorded on Azerbaijani state television on June 2011.

5.4.7. *Capitalizing on experience in cultural heritage approach: a development Log Book for the AACH and AICH portals*

The creation of a portal for cultural heritage and the cultural heritage initiative that it involves represents a wealth of experience to capitalize on for analyzing, revising previous work, and altering the theory to fit into reality as well as valorizing and sharing experiences. The experience gained through the creation of cultural heritage portals also enables comparative analysis and highlights their shared features and characteristics to develop a general model for cultural heritage initiatives and portals.

---

24 For other ways of promoting a Web portal, see Chapters 6, 7 and 8.

On the basis of these considerations, we have created, together with Valérie Legrand, a *Log Book*[25], which is a virtual collection of our respective experiences in developing Azerbaijani and Andean cultural heritage portals.

Figure 5.1. *Log Book – ASW-HSS project (in French)*

The Log Book includes nine major sections. In the *working documents* section, administrative and relevant documents are included, such as reports, minutes, lists of tasks, work procedures, and so on. The *Ethics* section includes the legal documents used to collect corpora and establish partnerships. Our work on cultural heritage portals also includes researching resources on Azerbaijani and Andean cultural heritage, as well as the general information linked to cultural heritage and practices for diffusing cultural heritage via the Web. As such, we have created a virtual bibliography under the heading *Links*. Events watch on Azerbaijani and Andean culture were also used when creating these portals. The corresponding section *Events* is therefore designed to show Azerbaijani and Andean

25 The Log Book of the ASW project can be found at: http://semioweb.msh-paris.fr:8080/site/projets/logasa/

cultural events in France. The section, *Publications, communications* contains publications and communications which have taken place during the ASW-HSS project.

The concrete results of our work, XML descriptions of our corpora, video publications, and portals are also listed in the Log Book.

Two special sections focus on our research on the ASW environment, including software testing and ASW analysis schemes with suggestions for modifications to ASW tools and ontologies as well as the schemes, ontologies, and thesauri which we have developed for the semiotic description of our respective corpora (AACH and AICH).

5.5. Analyzing audiovisual corpora for AACH in ASA

This section (5.5) presents our work on the semiotic description framework for the AACH portal's corpus in more detail. Semiotic description is the most innovative feature of our Audiovisual Azerbaijani cultural heritage portal.

5.5.1. *Identifying areas of knowledge for the AACHP*

We have defined the aim for developing the AACH portal, the next stage consists of defining its themes. This task has led us to research the concept of Azerbaijani cultural heritage.

In the BnF's words, "Comme le rappelle l'UNESCO, le patrimoine culturel ne se limite pas à ses seules manifestations tangibles, comme les monuments et les objets qui ont été préservés à travers le temps. Il embrasse aussi les expressions vivantes, les traditions que d'innombrables groupes et communautés du monde entier ont reçues de leurs ancêtres et transmettent à leurs descendants, souvent oralement" [as UNESCO states, cultural heritage is not only limited to tangible manifestations but also to monuments and objects which have been preserved over time. It also encompasses living expressions and traditions which countless groups and communities around the world have received from their ancestors and passed on to their descendants, often orally][26]. As such, every country and people have their own interpretation of the concept of cultural heritage "si pour les Français ce sont d'abord les châteaux, les Allemands, quant à eux, citent l'histoire tandis que pour les Finlandais ce sont les traditions, les Italiens eux privilégient l'architecture et l'archéologie puis la peinture et le cinéma" [If, for the French, this is primarily palaces and castles, the Germans have history, the Finnish have their traditions, the Italians have architecture, archeology, painting, and cinema][27].

Our research has the main elements of Azerbaijani cultural identity, we referred to official organizations, both international and national as well as experts' opinions.

The principal features of Azerbaijani cultural heritage of international importance are found in UNESCOs Intangible Cultural Heritage of Humanity list. These include Azerbaijani mugham, Ashik art, the celebration of Norwuz (also practiced in a number of other countries), and the art of Azerbaijani carpet weaving[28]. Two other elements of Azerbaijani culture have also been included in the UNESCO list due to their exceptional universal value, both architectural and natural, such as the fortified city of Baku (Icheri Sheher) and the Gobustan Rock Art Cultural Landscape. Ten other features of Azerbaijani architectural and natural heritage are also included in UNESCOs list of Intangible Cultural Heritage.

In Azerbaijan, the study, preservation, development, and promotion of Azerbaijani cultural heritage are mostly created by two official institutions, the Minister for Culture and Tourism and the Heydar Foundation directed by the First Lady of Azerbaijan and UNESCO good-will ambassador, Mehriban Aliyeva. In 2010, the Ministry of Culture and Tourism of Azerbaijan drew up an inventory of Azerbaijani Intangible Cultural Heritage including national traditions, traditional arts, and folklore. This initial list contained over

---

26 Bibliothèque nationale de France (BnF), *Patrimoine: une notion plurielle à visiter* [Heritage: a plural concept to examine]: http://www.bnf.fr/documents/biblio_patrimoine_notion.pdf [Last accessed 17/06/2011].
27 See footnote 26.
28 UNESCO *Intangible Heritage lists*: http://www.unesco.org/culture/ich/index.php?lg=fr&pg=00011#results [Last accessed 18/06/2011].

10,000 components[29]. The principal areas of Azerbaijani heritage feature on the lists introduced in the *Azerbaijan* portal run by the Heydar Aliyev Foundation[30] and on the portal of the Ministry of Culture and Tourism of Azerbaijan[31].

To determine our focus areas in Azerbaijani cultural heritage for the AACH portal, we have also consulted Azerbaijani experts such as Azerbaijani cultural researcher, Fuad Mamedov, professor and president of the Association of Azerbaijani Culture[32].

Accounting for the results of our study and based on the areas of knowledge cited by UNESCO[33], we have created an initial but non-exhaustive thematic list of Azerbaijani cultural heritage to be covered by the AACH portal:

– *Music*: Azerbaijani musical heritage is primarily represented by the traditional genre *mugham* (classical, scholarly, academic traditional music). Mugham is the original Azerbaijani national music. It also represents general Azerbaijani cultural heritage and is considered as a basic value of their national identity by Azerbaijanis. All the main genres of world music, particularly classical music, jazz, and opera, are represented in Azerbaijani music. This is due to the synthesis of ordinarily "European" musical genres with Mugham, borrowing their originality and overall character. Ashik music (performed by mystic troubadours or traveling bards) is a popular genre of Azerbaijani culture. Popular songs and instrumental dance music are also part of traditional music. Instruments are used to interpret traditional genres of Azerbaijani music and are part of Azerbaijani cultural heritage.

---

29 Medeniyyet gezeti ("Culture" publication), 21/05/2010: http://medeniyyet.az/new/?name=content&content=5504 [Last accessed 18/06/2011].

30 Heydar Aliyev Foundation, *Azerbaijan, General information on azeri culture*: http://www.azerbaijan.az/portal/Culture/General/general_e.html   [Last   accessed 18/06/2011].

31 Ministry of Culture and Tourism of Azerbaijan, *Azerbaijani Culture*: http://www.mct.gov.az/?/az/azculture [Last accessed 18/06/2011].

32 See above in this chapter.

33 UNESCO, *Intangible Heritage Domains in the 2003 Convention*: http://www.unesco.org/culture/ich/index.php?lg=en&pg=00052 [Last accessed 29/06/2011].

– *Living performing arts*: among living performing arts, traditional and historico-social Azerbaijani characteristics are most often not only expressed in national theater and traditional dance, but are also represented in ballet and opera. For example, it was in Azerbaijan that the first composition and staging of the Eastern opera "Layla and Majnoon" took place (1908). Ballet and national opera represent the combination of European and Azerbaijani styles.

– *Visual arts – painting*: the rock art and petroglyphs in the Gobustan National Park date back to the Paleolithic period and are the most famous Azerbaijani prehistoric visual art. They are exceptional resources for studying prehistoric man's way of life. In the Middle Ages, visual art in Azerbaijan was mostly expressed by decorative art. The most notable expression of visual art in Azerbaijan during this period is that of miniatures (illuminated manuscripts) in Tabriz, where they are not only the most famous miniatures in Azerbaijan but also in the whole of the Orient. In the 19th Century, parallel to the development of Western style painting in Azerbaijan, caricature also entered into Azerbaijani cultural heritage with the publication of the eminent satirical socio-political publication *Molla Nasreddin* (1906–1931).

– *Visual arts – architecture and historical heritage*: Azerbaijani culture straddles both Western and Eastern civilization in almost all areas. This duality is clearly expressed in the architecture of Baku where the historical site of Icheri Sheher coexists harmoniously with buildings in classical, neo-renaissance, baroque, neo-classical, and neogothic styles from the first oil boom (between the end and beginning of the 19th and 20th Centuries) as well as in modern ones including, like European local musical genres, both national and oriental motifs.

– *Audiovisual-visual arts*: In 1898, cinema was introduced in Azerbaijan. Ever since the 20th Century, cinema constitutes a real cultural heritage which currently represents a precious source for historical, cultural, and anthropological study of the Azerbaijani people, and also enables us to trace the ideological evolution of the country under different political regimes. Azerbaijani cartoons, alongside fictional films, depict the cultural values of the Azerbaijani people.

– *Arts and crafts and decorative art*: Azerbaijani arts and crafts are represented by several areas of which art and weaving are the most well known. Being historically secular, Azerbaijani arts and crafts represent a rich heritage which includes knowledge and collections of artisan products.

– Social practices, celebratory rituals and events: people's rituals and ceremonial traditions are vectors of their historical evolution as well as their cultural and spiritual identities. The celebration of Norwuz symbolizes the arrival of spring and is the most representative example of Azerbaijani festive traditions as well as the expression of the authentic cultural identity of the Azerbaijani people.

– Oral and written traditions and expressions: the heritage of oral and written expression in Azerbaijan is represented by a rich literary heritage including numerous oral and written genres, as well as by traditional folklore.

– Linguistic diversity in Azerbaijan: the linguistic heritage of Azerbaijan includes not only the Azerbaijani language but also dozens of other languages belonging to different language families.

– Transmitting and preserving Azerbaijani language and culture: this subject is introduced, in the form of lessons, academic events, interviews as well as exhibitions, art galleries, organizations, and people involved in transmitting and preserving (i.e. presenting, disseminating, and teaching) Azerbaijani cultural heritage.

– Research into Azerbaijani culture: this area will introduce the research conducted into different areas of Azerbaijani cultural heritage.

5.5.2. *Library of thematic analysis schemes in AACH*

The areas of knowledge covered by the AACH portal which we have identified below are expressed in the thematic analysis schemes of the AACH domain. To design the library of thematic analysis schemes, we used the areas of knowledge defined in the previous section.

To structure our analysis schemes, we have used the CCA (Culture Crossroads Archive[34]) schemes which have been adapted and developed for the AACH such as, for example, *Linguistic Diversity in Azerbaijan Music* to which we have added new schemes specific to the AACH, for

---

34 See http://semiolive.ext.msh-paris.fr/arc/.

example *Visual arts*, Azerbaijani *musical instruments*, *Visual arts (painting, audiovisual arts* and *historical architecture and heritage).*

Music	Mugham	*Traditional Azerbaijani academic music genre*
	Ashik	*Traditional Azerbaijani genre of popular music*
	Classical	*Classical music incorporating traditional themes*
	Jazz	*Jazz music incorporating traditional motifs*
	Popular songs and instrumental dance music	*Popular songs of the 20th Century; traditional dance music*
	Musical instruments	*Introduction to instruments, their areas of use (genres)*
Living performing arts	*Opera*	*"Layla and Majnoon" and others*
	Theater	*Dramatic theater, puppetry*
	Ballet	*"Seven beauties", "A Thousand and One Nights" and others*
	Dance	*Traditional dance*
Visual arts – painting	*Painting*	*Painting from the 19th and 20th Centuries and more modern work*
	Floral art	*Painting flowers, floral art*
	Rock art and petroglyphs	*Art of drawing/carving on rocks practices by Neolithic man (Gobustan)*
	Miniatures	*Medieval style of painting*
	Caricatures	*Satirical publication "Molla Nasredin" (1906–1931), modern caricatures*
Visual arts and historical heritage		*Icheri Sheher*

Table 5.1. *Areas to be included in the Azerbaijan cultural heritage portal*

Visual – audiovisual arts	*Films*	*Cult films from the 20th Century with humanist ideas and values, study of dominant ideologies in films, national cinematic industry*
	Children's films	
	Cartoons	
	Documentaries	
Arts and crafts and decorative arts	*Ceramics and pottery*	*Decorative ceramics, artisan pottery*
	Glass art	*Manufacture of glass products*
	Weaving	*Rugs, kilims, other woven materials: bed-covers, slippers, tablecloths*
	Textiles, silk	*Artisan textile production, national costume*
	Metallurgy	*Utensils, weapons, jewelry*
	Baking	*Tandir – traditional bread, traditional sweets*
Social practices, celebratory rituals and events		*Norwuz – celebration of Spring*
Linguistic diversity in Azerbaijan	*Azerbaijani language*	*Introduction to the Azerbaijani language, language registers and different social contexts*
	Languages of Azerbaijan	*Turkic languages, Caucasian languages Iranian languages, other languages*
Oral and written traditions and expressions	*Literature*	*Ruba'i, gazels*
	Folklore	*Stories, rhymes, songs*
Transmitting and preserving Azerbaijani language and culture		*Interviews, seminars, talks, classes, institutions and people involved in transmitting and preserving Azerbaijani culture (universities, museums, research centers, etc.)*
Research into Azerbaijani culture		*Interviews, conferences, talks, round tables*

Table 5.1. *(continued) Areas to be included in the Azerbaijan cultural heritage portal*

5.5.3. *The AACH thesaurus*

The creation of thematic analysis schemes for Azerbaijani audiovisual cultural heritage also required creation of new corresponding thesauri[35] and categories. For example, creating the category *Public figures in Azerbaijan* meant that we had to specify the figures from different spheres of social and cultural life in Azerbaijan in the same category. The list in this category also includes names of universities, musicians, artists, artisans, professors and academics, public officials, as well as normal citizens who have contributed to our research.

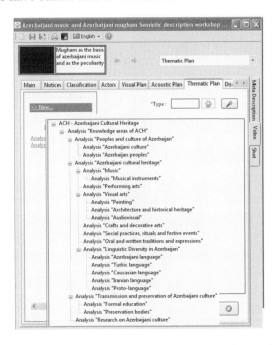

Figure 5.2. *Library of thematic analysis schemes in the Audiovisual Azerbaijani cultural heritage portal (AACH)*

We created the category *Languages of Azerbaijan* which has in turn enabled us to add a thesaurus of the three language families existing in Azerbaijan.

---

35 See Chapter 5 [STO 11a].

The thesaurus *Azerbaijani musical instruments* introduces traditional musical instruments used in Azerbaijani music while the thesaurus *Azerbaijani literary genres* includes the names of specific literary genres existing in Azerbaijan.

These initial thesauri used in the AACH portal are completed during the development of the audiovisual corpus.

Figure 5.3. *Thesaurus from the AACH portal*

When building the AACH thesaurus, the choice of spelling of the terminology specific to Azerbaijani culture, which does not have exact equivalents in French or English, has often required multisource study to identify the most commonly used orthographic transcription by comparing them with those used in official documents (i.e. dictionaries, encyclopedias, official organizations). As such, for Azerbaijani Mugham, we have adopted the spelling used by UNESCO. In the absence of a reference point, we have simply phonetically transcrebed Azerbaijani terms. For example, the term *bayati* (a literary genre specific to Azerbaijan).

5.5.4. *Pragmatic analysis of semiotic descriptions of the AACH audiovisual corpus*

As the primary aim of developing the AACH portal is for educational and academic purposes, in this sub-section we will examine and evaluate the procedure of semiotic analysis the AACH corpus in view of their various potential advantages for educational and academic use. With this in mind, the most interesting analysis schemes in ASW Studio for the AACH corpus are *themes, acoustics, visuals, uses, classification, and translation.*

5.5.4.1. *A representative video of the AACH corpus*

For our demonstration we have chosen a video, *Azerbaijani music and Mugham*, which is indicative of the AACH portal[36]. It is an interview of three well-known Azerbaijani musicians who explain the main characteristics of Azerbaijani music and mugham, and provide a demonstration by interpreting the extracts of Azerbaijani music and show their traditional instruments. As such, the content of this video enables its description and use not only in terms of themes but also in terms of visuals and acoustics[37].

5.5.4.2. *Segmentation for focused analysis using the ASW Segmentation Workshop*

The first stage of analysis in the ASW Studio[38], thematic segmentation of the video, will enable the user to search for a video extract responding precisely to their criteria. As such, due to the thematic indexation of our video segments (which cover several subjects such as Azerbaijani music, Mugham, Azerbaijani musical instruments, etc.), a search related to Azerbaijani musical instruments will only return videos where its sections are directly linked to this subject. As such, segmentation also enables us to find excerpts that focus on a precise subject in all the videos of the corpus.

---

36 See the Azerbaijani culture portal: http://semioweb.msh-paris.fr/corpus/azeributa/FR.
37 See Chapter 4 [STO 11a].
38 See Chapter 2 [STO 11a].

5.5.4.3. *Analyzing themes for exploring the thematic richness of an AACH audiovisual text*

Several analysis schemes for *Themes* enable us to describe the same event according to several themes. As such, the video *Azerbaijani music and mugham*, featuring many of the subjects covered, can be described according to at least four themes: Azerbaijani music, mugham as an intercultural musical genre, Azerbaijani mugham, and Azerbaijani musical instruments. It is in the themes section that we find the library of the previously identified thematic description schemes.

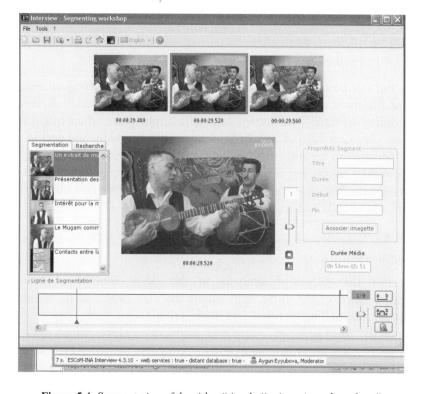

Figure 5.4. *Segmentation of the video "Azerbaijani music and mugham"*

The formulas for analyzing the themes enable us to describe the event in detail from several perspectives. As such, the *Musical instrument* section enables us not only to identify the instrument in question but also its place of origin and where it is used. This also applies to the *Music* section which enables us to identify the genre of music in question as well as its sphere of use and origins.

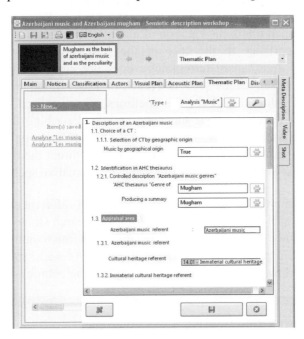

Figure 5.5. *Analysis of the themes in an AACH video*

Thematically describing videos focusing on one subject enables us to create a thematic audiovisual file on this subject. As such, for example, the theme of mugham is covered in several parts of the AACH portal such as *Azerbaijani music and mugham, Interview with the researcher, Sanubar Baghirova,* or even *On the streets of Icheri Sheher*[39], and is only represented in the acoustics section. Due to thematic description, it is therefore possible to present these videos or segments in the form of a thematic file on Azerbaijani mugham.

Thematic description therefore enables us to provide the user all the videos and segments corresponding to the subject of their research.

---

39 See the Azerbaijani Culture portal: http://semioweb.msh-paris.fr/corpus/azeributa/ FR.

5.5.4.4. *A thesaurus showing the terminological richness of the AACH*

The detailed description of a topic in the *themes* section enables us to indicate all the orthographic variants of the word.

With this in mind, the creation of a controlled thesaurus assumes a special importance in the case of the AACH corpus. Given that specifically Azerbaijani terminology does not always have a stable equivalent in languages such as French or English, the creation of a thesaurus enables us to fix the spellings of specialized terms and standardize them and their meanings, while describing the texts in question. Simultaneously, it is also advisable to indicate any other spelling variants so that the search engine can direct the user toward the right text even with a key word using an alternative spelling.

For example, the word *mugham* has several different spellings in French, as well as in English. Etymological research shows that it can indicate either the concept of mugham as an intercultural musical genre or as a precise cultural musical genre. As such, spelling may vary depending on the meaning and its underlying culture.

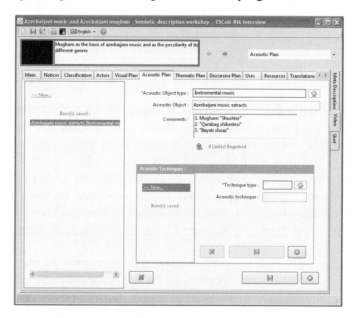

Figure 5.6. *Analyzing the acoustics in an AACH video*

5.5.4.5. *Visuals and acoustics for exploring the maximum cognitive potential of the AACH corpus*

In audiovisual videos or segments of cultural heritage, including views of surroundings, scenes showing performing arts, visual arts, arts and crafts, or even social practices, the cognitive purpose of describing the video's themes is highlighted. This is also applicable to describing acoustics in audiovisual videos or segments as a musical source or containing scenes of musical practices. This is the case with the video *Azerbaijani music and mugham* which contains scenes of Azerbaijani music. The description of the visuals and acoustics in the extracts and musical performances contained in the AACH corpus enables us to create a thematic file of Azerbaijani musical practices to provide an entertaining resource for teaching Azerbaijani culture.

5.5.4.6. *Multilingual adaptation of the AACH portal for intercultural studies*

As indicated in previous chapters, the ASW Studio provides several means of multilingual adaptation for audiovisual texts and their descriptions.

First of all the options of multiple linguistic indexing proposed in the list of *Languages* in the *Video* section[40] of the ASW Studio enables us to identify all the languages used in a multilingual video. Due to this option, a francophone user can, for example, find all the videos containing French in the AACH portal. Similarly, an Azeriphone can obtain a list of all the videos in Azerbaijani.

The advantage of focusing on language is further demonstrated due to the segmentation procedure that we examined in section 5.5.4.2. Identifying the language of each extract from a video also enables the user to locate not only videos containing their language but also concrete video extracts recorded in their language.

For example, the videos of interviews with researchers Fuad Mamedov and Sanubar Baghirov contain both French and Azerbaijani and Azerbaijani and English, respectively. The extracts in French and

40 See Chapter 3 [STO 11a].

English are brief introductions for the researchers and their areas of interest. Due to multilingual indexing, a French researcher, for example, can locate not only these bilingual videos but also access precise extracts containing discourse in French or English, enabling them to find out more about their colleagues' areas of research.

The *translation* option proposed by the ASW Studio provides access to the audiovisual text's content to audiences who do not speak the language used in the video. In the case of the AACH portal, multilingual adaptation of an audiovisual text enables it to be used as an educational support in teaching foreigners about Azerbaijani culture. This offers them the possibility of learning about Azerbaijani cultural heritage independently. As such, for example, the translation into French of the video *Azerbaijani music and mugham* summarizes the contents of the video segment.

Figure 5.7. *Translation of an AACH video segment*

Finally, the ASW environment also enables the user to write semiotic descriptions in any language selected from the *Languages* list of the *Meta-description* section[41]. As such, for example, descriptions of the same AACH video are available in French, Azerbaijani and Russian.

In this way, the multilingual indexation ASW mechanisms therefore enable us to optimize the cognitive use of an audiovisual text.

5.5.4.7. *Types of discourse for learning foreign languages*

Indexing discourse is particularly useful for teaching a foreign language. Due to a search in the AACH portal's corpus according to the criteria of the discourse genres, a teacher of Azerbaijani can locate videos containing discourse of different genres including dialog, conversations, negotiations, debates, and so on. Using them will enable the foreign students to observe how the language functions in real situations and improve their linguistic abilities.

Besides, watching videos containing familiar and official discourse enables the students to differentiate among various registers, select appropriate styles and vocabulary, and expressions for given contexts.

The types of genres of indexed discourse are, in turn, useful for specialized learning of Azerbaijani. For example, students could use it to learn legal, business, travel, or other types of vocabulary. For example, the video *Azerbaijani music and mugham* indexed under the genre *Musical discourse* enables the students to learn musical vocabulary in Azerbaijani, specifically the names of different musical genres and Azerbaijani musical instruments.

5.5.4.8. *Scientific disciplines in the AACH for research and teaching*

As we have already seen in previous chapters, the *Classification* field enables us to index videos according to academic disciplines. This function represents a real advantage for both researchers and students. Due to the possibility offered by the AACH portal to access the corpus by academic discipline, researchers can locate videos corresponding to their areas of research. With respect to students, classifying videos by academic discipline provides material that is

---

41 See Chapter 6 [STO 11a].

complimentary to their studies. For example, the video *Azerbaijani music and mugham* can be useful for both researchers and students of ethnic musicology. We have created a thesaurus of academic disciplines featured in the AACH portal's corpus.

AACH scientific disciplines
Anthropology
    Cultural and social anthropology/Culturology
    Anthropology of art
    Ethnography
    Ethnomusicology
    Archeology
     Epigraphy
     Paleography
   Architecture, design, applied arts
     Performing arts
  Literature
  Philosophy
  Economy
  Geography
   History
Cultural history
   History of art
   Musicology
  Philology
  Linguistics
  Psychology
  Musicology
   Ethnomusicology
Education sciences
   Teaching aids for learning Azerbaijani
   Teaching aids for Azerbaijani culture
   Exercises
    Sociology

Table 5.2. *Academic disciplines in the AACH portal*

5.5.4.9. *Suggestions of use for audiovisual documents/materials in the AACH*

The index *Uses* includes the aims and immediate uses of its portals such as teaching, learning, cultural education, and research. The ASW project suggests potential ways for educational and academic use of videos and extracts. For example, the video *Azerbaijani music and mugham* could be used in a formal teaching context or even for ethnomusical research, for example, on the general theme of mugham or on geographic varieties of mugham.

The video could also be used for intercultural education by the people who are interested in Azerbaijani culture. This recording is an ideal means of introducing Azerbaijani music and mugham which are presented in an entertaining way, interspersed with performances of traditional musical instruments.

The video is also useful for the specialists, specifically foreign musicians who want to find out more about Azerbaijani music and instruments.

5.6. Applications for the AACH portal and the ASW environment

From the summary of possible uses for the AACH portal's corpus which was analyzed and indexed from different perspectives in the ASW studio, we can identify five overall areas of application for the portal:

1) *Teaching Azerbaijani language and civilization to foreigners, specifically francophones*: the AACH portal developed by using the ASW approach provides educational material for teaching Azerbaijani, and is a particularly good support for teaching about Azerbaijani civilization. The advantages of audiovisual material in comparison with the traditional paper or audio sources lie in their entertainment value and the possibility of, for example, seeing authentic cultural practices or hearing different specialists speak about their work or different areas of study and activities. Audiovisual documents enable us to gain authentic samples of discourse related to the language in question.

2) *Teaching about Azerbaijani civilization in the context of university or school courses*: the AACH portal can serve as an educational support as well as a potential resource for thematic lessons on Azerbaijan or an area of Azerbaijani culture as a general university discipline[42] or even teaching programs in secondary education. As such, we have statements about the portal's use for creating a folder on Azerbaijan in a French high school as well as for university courses on the linguistic make up of the Caucasus.

3) *Intercultural education: initiation, discovering Azerbaijani culture*: the AACH portal can also be used as an entertainment tool for intercultural education for discovering Azerbaijani culture. Some of the videos from the corpus represent a means of introducing users to Azerbaijani culture, for example, the video entitled *Azerbaijani music and mugham*.

4) *Foreign research into different areas of Azerbaijani culture*: on the one hand, the corpus of the AACH portal introduces different official sources, trade specialists, researchers, academics, and represents an excellent resource for researchers, both French and Azerbaijani in their research related to Azerbaijan and its history and cultural heritage. On the other hand, by capitalizing the results of academic research in these fields, the AACH portal also creates a base for exchanges among Francophone, Anglophone, and Azerbaijani researchers.

5) *Art, culture, and performing arts:* the AACH portal also enables French specialists in art, culture, and performing arts to familiarize with fellow specialists' work techniques. It also contributes to sharing experience between culture specialists.

Outside of the AACH portal, the ASW environment has other applications apart from the fields discussed here.

By proposing multicriteria classification and analysis of information, the ASW studio makes search results more precise and information more accessible and adapted to educational, academic, and specialized applications. Due to the ASW environment, the creation of portals can also help the institutions such as universities, or

---

42 See Table 5.2.

research and cultural institutions to capitalize on and use their archives of information.

As such, the cultural heritage initiative developed in our project will enable teachers, researchers, and cultural figures to manage the process of organizing their own archives better.

5.7. Conclusion: advantages, benefits and perspectives

A review on our research and development project in the form of the AACH portal in the ASW project reveals the following conclusions.

The originality of this project lies in the fact that theoretical reflection goes hand in hand with practical development. Theoretical reflection has enabled us to construct a cultural heritage approach to create an audiovisual cultural heritage portal. The practical development and building of a concrete archive have enabled us to expand this approach and have also become its concrete result.

The development of the AACH portal has not only brought a concrete solution to the problem outlined at the beginning of this chapter but has also revealed applications beyond that of teaching.

First of all, the collection of resources and multimedia educational resources proposed by the AACH portal are highly valuable for teaching Azerbaijani language and civilization in a context lacking educational material.

One of the major advantages of the audiovisual archive of the AACH portal is its universal accessibility. As it offers a rich collection of online resources, it can be used not only by teachers, students, researchers, or specialists but also by anyone who wants to learn Azerbaijani culture.

As such, the ASW approach and environment offers teachers, researchers, and participants in Azerbaijani culture the chance to archive, use, disseminate, and benefit from the teaching and research of their knowledge, as well as having the results of their research and cultural archives at their disposal.

The development of the AACH portal has also led to more general reflection on the role of the teacher and researcher nowadays. Their roles are no longer limited to completing their traditional tasks. The current information society and the context of globalization offer the teacher and researcher an active role in collecting, disseminating, and using information with the application of new technologies, notably the Web, one of the major tools of knowledge internationalization. This new role requires both researchers and teachers to have computer training. Our work at ESCoM and our participation in the ASW-HSS project have enabled us to acquire new IT skills. As such, with the ASW project, we were quite fortunate to find ourselves at the forefront of innovation in terms of applications and disseminating knowledge using new technologies, specifically in their most evolved form, that of audiovisual media.

The development of the AACH portal has also introduced new requirements and has traced the subsequent evolution of the ASW Studio. Its use by figures in teaching, research, and culture necessitates its independent use. The flexibility of ASW Studio offers the users independence throughout the process of creating their online archives and will also provide them an opportunity to adapt the current ASW Studio ontologies and schemes as well as creating new ones. The autonomy brought by using ASW Studio should also be ensured by providing technical training and a guide for beginners. We make the portal more intuitive which will also be one of the areas for reflection in the future.

The potential of the AACH portal, reinforced by the development of the ASW Studio, gives us hope that it will emerge as a significant model for preserving, valorizing, and teaching about Azerbaijani cultural heritage and also contributing to intercultural dialog.

PART 3

Social Networks, Web 2.0 and Mobile Communication

Chapter 6

Academic Communication via Facebook and Twitter

6.1. Introduction

Thanks to the ASW Studio (see [STO 11a]), we have a corpus of academic and cultural audiovisual resources which are analyzed and indexed in detail and which could be used by people such as researchers, teachers, students, parents, "beginners" in a specific area of study, media professionals and other specialists (i.e. in tourism or in cultural mediation) and so on. These analyzed corpora are published online in the context of the ASW-HSS[1] project as Web portals.

One of the initial issues in the ASW-HSS project concerns the dissemination and circulation of academic and/or cultural content in new information networks. However, how can we ensure that these audiovisual resources are made available to potentially interested audiences? Similarly, how can we ensure that these resources are shared by interested groups or communities while accounting for the fact that these groups are geographically and even temporarily sparsely "distributed"?

Chapter written by Jirasri DESLIS.
1 http://www.asa-shs.fr/.

The use of social media, whose applications are based on the concept and technology of Web 2.0 that allows user generated exchange [KAP 11], seem to be a potential technological solution to this issue.

In this section, we will describe a series of concrete experiments with different Web 2.0 "applications" that aim to explore new means of circulating, providing access, and sharing academic and cultural information using the technical features offered by these applications.

To do so, we have used a corpus of 146 hours of audiovisual resources documenting archeological research. This corpus has been analyzed and indexed using the tools developed in the ASW-HSS project and which have been published in the ArkWork portal. This portal is one of the main drivers of this research project.

Part 3 is divided into four chapters. In this chapter, we will briefly introduce the ArkWork portal before examining a series of experiments that deal with new means of disseminating and sharing academic content using Facebook and Twitter.

Chapter 7 will focus on a series of investigations in the digital content sharing platforms such as Flickr and TwitPic designed for disseminating photographic content while YouTube and Dailymotion are the two video sharing platforms. We will also examine how to exploit the new potentials offered by the mobile technology for circulating academic content in a world of "nomads".

Chapter 8 will discuss the examples that show how to use the content aggregation platforms and community portals for more effective distribution of academic content via digital video. Finally, Chapter 9 will focus on the tractability of uses of a video on the Web.

6.2. The ArkWork portal

6.2.1. *Nature of the resource*

The ArkWork portal is one of the major drivers of the ASW project that focuses on describing, publishing, and diffusing audiovisual resources dedicated to thematically organized academic and cultural heritages. This portal focuses on the field of archeology and is divided into five main areas:

– archeological models, methods, and techniques;

– fields of specialism in archeology;

– archeology of world civilizations;

– field work in archeology;

– the cultural role of archeology.

It also includes an online video library composed of 146 hours of videos in 5 languages taken from 19 interviews, 7 talks, 1 research seminar, and 7 reports. All these videos are described and indexed in detail using a metalinguistic system (see Figure 6.1) developed in the ASW-HSS project [STO 11a].

Figure 6.1. *Prototype of the new ArkWork portal showing the different types of access, developed using the metalinguistic system (access by theme, thesaurus, geographic location, date, and so on.)* [2]

6.2.2. Example of video analysis and adaptation

The videos in our corpus were described and analyzed in detail. We will study a video entitled "From (Different) Horizons of

2 For more information on the prototype of the new ArkWork portal, see Chapter 7 [STO 11a].

Rockshelter"[3] in Thai. This documentary was created using a series of research notes from the "Archéologie du haut plateau à Pang Mapha" [Archeology at the High Plateau at Pang Mapha] project in the Mae Hong Song province (Thailand) (Phase 1–2, 2001–2006). The description of this documentary was carried out at two levels; as a complete video and as different sections within the video.

Figure 6.2. *Description of the whole video in Thai and French*

The description of the complete video content involves synthetic analysis of the video's content (see Figure 6.2). This description was carried out in Thai and then translated into French. In order to make the content as accessible as possible to our users, the majority of whom

3 http://semioweb.msh-paris.fr/corpus/ArkWork/1909/home.asp.

were French speakers, the video was segmented into 27 chapters. The title of each chapter was provided in French and each segment was accompanied by a synthetic translation in French (Figure 6.3).

This raises obvious questions about the significant change over recent years in the manner in which the Web is used. How do we integrate this kind of portal into social networks using Web 2.0? Similarly, how do we ensure that this description, analysis, and linguistic adaptation can be shared by virtual communities? How can indexing and analyzing serve as a point of departure for generating new knowledge using the contributions of people and groups interested in fields such as that covered in the ArkWork workshop?

We have therefore decided initially to focus our investigation on the most popular information sharing platform, Facebook.

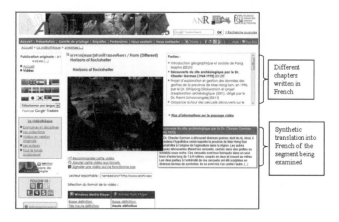

Figure 6.3. *Different segments of the video with the titles and synthetic translation in French*

6.3. Facebook for sharing various types of information

The ArkWork page[4] on Facebook, created in October 2010, is chosen due to its multiple functions which can help us to fulfill our objectives:

---

4 The ArkWork page on Facebook can be found at the following address: http://www. facebook.com/atelierdesarkeonautes.

– creating a profile and publishing information;

– sharing the information in various forms (texts, URL links, photographs, videos etc.);

– creating pages and groups to promote various organizations.

Hence, two types of information are used for the ArkWork Facebook profile, resources from the ArkWork portal and academic information from archeology and heritage studies (Figure 6.4).

Figure 6.4. *The ArkWork profile page on Facebook*

6.3.1. *Valorizing the ArkWork resources: sequences and images taken from the video source*

The choice of resources to be published from the ArkWork portal is based on two axes. The first axis involves making a specific and short video sequence promoting the whole video by inviting subscribers, or "friends"[5] to view it via the address leading to the video's cover page on the official ArkWork site (Figure 6.5). With the

5 Term employed by Facebook.

"Share this" function provided by Facebook, we can publicize that a video sequence has been uploaded specifically to "friends" who are interested in the themes found in our videos (deduced from the information provided in their "Infos" or "Wall").

Figure 6.5. *A sequence of the video "Nouvelles données sur la chronologie des rois de Nashshân" [New information on the chronology of the kings of Nashshân] from the seminar "Rencontres Sabéennes" [Sabean Meetings], recorded on 4th June 2009*

The second axis involves uploading an excerpt of a video as a "preview" with the aim of promoting the whole film found on the ArkWork site. This is the case with the promotion of the report entitled "Visite du chantier de fouilles archéologiques à Noisy-le-Grand avec Cyrille Le Forestier" [Visiting the archeological digs at Noisy-le-Grand with Cyrille Le Forestier][6] (Figure 6.6), which was shared a month before the whole video was uploaded onto the official ArkWork Website on 15th December 2010. Similarly, ArkWork had proposed collections of images taken from its videos on Facebook. These images were published in the same way as promoting the video sequences followed by the whole video uploading (Figure 6.7), or by promoting the existing videos on the ArkWork portal (Figure 6.8).

---

6 http://semioweb.msh-paris.fr/corpus/ADA/2101/home.asp.

Figure 6.6. *Extract of the report "Visite du chantier de fouilles archéologiques à Noisy-le-Grand avec Cyrille Le Forestier" [Visiting the archeological digs at Noisy-le-Grand with Cyrille Le Forestier] to announce its publication on the ArkWork site*

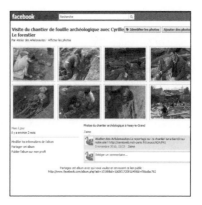

Figure 6.7. *Extracts of the images from "Visite du chantier de fouilles archéologiques à Noisy-le-Grand (Ile-de-France) avec Cyrille Le Forestier" [Visiting the archeological digs at Noisy-le-Grand (Ile-de-France) with Cyrille Le Forestier] to announce its publication*

The creation of photo albums on Facebook not only enables us to have a collection of images taken from the video source but also use these photos as markers for each sequence in the video. This therefore enables the ArkWork friends to view a corresponding specific sequence on the official ArkWork portal which had previously been segmented using the ASW Segmentation Workshop[7].

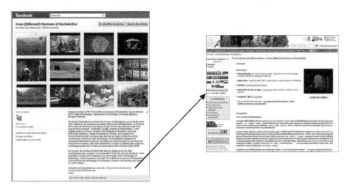

Figure 6.8. *Photo Album page "From (Different) Horizons of Rockshelter", taken from images from the source video, archived on the ArkWork site*

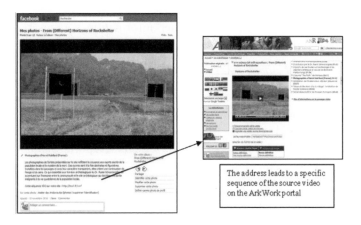

Figure 6.9. *Image taken from a sequence from the source video with the description, "synthetic translation" from Thai into French*

The example that we are using is the report, in Thai, entitled "From (Different) Horizons of Rockshelter" which we have previously introduced. The importance of this example is the reuse of the video's description and synthetic translation of different segments in French to contextualize the images extracted from the video (Figure 6.9). Hence,

---

7 For further information, see Chapters 2, 4, and 6 in [STO 11a].

an image in this photo album represents a segment and is accompanied by a synthetic translation and a URL link leading to this specific section on the official ArkWork site. French speaking users can therefore appreciate the overall theme of the content before viewing this audiovisual resource completely on our Website.

6.3.2. *Type of information to be communicated via profile "Walls"*

As we know, each profile has a "Wall" where its owner can communicate information and his/her "friends" can post comments. The "Wall" can be seen by all "friends" and the information on this space is considered as a public conversation.

We can classify the information communicated by the "ArkWork" profile on Facebook as follows:

– selected videos from the ArkWork Portal;

– relevant information from other information sources regarding archeology and heritage.

6.3.2.1. *Selected videos from the ArkWork portal*

There is a wide choice of videos. These videos are found in the monthly updated section "Top Videos" on the ArkWork portal (Figure 6.10) and videos from our collections which are rotated according to different genres (interviews, talks, reports, seminars etc.) and languages.

We can also select videos from our archive according to an academic event linked to the current affairs. These are videos specifically selected to accompany the recent academic news communicated by the ArkWork "friends" on Facebook (Figure 6.11).

We have therefore highlighted the discovery by a team of French researchers of a new hominid in Eritrea on the professional Facebook page of the National Natural History Museum by inviting its members to view an audiovisual recording of an interview with the great French archeologist Henry de Lumley, titled "Les grandes étapes de l'aventure humaine" [The main stages of human adventure][8].

8 http://semioweb.msh-paris.fr/corpus/ada/2069/.

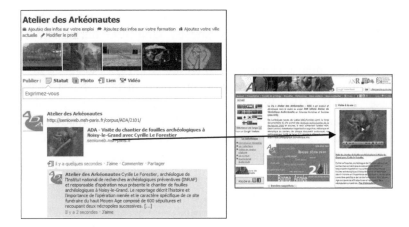

Figure 6.10. *The video promoting the "Top Videos" section on the ArkWork home page*

Figure 6.11. *A video selected to accompany an academic event*

6.3.2.2. *Important information from other sources regarding archeology and heritage*

The ArkWork profile on Facebook also plays a kind of "information transfer" role. It communicates relevant information from other sources regarding archeology and heritage which are useful for "friends". We have, for example, downloaded and uploaded a video sequence about the archeological site at Sarazm (Tajikistan) from the *B-roll*[9] collection from the UNESCO press service[10]. This site was listed as a World Heritage site by UNESCO during the 34th session of the World Heritage Committee (25th July – 3rd August 2010). This sequence (Figure 6.12) on the ArkWork Facebook profile is accompanied by the description proposed in the UNESCO press release[11] and the URL linking to more detailed information about the World Heritage site[12]. Communicating this kind of information on our "profile" enables us to reinforce our active approach and closely follow the international events in archeology.

Figure 6.12. *A video provided by UNESCO uploaded to the ArkWork profile with a description and link to the information source*

6.3.3. *From profile pages to professional (fan) pages: personalizing and adding other applications*

At the beginning of 2011, a professional page for the ArkWork portal was created on Facebook in order to use the applications that are

9 The video sequences are provided for free as a means of communication.
10 http://www.unesco.org/new/fr/media-services/multimedia/news-videos/b-roll/.
11 http://www.unesco.org/new/fr/media-services/single-view/news/world_heritage_committee_inscribes_five_new_cultural_sites_on_world_heritage_list_and_approves_two_extensions_to_existing_properties/.
12 http://whc.unesco.org/fr/list/1141.

not available on the profile pages. This also provides the Internet users an opportunity to view the information posted without necessarily having to be a member of the community, since it is a public page. A professional page also enables us to view the statistics of users ("fans", the term used by Facebook) and their interactions about the information we have posted. These statistics are highly useful for understanding the real interests of the users, undeniably one of the main criteria for selecting our audiovisual resources and making them available to our "fans". For example, we have shared information on our professional page about the live coverage of the 40th anniversary celebration of the 1970 Convention on the Illicit Traffic of Cultural Property (15th March 2011) communicated by the UNESCO professional Facebook page. This information on our professional page has gained 44 "impressions"[13]. On the 16th March (last day of the event), we have posted a video about the conference entitled "Un Inédit du Jawf" [Preview to Jawf] by Rémy Audouin, archeologist and ex-head of the *Centre français d'archéologie et de sciences sociales* in Sana'a in Yemen. In this, the speaker introduces the results of the protection project for endangered sites and objects in the Jawf region (2004–2009) under the context of guidance by UNESCO, the French *Fonds Social de Développement* [Social Development Fund], the Yemen government, and the status of illicit traffic of cultural property in this country (Figure 6.13). This video has gained 73 "likes".

We will now explore different applications available for integrating these videos into the ArkWork professional page. There are three objectives:

– creating a digital identity for the professional page and making it more attractive;

– automatically relaying content from the official portal and other ArkWork social networks;

– creating a specific space for promoting cultural and academic institutions in archeology and heritage.

13 The impressions are recorded each time a message is seen by a user, either on the professional page, or in the news feed of his Facebook profile page.

To respond to the first objective, we have created a personalized home page (Figure 6.14) developed using the Pagemodo application[14]. This provides a more attractive view than the "Wall". A default home page is created using the images taken from our videos and a short description of the official ArkWork portal. It is also designed to encourage Internet users in general and specifically our "friends" to press the "like" button at the top of the page, indicated by a 'thumbs up' sign. This approach is also used on the professional Facebook pages of other cultural institutions such as the *Institut National de l'Audiovisuel* [National Audiovisual Institute][15].

Figure 6.13. *Conference, entitled "An unpublished Jawf", specially selected to accompany the celebration of the 40th anniversary of the 1970 Convention against Illicit Traffic of Cultural Property UNESCO*

14 http://www.pagemodo.com/.
15 http://www.facebook.com/Ina.fr?sk=app_10442206389.

Figure 6.14. *Personalized home page on the ArkWork professional page*

Figure 6.15. *Two applications on the ArkWork professional page, designed to relay information from the official portal (left) and video extracts from the YouTube channel (right)*

For the second objective (automatically relaying content from the official portal and other social networks), we have provided a choice of two applications on the ArkWork professional page. The first is a tab entitled "News" including the RSS reader from the official ArkWork portal. This function allows the subscribers (Fans) to automatically view the latest updates from our official portal (Figure 6.15 – left). The second is an application that aims to combine the extracts of the videos from our YouTube channel[16] (Figure 6.15 – right). This YouTube application allows the subscribers (Fans) to view these extracts (the majority of which are in English with the possibility of using a multilingual sub-titling function provided by YouTube) without leaving the Facebook.

In order to achieve our third objective, creating a space dedicated to promoting cultural and academic institutions in archeology and heritage, we have developed a tab called "Extended Info". This application enables us to create a mini Web page inside the professional page and also enables us to add several media (text, photographs, videos). We have used this to promote the UNESCO Convention on the Protection of the Underwater Cultural Heritage by integrating the video *UNESCO Convention on the Protection of the Underwater Heritage[17]*, photographs, a short description, and the Web address of the Convention's official site[18]. This initiative was carried out on the occasion of the Convention's 10th anniversary (Figure 6.16).

The ArkWork Facebook profile account currently represents an international community of 866 "friends" and the professional page has 77 "fans". The exercise of promoting the professional page to our "friends" is under process.

Quantitatively, we can distinguish between four types of "friends" on our Facebook profile:

– individuals interested in archeology, art and culture from different continents. However, it should be noted that there is a strong concentration of this type of "friend" in Europe;

– groups and professional networks (both national and international), particularly in the fields of archeology and heritage, museums, digital culture, and the media, for example, Rempart[19] (*Réseau d'associations au service du patrimoine*), the *Société*

16 Our YouTube channel can be found at the following address: http://www. YouTube.com/user/LesArkeonautes?feature=mhum.
17 http://www.YouTube.com/watch?v=aoNV8tRVRqo&feature=player_embedded.
18 http://www.unesco.org/new/fr/culture/themes/underwater-cultural-heritage/the-2001-convention/.
19 http://www.rempart.com/.

d'Etudes en Archéologie Subaquatique[20], the *Réseau muséal du Saguenay-Lac-Saint-Jean* representing 17 Canadian institutions[21], the *Amici del Museo Civico Archeologico di Bologna – Esagono*[22] in Italy, *ArchéoPass*[23] (Archeological network in Southern Belgium) and the *Observatoire des médias Arcimed*[24], and so on;

– administrative (regional, national, international), cultural, and academic institutions. These include, for example, the Center *Archéologique du Var*[25], the *Délégation de la mémoire, du patrimoine et des* archives (French Ministry of Defense)[26], the French ambassador for Yerevan in Armenia[27], and so on;

– private companies in the consulting, publishing, communication, tourism, and hospitality sectors. This includes, for example, *Le Guide du Routard*[28], *Les éditions de l'Homme*[29], *Château de la Plumasserie, Château de Verrières*[30], and so on.

6.4. Twitter as a means of publicizing short information

The use of Twitter began at the same time as that of Facebook. Twitter is a social network and microblogging tool which allows users to publish short messages (a *tweet* of not more than 140 characters) on their personal page (*timeline*) via the Internet, instant messaging, or text message. This can then be seen by the subscribers (followers) while following streams produced by other users (*following*). Beyond this basic function, a number of more or less sophisticated features are available. For example, the user can send a *direct message* to another member,

20 http://www.archeo-seas.org/index.php?page=accueil&lg=fr.
21 http://www.reseaumuseal.com/index.php.
22 http://www.amicimuseo-esagono.it/.
23 http://www.archeopass.be/.
24 http://www.acrimed.org/.
25 http://centrearcheologiqueduvar.over-blog.com/.
26 http://www.defense.gouv.fr/sga/le-sga/son-organisation/direction-de-la-memoire-du-patrimoine-et-des-archives-dmpa/direction-de-la-memoire-du-patrimoine-et-des-archives-sga-dmpa.
27 http://www.ambafrance-am.org/.
28 http://www.routard.com/.
29 http://www.edhomme.com/.
30 http://www.chateau-verrieres.com/.

retransmit a message from another user (*retweet*), create, follow, and share lists of accounts, advanced searches, and so on [SMY 11a].

With respect to the ArkWork Twitter account, the information communicated mainly concerns new updates, links to the official ArkWork site's collections as well as other cultural and academic information linked to archeology and heritage.

Figure 6.16. *The "Extended Info" tab for the UNESCO 2001 Convention for the Protection of the underwater Cultural Heritage*

6.4.1. *Twitter and sequential communication*

Similar to Facebook, in order to encourage the subscribers to our Twitter account to view a specific audiovisual segment of a video from our collection, we publish information containing the name of the chapter and the shortened Web address linking to the ArkWork portal (Figure 6.17, left). The use of the exact URL for each segment is possible owing to the ASW Segmentation Workshop. Hence, communicating this kind of information enables us to promote audiovisual passages from the middle or end of an academic event, which are often ignored by Internet users due to their length. For example, we have published a segment called *"Distribution spatio-temporelle des vestiges archéologiques et démodynamiques d'une métapopulation* [Spatial and temporal distribution of archeological remains and demodynamics of a metapopulation]"[31] which lasts around 18 minutes (Figure 6.17, right). This segment is part of the talk *Les distributions spatio-temporelles de marqueurs populationnels* [spatio-temporal distributions of population markers] given by Jean-Pierre Bocquet-Appel, Head of Research at the CNRS (*Centre National de la Recherche Scientifique* - UPR 2147 – *Dynamique de l'Evolution Humaine*).

ArkWork Twitter account

Specific segment of the video
on the ArkWork portal

Figure 6.17. *Announcement of the title and shortened URL of the video's specific segment from the ArkWork portal via Twitter*

Therefore, we can create a specific theme for disseminating the resources of differing lengths, over either a day or a week. This depends on different factors such as the video's length or the variety of its content, and so on.

To publish the video sequences over a day via the Twitter account, we have experimented by uploading a document called *"Des bracelets*

31 http://semioweb.msh-paris.fr/corpus/ADA/FR/_video.asp?id=2064&ress=6855& video=136756&format=84#26050.

en verre pour nos Gauloises: archéologie, expérimentation, fabrication" [Glass bracelets for our Gauls: archeology, experimentation, production][32], lasting around 17 minutes, directed by *Yves Le Bechennec*, archeologist from the *Seine-Saint-Denis Conseil Général* and member of the board of the ArkWork portal. This documentary introduces an academic investigation aimed at understanding the methods used to make glass bracelets in the Gaulish period.

To accompany this event and provide as much context as possible for this video, we have chosen a geographic framework to promote and lead communication campaigns in relation to the Audiovisual Research Archives (ARA) portal. The section "Videos of the week" in the ARA portal suggests two other archeological field documentaries about the Seine-Saint-Denis *départment*, *"Visite du chantier de fouilles archéologiques à Noisy-le-Grand avec Cyrille Le Forestier"* [Visiting the archeological excavations at Noisy-le-Grand with Cyrille Le Forestier][33] and *"Sauvetage archéologique en Seine-Saint-Denis"* [Archeological safeguarding in Seine-Saint-Denis][34] (Figure 6.18).

Figure 6.18. *Videos about the Seine-Saint-Denis region in the "Videos of the week" section on the Audiovisual Research Archives site*

---

32 This documentary introduces an investigation method of making glass bracelets during the Gaulish/ Roman period. For further information, see: http://semioweb.msh paris. fr/corpus/ADA/2131/home.asp.
33 http://semioweb.msh-paris.fr/corpus/ADA/2101/home.asp.
34 http://semioweb.msh-paris.fr/corpus/ADA/1668/presentation.asp.

Figure 6.19. *The film "Des bracelets en verre pour nos Gauloises: archéologie, expérimentation, fabrication" [Glass bracelets for our Gauls: archeology, experimentation, production] in the "Top Videos" section at the top right of the ArkWork home page*

At the same time, the ArkWork portal has also promoted the documentary "*Des bracelets en verre pour nos Gauloises: archéologie, expérimentation, fabrication*" [Glass bracelets for our Gauls: archeology, experimentation, production] in the "Top Videos" section (Figure 6.19).

We have promoted this via our Twitter account (Figure 6.20) with the first announcement "*Des bracelets en verre pour nos Gauloises: archéologie, expérimentation, fabrication* > http://bit.ly/eAqMHN". This shortened URL leads to the cover page of this video on our official site giving a precise description of the whole video. During the rest of the day, we have then posted all the current sequences of this video to our subscribers. For example, the second post includes the following text: "*Des bracelets en verre pour nos Gauloises: Résultats après les fouilles archéologiques en Seine-Saint-Denis* > http://bit.ly/eAqMHN". [Glass bracelets for our Gauls: results after the archeological excavation in Seine-Saint-Denis] Due to the limited nature of messages on Twitter, these texts also include a summary of the film's title, the title of the first sequence, and the Web address leading to the first sequence on our official site. All the sequences from the documentary are shown in chronological order over the course of the day.

Figure 6.20. *The first post promoting the film "Des bracelets
en verre pour nos Gauloises: archéologie, expérimentation, fabrication"
[Glass bracelets for our Gauls: archeology, experimentation, production]
to encourage the subscribers to view the whole video on our official site*

In terms of disseminating video sequences over a week, we have
experimented using the interview *"Les grandes étapes de l'aventure
humaine"* [The main stages of human adventure] with Henri de
Lumley, director of the *laboratoire de Préhistoire du Musée de
l'Homme et de l'Institut de paléontologie humaine* in Paris. This
53 minute interview has been chosen, since de Lumley was recently
awarded the title of *Grand Officier de la Légion d'Honneur*. Using the
same communication strategy as our previous example, this interview
was promoted under the "Videos of the week" section on the
Audiovisual Research Archives portal and in the "Top videos" on the
ArkWork portal during the week (10th–14th January 2011).

We have then published the information about this interview
(encouraging people to visit the video's home page) and its different
sequences via our Twitter account. This information was published in a
particular week, starting from Monday to Sunday of that week
(Figure 6.21). Our choice of publishing this information over a week

and not a day was due to the length of the video and the lack of diversity in the visual scenes in the interview (a plain recording focusing on one person only). The richness of the document stems from the oral discourse provided by the interviewee, in contrast to our previous example. Providing all the video sequences over the course of a day would give an impression that the document is boring whereas releasing a single sequence daily would be a better option for capturing subscribers' attention. This communication strategy therefore enables the document to have a longer life span with our audience.

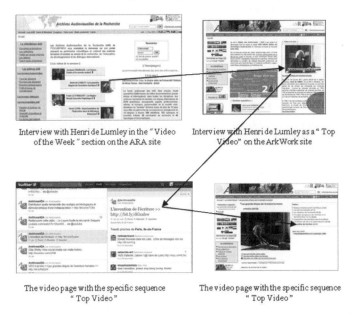

Interview with Henri de Lumley in the "Video of the Week" section on the ARA site

Interview with Henri de Lumley as a "Top Video" on the ArkWork site

The video page with the specific sequence "Top Video"

The video page with the specific sequence "Top Video"

Figure 6.21. *The promotion campaign for the interview "Les grandes étapes de l'aventure humaine", to celebrate Henri De Lumley's title of Grand Officier de la Légion d'Honneur*

In addition, the strategy of proposing a nonlinear, even fragmented reading, guided by the portal's administrator has three advantages. First, this increases access to audiovisual documents, respecting the administrator's programming at the same time. Second, it fits with the Internet users' tendency toward "zapping" when reading [BEL 01] and provides them with a quick access to information. Third, it provides a more adapted and dynamic means of access which encourages non-specialist users to find out more about academic events of a longer duration whose subjects are often difficult to access.

This question of finding a means of making our resources more exciting is also an issue in the Question-Answer section aimed at our subscribers. This involves posting a text such as: "Question: des Khunnu ? Réponse >> http://bit.ly/miwLFc" on Twitter. This short URL leads to our cover page for the video "*Que savons-nous des Khunnu, maîtres de la Mongolie du iiie siècle avant notre ère au iie siècle de notre ère?*" [What do we know about the Khunnu, rulers of 3rd Century Mongolia before the 2nd Century of our era?]. For this, a talk given by Jean-Paul Desroches, general heritage curator, provides answers to the questions we have posted via Twitter.

6.4.2. *Twitter and video extracts spread through ArkWork video sharing platforms*

The other form of information communicated via the ArkWork Twitter account is an invitation to view the video extracts from the ArkWork portal, made available using the video sharing platforms YouTube and Vimeo. We will examine the significance of these video sharing platforms for academic communication, specifically our audiovisual resources, in more detail.

The advantage of posting these extracts lies in the fact that it makes it easier for subscribers to immediately view them without having to leave the Twitter page (Figure 6.22). In addition, if the subscribers want to know more about these extracts, they can consult the short description of each video on YouTube or Vimeo. There are two potential scenarios that arise from this situation. Firstly, if the subscribers want to get into further detail about the same topic and to view all the academic events, they can click on the URL link leading to the cover page of the event on the official ArkWork portal. In the second case, just getting subscribers to visit our YouTube or Vimeo channels enables the subscribers to discover different video extracts from our collection with different themes. This could encourage them to go and view the complete video on the official ArkWork portal.

Figure 6.22. *Post of the extract entitled "Changing Landscapes" given by Margaret Faull, director of the "National Coal Mining Museum for England"*

6.4.3. *Twitter and paper.li, an automatic publication platform*

In this section we will study other advantages of publishing video extracts from our YouTube and Dailymotion channels via Twitter.

These extracts, released through our Twitter account, can be automatically reused owing to the "*Paper.li*" application which is a collaborative newspaper. This enables us to create a personalized public daily newspaper composed of articles by automatically collating information published on Twitter accounts. There are several ways of creating this newspaper:

– from a Twitter user's account (and their following accounts);

– from a key word (also called "hashtag"[35]) used in tweets as #keyword;

---

35 This is a method of adding metadata to the tweet, additional information which allows us to regroup the messages around a single theme, place, or event.

– from a list of Twitter users created using the Twitter "list" tool (which enables us to organize our Paper.li according to different themes).

Paper.li is sent every 24 hours and is indicated by a tweet published on the Twitter account of the user with the application. The result takes the form of an online daily newspaper with pages of articles (including text, photos, videos etc.) [RAY 10].

Hence, the ArkWork video extracts on YouTube, Vimeo, or Dailymotion published on Twitter are automatically integrated into our daily Paper.li called *Les Arkéonautes Daily* (Figure 6.23).

Figure 6.23. *Extract from the interview "Images Médiévales"[Medieval Images] with Jean-Claude Schmitt (Directeur of studies at the Ecole des Hautes Etudes en Sciences Sociales and Director of the Groupe d'Anthropologie Historique de l'Occident Médiéval) on DailyMotion, announced* via *the ArkWork Twitter account and integrated into our Paper.li collaborative newspaper*

Promotion of the newspaper is done in two ways:

– using our social networks. We have posted the Web address of the newspaper in the "Info" section on the ArkWork profile and professional Facebook pages;

– on the official ArkWork portal home page. This includes the *"Les Arkéonautes Daily" widget*[36] provided by Paper.li and the *Pearltrees*[37] platform which contains a "pearl of information" about our newspaper (Figure 6.24).

The "Les Arkéonautes Daily" widget

Pearltrees Platform

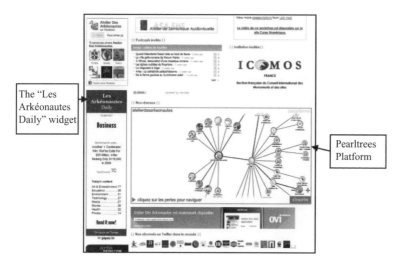

Figure 6.24. *The Pearltrees platform and the "Les Arkéonautes Daily" widget built into the ArkWork official portal's home page*

6.4.4. *Communication between Twitter and Facebook*

The last important point about the flow of information communicated via Twitter is the possibility of transmitting this information automatically via the Facebook account in real time. This application is activated on the Facebook account. Information is shown both on our profile and professional pages on Facebook (Figure 6.25). This point of communication enables us to save time and use the same information to reach two types of audience ("friends" and "fans" on Facebook and subscribers on Twitter) which are not necessarily the same for both accounts.

---

36 A graphic interface component.
37 Pearltrees is a platform for curating content allowing each member to organize and share information on the Internet. We will study this subject in Chapter 8.

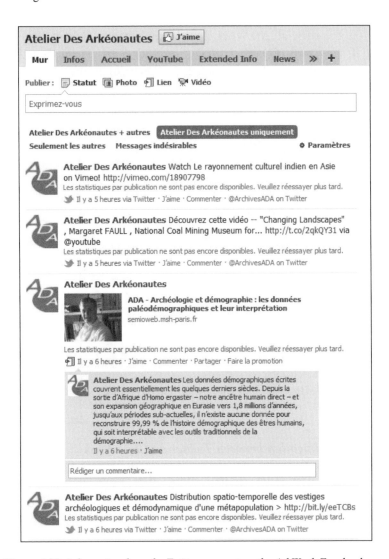

Figure 6.25. *Information from the Twitter account on the ArkWork Facebook page*

Chapter 7

Uses for Digital Content Sharing Platforms

7.1. Introduction

The aim of our investigation of photo sharing platforms is to reuse the images taken from our audiovisual resources as we have done with the photo album on our Facebook account[1]. This is because we want to attract users from these platforms to visit our archives on the ArkWork portal. As part of this investigation, we have decided to use the two most popular image sharing platforms, namely Flickr and Twitpic.

As we have already seen (see Chapter 6), the ArkWork portal contains a collection of videos which were analyzed and indexed in detail. There are several ways of accessing these resources, for example, by subject, location, chronology, and so on.

Using video sharing platforms is a possible solution for promoting this archive and enabling different users such as amateurs, professionals, teachers, students, and researchers to view, work with and use this corpus. We will experiment using the three most popular platforms (YouTube, Dailymotion, and Vimeo) to compare their

Chapter written by Jirasri DESLIS.
1 See Chapter 6.

different features and make our videos more accessible and employable in different contexts.

7.2. Flickr

The hosting site Flickr enables the users to upload images and videos and categorize them, attach descriptions, and link (or tag) them using key words. This can then be used in advanced searches by, for example, place or subject. Flickr also enables us to geographically index (or geotag) images and videos (for 90 seconds) by placing them on a map.

Figure 7.1. *Gallery of images taken from a documentary entitled "From (Different) Horizons of Rockshelter" with a description and Web address leading to the video's page on the ArkWork portal*

To experiment with the features offered by Flickr, we have created an album containing a series of images from the documentary entitled "From (Different) Horizons of Rockshelter" (Figure 7.1), created using research notes from the "Archéologie du haut plateau à Pang Mapha" [Archeology at the High Plateau at Pang Mapha] project in the Mae Hong Song province (Thailand). Similar to the case of Facebook photo albums, each image represents a single sequence from the documentary and is accompanied by a short description as well as a URL leading to the sequence on the ArkWork portal. However, the Flickr photo albums have some features that are not available in the Facebook photo albums. This includes the ability to note the geographic locations featured in the photographs on a map and attach key words to them.

We have therefore integrated the coordinates of each image to enable the users to know more about the geographical location and better understand the content when they decide to view the video on the ArkWork portal (see Figure 7.2). We have also attached key words such as Mae Hong Song, Thailand, archeology, anthropology, artistic installation, and so on. This means that our album can be classified in different Flickr databases and can be easily found through search results.

Figure 7.2. *Short description and Web address leading to the specific segment on the ArkWork portal and the geographic location where the photo was taken*

7.3. Twitpic

Twitpic is a site which enables the users to upload photos easily and share them in almost real time on the microblogging network Twitter and other social networks. Similar to Flickr, it can be used independently of Twitter. However, a certain number of features make it an ideal complimentary tool to Twitter. For example, the names of users and passwords on Twitpic are identical to those for Twitter, and photo comments are also retweeted. In addition, the URLs on Twitpic are already short. Searches on Flickr and Twitpic are done via keywords or *tags*. However, the platform Flickr does not have a shared real-time search tool such as that found on Twitpic (done using # followed by a word). Twitpic's search tool therefore enables us to find series of photos linked to a particular event.

As the ArkWork portal already has a Twitter account, it seemed logical to use the Twitpic service to share the images from our videos. This experiment aimed essentially to encourage our Twitter followers to visit our existing audiovisual collection and inform them about future uploads related to new events on the ArkWork portal.

Image taken from a report to go onto the ArkWork portal with the description and URL leading to the portal

Automatic update of the Twitpic account to Twitter. Subscribers to the Twitter account can see the image directly without leaving Twitter

Figure 7.3. *Automatic communication between Twitpic and Twitter*

For this purpose, in December 2010, we have created an event called "Avant-première pour le documentaire Des bracelets en verre pour nos Gauloises: archéologie, expérimentation, fabrication" [Preview to the documentary Glass bracelets for our Gauls: archeology, experimentation, production] by posting pictures from it to publicize its next upload to the ArkWork portal to our Twitter subscribers (Figure 7.3). Uploading this event onto Twitpic results in automatic posting on our Twitter account. In addition, all the photos accompanied by the tag #archéologie were linked to both the Twitter and Twitpic accounts when the subscribers search for this theme.

We also informed ArkWork portal visitors about our Twitpic account using the widget that links the Twitpic gallery of images to the ArkWork portal's homepage.

7.4. ArkWork on YouTube

YouTube is a video hosting platform where the users can upload, view, and share their video sequences. Videos can be accessed via categories using keywords (or tags) as in Flickr. This platform also allows the users to export videos to blogs or Websites. This platform is also very significant since it suggests other related videos by using the title and tags at the right side of the screen in a scrolling side bar. This function is particularly useful for viewing videos thematically.

However, we will also examine other specific functions of YouTube in relation to the ArkWork collection enabling us to use video extracts from our collection in different contexts.

7.4.1. *Multilingual accessibility*

As our video corpuses are multilingual (French, English, Spanish, German, and Thai), we have investigated the possibility of making these resources available to our international audiences. One of the technical features provided by YouTube which could solve this issue is the ability to automatically transcribe oral discourse as sub-titles using voice recognition (Figure 7.4).

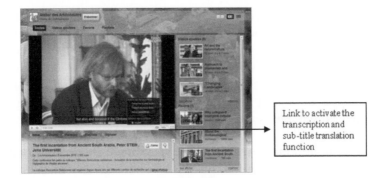

Figure 7.4. *Automatic transcription proposed by YouTube of the video entitled "The first incantation from Ancient South Arabia"* [2] *by Peer Stein (University of Jena, Germany)*

This function was initially designed for hearing impaired users, but has evolved to introduce translations as sub-titles in different languages. Currently, the automatic generation of sub-titles using voice recognition applies only to English language videos. Hence, we have used only English language videos from the ArkWork archive to carry out this investigation. Once the video has been uploaded, YouTube enables us to automatically transcribe the sound from the video. However, this transcription is not done in real time and can take from an hour to a whole day to complete.

YouTube also enables us to download the transcription file (in.sbv format, compatible with WordPad) to correct and upload back onto the server if necessary (Figure 7.5). This feature also enables us to import transcriptions of videos which were written by the creator. Automated tools are used to synchronize the subtitles so that they appear with the right timing when the video is played.

In spite of the fact that the transcription function offered by YouTube supports videos in English only by default, this platform can propose sub-title translations in 50 different languages (Figure 7.6). This means that the videos are more accessible to Internet users who do not understand the video's language of production.

2 See the whole video at: http://semioweb.msh-paris.fr/corpus/ADA/FR/video.asp? id =2020&ress=6637&video=11033&format=82.

Page showing the possibility of downloading   "Caption sbv " file reworked in
the transcription for correction   WordPad

Figure 7.5. *Altering automatic transcriptions on YouTube*

Figure 7.6. *Translating sub-titles from English into Chinese*

YouTube also offers the possibility of interactive transcription where the user can click on a sentence of their choice to move the video to that place (Figure 7.7).

Figure 7.7. *Interactive transcription with the automatic sequence of the video's timeline*

7.4.2. *Geographically contextualizing video content*

The other advantage of YouTube is that it enables us to include information on the date or place of production. This can be communicated using Google Maps and can also show the video on a map (Figure 7.8). This way of integrating and representing this kind of information is interesting for contextualizing videos both geographically and temporally.

Figure 7.8. *Marking the video's date and place of production*

In our example, we have uploaded a video segment entitled "On the podium of the Temple of Jupiter" by John Dobbins, Professor of Classical Art and History at the University of Virginia, Charlottesville onto YouTube. This segment is part of the interview "The Pompeii Forum Project"[3] which is archived on the ArkWork portal. Once the

---

3 http://semioweb.msh-paris.fr/corpus/ADA/1881/home.asp.

information about the location has been entered (i.e. geo-tagged), the video can be linked to Google Earth and Google Maps.

7.4.3. *An interactive video with annotation*

Another feature provided by YouTube is that of linking videos using annotations. For example, we have uploaded onto YouTube two videos called "L'influence de l'industrie minière et sidérurgique sur le paysage de Banska Štiavnica" [The influence of the coal and steel industry on the landscape of Banska Štiavnica][4] and "Changing Landscapes"[5]. These two talks are part of the seminar "Les paysages de la mine, un patrimoine contesté" [The landscape of the mine, a disputed heritage], filmed in 2008 and uploaded to YouTube. We have annotated the end of the first video to encourage the users to watch the second video from the same academic event (Figure 7.9).

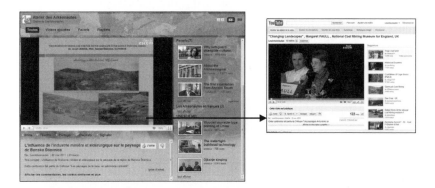

Figure 7.9. *Text saying "See related VDO" attached to the end of the video "L'influence de l'industrie minière et sidérurgique sur le paysage de Banska Štiavnica" [The influence of the coal and steel industry on the landscape of Banska Štiavnica] sending viewers to the video "Changing Landscapes" from the same event*

---

4 http://semioweb.msh-paris.fr/corpus/ADA/FR/_video.asp?id=1851&ress=5909& video=9588 &format=82.
5 http://www.archivesaudiovisuelles.fr/FR/_video.asp?id=1601&ress=5213&video=8 305&format=69.

This annotation not only enables us to create links between videos on our channel, but also to propose other video resources on YouTube whose content has a direct link to our video. For example, in our case, we have tested this with the video "Changing Landscape" by Margaret Lindsay Faull (National Coal Mining Museum of England). At the seventh minute and fifteen seconds of her contribution, a photograph is used to illustrate her point about miners' lives. We have therefore integrated a "stop on this image" function where the video can also be paused.

We have also inserted the text "A coal testimony" here and paused the video for about a minute (Figure 7.10 – left). We have then inserted a URL address to this text linking to another YouTube link of a series of videos called "Coal Mining Story" told by an ex-miner relating the history and significance of this industry in the United Kingdom. These videos are primarily composed of images from archives and various interviews showing the variety of discourses on this subject. The people involved include, for example, miners and their families, operations managers, and public officials.

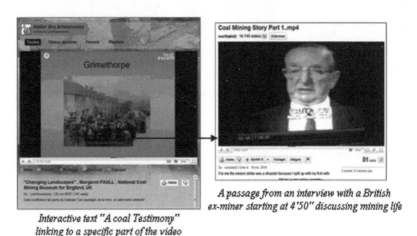

Interactive text "A coal Testimony" linking to a specific part of the video

A passage from an interview with a British ex-miner starting at 4'50" discussing mining life

Figure 7.10. *Creating interactive videos, as found on YouTube*

In our case, we have linked the passage of our video with the first video from this series at the fourth minute and fifty seconds. The video begins with an interview with a British miner (Figure 7.10 – right), preceded by a series of several images from the archive contextualizing the subject. The use of this annotation technique not only enables us to enrich our video using precise audiovisual references but also to create a new type of nonlinear narration integrated into the video, if not the creation of interactive videos.

7.4.4. *YouTube and Apture videos*

The use of video on YouTube to accompany text on Internet pages is also found in the Apture application. This is a contextual semantic search tool which the user activates by highlighting a word or sentence which then becomes rich-media hyperlinks[6]. To use this service, the user has to install Apture as a browser extension (available on Firefox, Chrome, and Safari). Apture suggests various types of content (e.g. Websites, videos, images) and enables the user to explore a subject in further detail without having to navigate away from the page they are already on.

In our case, for example, we have installed the Apture extension onto the browser Chrome (by Google). A possible example of use for this service in relation to our YouTube videos could be as follows. The user searches for the subject "Mining heritage in Europe" on the site *Encyclopedia Universalis*, run by Louis Bergeron, Honorary Director of Studies at the *Ecole des hautes études en sciences sociales*. The application highlights the words "Mining heritage" to obtain results suggested by this service (Figure 7.11). The "Learn More" tool then links onto these words. Once the bubble is activated, a side bar suggests three types of information: search results from the search engine Bing, videos from YouTube, and pictures from Google Images.

---

6 *Rich-media* generally means a platform containing several different kinds of media (video and audio content, textual resources, animations etc.). *Rich-media* content therefore refers to a range of media synchronized with each other.

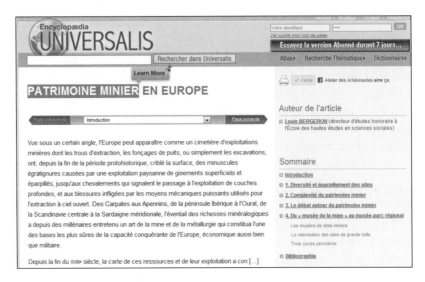

Figure 7.11. *The words "Mining Heritage" highlighted by the user and the display bubble "Learn more" activating the Apture application*

In our example (Figure 7.12 – left), the side bar opens and suggests various information about mining heritage. This service suggests two videos marked with the key words mining heritage, history, techniques, and so on, posted on our YouTube channel entitled "L'influence de l'industrie minière et sidérurgique sur le paysage de Banska Štiavnica" [The influence of the coal and steel industry on the landscape of Banska Štiavnica] by Jozef Labuda and "Changing Landscapes" by Margaret Lindsay Faull. These are videos of talks given during the conference "Les paysages de la mine, un patrimoine contesté" [The landscape of the mine, a disputed heritage][7], held at the *Centre historique minier* in Lewarde, Nord-Pas de Calais, France in 2008. When the user selects the video from this list, the video is shown in a pop up window (Figure 7.12 – right). The display of our video to accompany the article is a concrete example of using audiovisual resources to contextualize and illustrate the theme being researched.

---

7 http://semioweb.msh-paris.fr/corpus/ADA/1851/home.asp.

Figure 7.12. *The side bar displays different types of information about the subject "Mining heritage" (left) and the chosen video is shown in a pop up (right)*

7.5. ArkWork on Dailymotion

The Dailymotion platform is chosen to investigate sharing different video extracts from the ArkWork portal with two objectives in mind:

– to widen the audience using our resources;

– to valorize resources, particularly in French, from both the ArkWork portal and the Audiovisual Research Archives.

From a technical perspective and the manner in which they function, YouTube and Dailymotion are fairly similar. These two platforms enable us to organize the folders in categories (or "channels" on Dailymotion) and groups as well as key words. In terms of multilingual accessibility, Dailymotion also enables us to transcribe oral discourse and translate it into several languages. However, this has to be done manually and not automatically as on YouTube.

However, one of the advantages of Dailymotion is the length of the video which can be uploaded onto the platform. The ArkWork channel on Dailymotion is part of the Official User program which allows us to upload videos of unlimited length. Our aim is to make longer videos available to users of this platform and increase the range of our audience. As Rowe has underlined, "the greater the number of views of uploaded content, the greater the audience levels of the user" [ROW 11][8].

---

8 Higher the number of views of the uploaded content, higher is the audience share of the user.

In terms of programming, we have posted videos whose themes include archeology and human and social sciences (Figure 7.13).

Figure 7.13. *The home page for the ArkWork Archives on Dailymotion*

Like on YouTube, each video is accompanied by a description, a link to the home page for the academic event, key words (tags) as well as the geographical location of the content. An example of this would be our video extract entitled "Les enjeux de la conservation du patrimoine minier en Sardaigne" [The challenges of conserving mining heritage in Sardinia] which is part of the conference "Les paysages de la mine, un patrimoine contesté" [The landscape of the mine, a disputed heritage]. We have also noted the geographical location of Sardinia to contextualize this content (Figure 7.14 – left) with a link leading to the home page for this conference (Figure 7.14 – right).

The advantage of making these videos available more easily, owing to video sharing platforms such as YouTube and Dailymotion, is that it increases the chances of appearing high on the list of search engine results. For example, for the search of our video about the seminar "Les paysages de la mine, un patrimoine contesté" [The landscape of the mine, a disputed heritage], we have chosen to use the broadest key words "mining heritages". As a result, our video is shown in the second position on the first page of results on the "Web" tab of Google search and in first position in the "videos" tab.

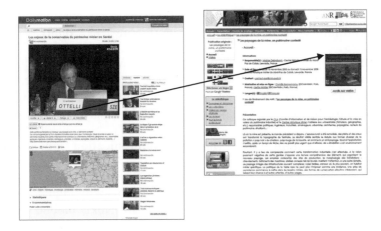

Figure 7.14. *The video page on Dailymotion with the description, a link to the ArkWork portal, and a map*

7.6. ArkWork on Vimeo

Initially, the "Vimeo" platform was selected due to the size of the videos that can be uploaded (500 Mb per week) onto it. The ArkWork channel on Vimeo (Figure 7.15 – left) suggests videos from the Audiovisual Research Archives with highly varied themes.

Figure 7.15. *The ArkWork channel on Vimeo (left) and the video page with its description and URL to the official ArkWork portal (right)*

There are, however, two interesting features provided by Vimeo which enable us to share our resources through various means. The first is the possibility of automatically converting our videos into MPEG-4 format[9] and downloading them (Figure 7.15 – right).

The user can use the URL of the video in MPEG-4 to watch later on various media players such as iTunes. iPod users can therefore synchronize this video content and watch it anywhere. This format is also compatible with mobile phones having video players.

7.7. Nomadic approaches: mobile communication for sharing academic content

To make our resources more accessible to roaming digital content users, we have launched an Ovi application for Nokia mobile phones for the ArkWork portal which is available on the Ovi Store[10] Website (Figure 7.16).

Figure 7.16. *Page for the ArkWork Application on Ovi Store*

Ovi Store allows customers to download mobile games, videos, images, and ringtones onto their Nokia handsets. Some of the software is free while others can be bought using credit or debit cards or via billing operators. The content of Ovi Store is sorted into the following categories: Featured, Applications, Games, Personalization, and Audio & Video[11].

---

9 MPEG-4, also called ISO/CEI 14496, is a standard for coding audio-visual objects designed by the Moving Picture Experts Group (MPEG). For further information, see: http://fr.wikipedia.org/wiki/Mpeg_4.

10 ArkWork on Ovi Store : http://store.ovi.com/content/94136.

11 See: http://fr.wikipedia.org/wiki/Ovi_(Nokia).

The ArkWork application also contains RSS feeds from our four communication mediums via social networks. To vary the type of content to be communicated, we suggest RSS feeds from our different social networking sites:

– Dailymotion[12] (Figure 7.17a and b) and Vimeo[13] for videos (Figure 7.17c);

– Twitter[14] for brief information (Figure 7.17d);

– Twitpic[15] for resources in the form of image extracts (Figure 7.17e).

a) Simulation linking the "Art-
Work" RSS feed on Dailymotion
on a Nokia phone

b) Simulation linking the chosen
video page with the description
on the Nokia phone

c) Simulation linking the RSS feed
from "ArtWork on Vimeo" on the
Nokia phone

d) Simulation of the RSS feed
from our Twitter account

e) Simulation of the RSS feed
from our Twitpic account

Figure 7.17. *Different simulations on the Nokia mobile phone*

---

12 The RSS feed for our Dailymotion channel can be found at: http://www.daily motion.com/rss/user/ArchivesADA/1.

13 The RSS feed for our Vimeo account can be seen at: http://vimeo.com/channels/ 151876/videos/rss.

14 The RSS feed for our Twitter account can be seen at: http://twitter.com/statuses/ user_timeline/ 202197475.rss.

15 The RSS feed for our Twitpic account can be seen at: http://twitpic.com/photos/ ArchivesADA/feed.rss.

Nokia phone users can download and install this application from the site or phone for free and view our resources and keep themselves updated with our news.

Similarly, several social networks where we have posted our audiovisual resources and shared information, have applications for roaming use on mobile devices (e.g. phones or tablets). For example, Dailymotion and YouTube have an application which users can install onto their device (iPad[16], iPhone[17], iPod touch[18]) to view the content on these platforms. As we saw previously in section 7.6, one of the features of this platform is the ability to convert our videos into MPEG-4 format and download them for offline viewing. By using iTunes to view these videos, the user can synchronize these resources with their multimedia players or iPod (Figure 7.18).

Figure 7.18. *Extract of the seminar "Archaeology and demography: paleodermographic data and its interpretation"[19], by Jean-Pierre Bocquet-Appel[20], in the iPod viewer using iTunes synchronization*

---

16 The iPad is an electronic tablet designed and developed by Apple. It is specifically designed for media such as books, newspapers, magazines, films, music, games as well as the internet and email access (see: http://fr.wikipedia.org/wiki/Ipad).

17 The iPhone is a GSM mobile phone with the same features as the iPod touch.

18 iPod touch is a music player with a multitouch compact touch screen, designed and marketed by Apple which can be used as a portable console due to the range of applications and games available. It is Wi-Fi compatible and has Web access through Safari. It also has an email client and access to an optimized version of iTunes Store for downloading music (downloaded files are automatically added to the iTunes library when synchronized with the user's computer). It can also be used to view videos and photos and has access to an optimized version of YouTube. (See http://fr.wikipedia.org/wiki/IPod_touch).

19 http://semioweb.msh-paris.fr/corpus/ADA/2064/home.asp.

20 Director of studies at the *Ecole Pratique des Hautes Etudes* (EPHE) and head of research at CNRS.

In terms of social networking applications for mobile devices, all smartphones, such as Blackberry®, offer these applications to their users. Our Facebook account can therefore be viewed using this device (Figure 7.19) and our "friends" and "fans" can interact (by sending messages, photos, and videos) with us directly without having to use a computer.

Figure 7.19. *ArkWork on Facebook on the Blackberry® phone*

This can also be extended to other methods of communication via social networks such as YouTube (Figure 7.20).

Homepage of our YouTube
account on the BlackBerry

Showing the video "On the podium of the
temple of Jupiter" by John DOBBINS from
our YouTube account on the Blackberry

Figure 7.20. *View of the ArkWork channel (on YouTube) on Blackberry®*

Chapter 8

Uses for Content Aggregators and Community Networks

8.1. Netvibes, a content aggregator

One of the objectives of the official ArkWork portal is to *share academic information from the archeology*[1] *domain*. Hence, our initial challenge involves creating an archeological information portal which collects and disseminates information from a variety of sources. However, this raises the question; which Web 2.0 technology should we use?

The *Netvibes*[2] platform seems to be the best means of achieving this objective. According to the investigation conducted by Christophe Robert, *"Netvibes est un service de portail Web personnalisable ... Reposant sur la technologie RSS*[3]*, il permet de consulter sur une unique interface les nouveautés parues sur les sites Internet de son choix, ainsi que le font d'autres agrégateurs (Google Reader, Bloglines...). L'avantage est, en premier lieu, de pouvoir suivre*

Chapter written by Jirasri DESLIS.

1 http://semioweb.msh-paris.fr/corpus//FR/Soutien.asp.

2 http://www.netvibes.com/fr.

3 RSS is a family of XML formats used for Web content syndication. For further details, see: http://en.wikipedia.org/wiki/RSS.

l'actualité de plusieurs sites de façon plus efficace et plus rapide (évitant de s'y rendre inutilement s'il n'y a pas de nouveautés), et ainsi d'élargir le nombre de sites surveillés. Cet outil sied donc aux sites à actualisation fréquente: sites de presse, blogs... A la différence des "favoris" (ou bookmarks, ou marque-pages), la veille est ainsi nomade, accessible depuis n'importe quel poste informatique. La spécificité de Netvibes tient à son organisation de l'information par onglets et par "briques", ce qui le place à mi-chemin entre l'agrégateur et la page personnalisée (ou "home page", comme MyYahoo, Pageflakes ou Symbaloo): l'utilisateur peut adopter sa page Netvibes (dite "univers") comme page d'accueil, et y regrouper les accès à ses comptes mails, ses favoris YouTube ou Deezer..." [Netvibes is a personalizable Web portal service.... Based on the RSS technology, it enables [us] to refer news on Internet sites of our choice, as other aggregators (Google Reader, Bloglines ...). The advantage is, initially, to be able to follow new events on several sites more efficiently and quickly (avoiding visiting them pointlessly if there are no new events) and thereby increasing the number of sites viewed. This tool is therefore appropriate for frequently updated sites: press Websites, blogs.... Unlike "favorites" (or bookmarks), this technology is highly portable, and accessible from any computer terminal. The specificity of Netvibes relates to its organization of information according to tabs and "bricks" which places it halfway between an aggregator and a personalized page (or "home page" such as MyYahoo, Pageflakes, or Symbaloo): the user can adopt their Netvibes page (called a "universe") as a homepage and consolidate access to email accounts, YouTube or Deezer favorites ...] [ROB 09].

In the field of archeology, some of the research laboratories, libraries, and research centers have created specialized thematic information portals using *Netvibes* technology such as:

– a specialist portal for archeology in the Mediterranean[4] created by the research laboratory UMR 5140 *"Archéologie des Sociétés Méditerranéennes"* (Lattes, France) and the Camille Jullian Center in Aix-en-Provence, France;

---

4 http://www.netvibes.com/archeodoc#Accueil-Actualites.

– a specialist portal for medieval Mediterranean history, art, and archeology[5], created by the library of the *Laboratoire d'Archéologie Médiévale Méditerranéenne* (LAMM), Aix-en-Provence;

– a thematic portal for archeology, archeosciences, and history related to research and studies by researchers[6], created by the SRA Bretagne and UMR 6566 "*Centre de Recherche en Archéologie, Archéosciences, Histoire*".

While not competing with specialist organizations in the field of archeology, the *Netvibes* ArkWork platform is designed to be a thematic educational tool for archeology, heritage, and academic communication, more generally. Information is arranged in six tabs that are classified according to different types of information.

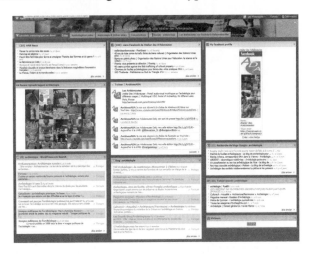

Figure 8.1. *ArkWork homepage on Netvibes*

The first tab (Figure 8.1), entitled "Archeology live", contains two main types of information. The first is provided by the Audiovisual Research Archives (using its RSS feed) and ArkWork portal as most recent posts via social networking pages (Facebook and Twitter). To distinguish these two types of information, the bars at the top of these

5 http://www.netvibes.com/biblamm#Accueil.
6 http://www.netvibes.com/centre-de-doc-sra#Accueil.

units are colored in yellow. Whereas there are bars colored in light brown, which show the search results that are automatically provided when the word "archeology" is entered in various search engines (e.g. WordPress.com, Bing, Google blogs, Yahoo!). The last tab of this type "Archeology Live" is a gallery of images that are recently "uploaded" and "labeled" with the word "archeology" on the photo sharing platform Flickr.

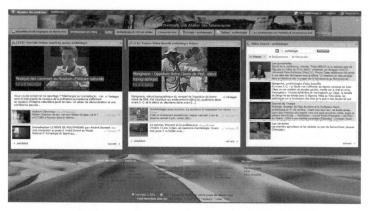

Figure 8.2. *The "Archeology in video" tab*

The second tab called "Archeology in video" (Figure 8.2) contains the latest information from the videos that are recently uploaded and tagged with the word "archeology". They are taken both from video sharing platforms such as YouTube (first column) or other specific video search engines such as *Truveo Video Search*[7] (second column) or the *Video search* application[8] (third column) hosted by Netvibes. This suggests videos as search results for the word "archeology" which have recently been posted online on three video sharing platforms (Vimeo, Dailymotion, and *Metacafe* [9]).

---

7 For more information on *Truveo Video Search*, see: http://en.wikipedia.org/wiki/ Truveo.

8 For general information about Video search engine see: http://en.wikipedia.org/wiki/ Video_search_engine.

9 *Metacafe* is a video sharing site where users can upload, view, and share short videos (of around 90 seconds duration). The platform accepts only original videos related to all forms of entertainment.

Figure 8.3. *The "Archeology and SSH in slides" tab*

The third tab called "Archeology and SSH" (Figure 8.3) contains a selection of PowerPoint presentations about archeology, cultural heritage, academic communication, and electronic resources in human and social sciences. These presentations are taken from different sources such as public or private institutions. We have used PowerPoint presentations which have been shared on the "Slideshare"[10] platform with the following themes:

– archeology (first column). These are presentations of research work from the department of Archeology and Ancient History at the Institution Française du Proche-Orient and the bibliographic resources provided by the *Fédération et Ressources sur l'Antiquité*;

– resources from human and social sciences (second column). These include presentations such as "revues.org" and "*Les TIC et l'art*" by INVISU (*Information Visuelle et Textuelle en Histoire de l'Art*), CNRS, and INHA;

– digital cultural heritage, cultural institutions, academic communication, and so on (third and fourth columns). This is a series of

10 *Slideshare* is a slide sharing platform with presentations in the following formats: PowerPoint, PDF, Keynote or Open Office.

presentations by J.P Dalbera of the *Direction des Musées de France*, the French Minister for Culture and Communication, and A. Defretin from the LEDEN Laboratory at the University of Paris VIII.

These presentations provide users with a quick overview of these subjects before they view other works by the same authors on their official sites or the *Slideshare* platform. The advantage for users consulting this platform is that it suggests other presentations of the same theme using associated key words.

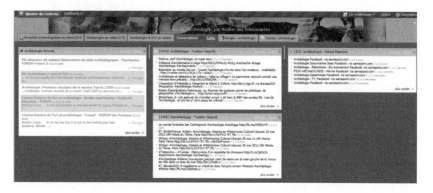

Figure 8.4. *The "Conversation" tab*

The fourth tab entitled "Conversation" (Figure 8.4) contains information taken from discussion forums. For example, we have included the "BoardReader" search engine which searches Web forums and electronic articles. The attached list of discussion forums in the first column shows the results for a search using the word "archeology". The second column is made up of two types of results from the search engine Search Twitter, which searches for subjects that are communicated in real time on Twitter. In our case, the first type of information contains the word "archeology" from the *Public Timeline* or the entire Twitter site (above). The second type relates to information containing #(*hashtag*) followed by the word "archeology". The third column includes information from a search for the word "archeology" on the search engine SocialMention which searches in real time. This search engine enables us to carry out searches of different social networks (blogs, microblogs, bookmarks, comments, images, news, videos, audio files etc. including trends). It also searches sources such as other search engines (Yahoo!, Google etc.) and services from social networks (Twitter, Facebook, *Friendfeed*[11], YouTube, *Identi.ca*[12], *Delicious*[13], etc.).

Figure 8.5. *The fifth tab called "Google: archeology"*

The fifth tab (Figure 8.5) called "Google: archeology" suggests results from Google search with the key word "archeology" in them. The results are classified according to the type of information involved: Web, video, blogs, current affairs, images, and books. Similarly, we have also provided search results with the word "archeology" from the digital library Gallica[14] (*Bibliothèque nationale de France* – BnF) in the sixth tab (Figure 8.6). These results include resources from heritage archives from the BnF in the form of books, manuscripts, cards, images, articles, and reviews.

---

11 FriendFeed is a real-time aggregator which consolidates updates from social media, social networks, blogs and other RSS sources. (See: http://fr.wikipedia.org/wiki/FriendFeed).

12 Identi.ca is a free social networking and microblogging solution. Users can add text of a maximum of 140 characters based on the principle of microblogging, the same limit as that on Twitter. (See also: http://fr.wikipedia.org/wiki/Identi.ca).

13 Delicious is a social Website which allows users to save their Internet bookmarks and classify them according to the principle of folksonomy by key words (or tags) (see also: http://fr.wikipedia.org/wiki/Delicious).

14 The Gallica digital library: http://gallica.bnf.fr/.

Figure 8.6. *The sixth tab showing the Gallica library*

8.2. Pearltrees, a content curation platform

We have also investigated the usage of the second content "curation" platform, "*Pearltrees*". This is a content curation platform organized according to the clusters of information developed by a "curator" and other users via sharing functions. The ingenuity of this platform lies in its spatial organization and tree navigation features for information which is shown as a mind map made up of "pearls". This platform is a complimentary tool for Netvibes to organize information clearly and quickly by creating thematic folders.

The information in our *Pearltrees* account (Figure 8.7) is organized as follows. Our avatar, in the form of our logo, is positioned in the center of the tree. It is connected by various "pearls" representing Web pages (including official pages from our various research projects and other cultural and educational institutions) with other groups of users whose themes are linked to archeology, heritage, culture, and the Web 2.0 community.

To deal with the Web pages arranged around our avatar, we have developed a highly detailed tree to promote our various research projects and bring together our research in one place. Our avatar is therefore connected with a "pearl" representing the official ArkWork page which, in turn, is linked to a "pearl" for the official ASW-HSS project. This also includes other portals in the project (Culture Crossroads Archive and the Literary Workshop of Here and Elsewhere).

Given that the ASW-HSS project uses videos from the Audiovisual Research Archives (ARA), the "pearl" for this project is therefore connected to the ARA "pearl". By following the tree from the ARA "pearl", the user comes across other research projects whose resources come from the ARA site: "Amsud", the Latin American media library[15], "Azeri Buta", a portal dedicated to Azerbaijani Culture[16], "*Averroès*", the media library on French-Maghreb culture[17], "*Diversité linguistique et culturelle*"[18], "*Mondialisation et développement durable*"[19], "*Peuples et cultures du monde*"[20].

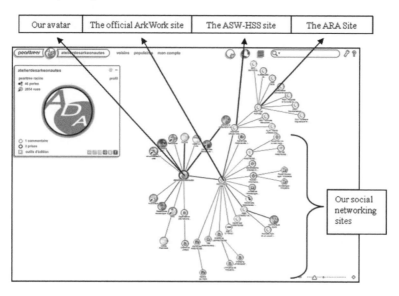

Figure 8.7. *The overall map of the information tree on the ArkWork Pearltrees platform*

---

15 A portal for sharing audiovisual resources about Latin America and the Caribbean: http://www.amsud.fr/ES/.

16 A portal on Azerbaijani culture: http://semioweb.msh-paris.fr/corpus/azeributa/FR/.

17 A portal on the language and culture of the Maghreb and their interactions with France and Europe in general: http://www.france-maghreb.fr/FR/Default.asp.

18 A portal dedicated to promoting and valorizing world linguistic and cultural heritage: http://www.languescultures.fr/FR/Default.asp.

19 A portal dedicated to globalization and sustainable development: http://www.evolutiondurable.fr/FR/Default.asp.

20 A portal dedicated to cultural heritage and people of the world: http://www.culturalheritage.fr/FR/Default.asp.

Around the official ArkWork pearl, we have created pearls representing our social networking sites (Facebook, Twitter, YouTube, Dailymotion, Vimeo, Storify[21], Vodpod[22], Netvibes, Livestream[23], Flickr, Tumblr[24], Scoop.it[25], etc.) as well as communication via other collaborative sites (the "Archeology"[26] page and the Wikipedia archeology portal[27] which we have integrated into our official site under the heading "Resources") and community sites (e.g. the Louvre Community).

With respect to the relationships with other Pearltrees users, we have selected pearls with previously examined themes and have placed them around our avatar. For example, the Pearltree for the *Collège des Bernardins*[28], UNESCO, *"Ressources Archéologie 10"*[29], and so on.

Since its creation, our Pearltrees platform has been viewed 3,195 times.

---

21 A platform that enables us to transform raw information posted on social networks (Twitter, YouTube, etc.) into articles. See Storify: http://storify.com/archives/les-arkeonautes.
22 A platform for creating collections of videos based on a subject or theme with other members. See Vodpod: http://vodpod.com/atelierdesarkeonautes.
23 A platform for disseminating videos directly with the community members in real time on Livestream, Facebook, and Twitter. See Livestream: http://www.livestream.com /atelierdesarkonautes.
24 Tumblr is a "microblogging" platform which enables users to post text, images, videos, audio, links, and quotes. As with Twitter, the user can follow other members from the community. See Tumblr: http://atelierdesarkeonautes.tumblr.com/.
25 Scoop.it is an information curation platform creating thematic media that we can follow. See Scoop.it: http://www.scoop.it/t/archeologie-et-patrimoine.
26 The "Archeology" page on Wikipedia can be found at (in French only): http://fr.wikipedia.org/wiki/Arch%C3%A9ologie.
27 The "Archeology" portal on Wikipedia: http://fr.wikipedia.org/wiki/Portail:Arch%C3%A9ologie.
28 Collège des Bernadins on Pearltrees: http://www.pearltrees.com/s/embed/createAccount#/N-fa=484276&N-u=1_39403&N-p=13493149&N-s=1_1885948&N-f=1_1885948.
29 Ressources Archéologie 10 on Pearltrees: http://www.pearltrees.com/#/N-fa=455338&N-u=1_33532&N-f=1_455338&N-s=1_455338&N-p=2699398&N-pw=19.

8.3. Sharing information on community portals: the Louvre Community portal (communauté.louvre.fr)

According to Wikipedia, *"Les plateformes communautaires se situent à la croisée entre le réseau social et une plateforme de diffusion de contenus. Un site communautaire n'est pas un blog ou une page perso, c'est un site rassemblant des internautes qui leur permet de partager des centres d'intérêts commun. Les internautes sont en mesure de communiquer de manière plus riche, c'est-à-dire en partageant, au sein d'un même espace, non seulement du texte mais également des photos, des vidéos"* [Community platforms are situated at the crossroads between a social network and a content sharing platform. A community site is not a blog or personal page. It is a site bringing together Internet users, which enables them to share common interests. Internet users can communicate in a richer manner, that is by sharing, in a single space, not only text but also photos and videos].

As our archive is concerned with archeology, we have subscribed to the Louvre museum community platform to share our resources. The audiences for this platform have both professional and personal interest (e.g. teachers) in the Louvre and its collections as well as in art, art history, and archeology [PRI 10].

We have therefore explored all the possibilities offered by this platform to its members which include:

– creating and publishing automatically-produced content;

– enhancing information about works in the Louvre by marking them and our resources with the same key words;

– debating and exchanging information by creating discussion groups.

8.3.1. *Building a profile: using our resources in cooperation with the Museum's collection*

We have initially created a profile page on this platform using our resources including extracts of images and integration codes from our videos, taken both from official portals (the ArkWork portal and the Audiovisual Research Archives) and video sharing platforms (Figure 8.8). These integration codes are accompanied by the description and the URL link to our official sites.

Regarding the policy for selecting videos to accompany our profile page on the Louvre Community portal, our choice was centered on complimenting the current resources in the Louvre. For example, we have decided to display a photograph of the "Seated scribe" exhibited by the Louvre in our photo gallery on our profile page. With the aim of creating a thematic consistency with the page that relates to Egyptian civilization, we have selected an extract from the interview called "*Le Delta égyptien d'après les textes grecs*" [The Egyptian Delta according to Greek texts][30] with André Bernand, respected University professor and specialist in Greek antiquity and Ancient Egypt.

Figure 8.8. *Our profile page on the Louvre Community site*

---

30 http://www.archivesaudiovisuelles.fr/191/.

Similarly, we have also selected another video from our archive to integrate on the platform. It is a conference entitled *"Un Inédit de Jawf"* [A preview to Jawf] given by Rémy Audouin, archeologist (at the *Centre Français d'Archéologie et de Sciences Sociales* in Sana'a, Yemen), with the talk entitled *"XIII* ^{e} *Rencontres sabéennes – Actualités de la recherche sur l'archéologie et l'épigraphie de l'Arabie ancienne"* [13th Sabean encounters – News in research on archeology and epigraphy in ancient Arabia][31], recorded in 2009. By introducing this research in the form of slide shows, the speaker shows various pieces from this civilization held at the Louvre Museum.

Integration of this resource into the Louvre Community platform offers a dual advantage. Firstly, regarding the Louvre, it is a case of the free exchange of information between institutions. Secondly, for members of this community, it can serve as a source of information preparing them for any future visits to the collection in question at the museum.

8.3.2. *Marking our resources in relation to Museum events*

Another criterion for selecting our sources involved choosing resources in relation to an event organized by the Louvre, advertised via the Louvre Community portal. For example, the Louvre Museum has organized evening events (throughout March 2011) around the theme of combat. For this event, the Louvre Community platform invited members to mark as many of the Louvre's posts with the word "combat" so that this word is shown in the *tag* clouds in the right hand column.

To create a link between this event and our resources, we have integrated two video extracts taken from the interview with professor André Bernand called *"La Joie des jeux: les Origines du sport olympique"* [The joy of games: the originals of Olympic sport] and *"Guerre et violence dans la Grèce antique"* [War and violence in Greek antiquity] (Figure 8.9). These two extracts are accompanied by a short description and encourage the community members to view the complete interview on the Audiovisual Research Archives[32] Website

31 http://semioweb.msh-paris.fr/corpus/ada/2020/home.asp.
32 http://www.archivesaudiovisuelles.fr/191/.

via the URL link. We have also included links to the three video extracts from the same interview on the Louvre Community platform.

Figure 8.9. *Extract of the interview entitled "Joie des jeux: les origines du sport olympique" [The joy of games, the origins of Olympic sport] with professor André Bernand with a combat related theme*

One of the themes in these two video extracts concerns combat. After choosing the selected themes "Greece and Rome", we have "labeled" the two extracts with the word "combat".

This means that when the community members search for pieces to "label" with the word "combat" as requested, our resources appear, alongside the exhibits of the Louvre Museum and resources from other members, labeled with the word (Figure 8.10). Our resources can therefore attract this community's members and prolong their interest when they visit our official site or use them to integrate into their own profiles. The positive results of this are undeniable, as there is a marked increase in visits to our site from this platform.

Figure 8.10. *Results for a search using the word "combat" showing our video extracts with the exhibits from the Louvre museum*

8.3.3. *Creating discussion groups*

To fulfill the object of complimenting the Louvre Community platform, we have created a public discussion group entitled "ArkWork Archives and the Louvre" (Figure 8.11). This creates a kind of "competition game" communication in this space. This communication technique enables us to animate the "client" relationship, to communicate messages and collect the profiles of participants. The mechanism for our "competition game" works in the following way.

Figure 8.11. *Group discussion page for the ArkWork archives and the Louvre*

Members of this group are invited to view the videos on our platform which share fixed key words in the posts written by the Louvre for their exhibits or with key words attached by the Louvre Community. For example, we have used an extract from the talk entitled "Portrait et devotion" [Portrait and devotion] by Albert Chatelet, professor at the University of Strasbourg II. This was part of the seminar *"Le portrait individuel: réflexions autour d'une forme de représentation du XIIIe au XVe siècle"* [Individual portraits: reflections in a form of representation of the 13th – 15th Centuries], filmed in 2003 (Figure 8.12). This video was therefore labeled with the words "Portrait" and "Devotion".

Figure 8.12. *Conference entitled "Portrait et devotion" [Portrait and devotion] by Albert Chatelet, made available to the group's members*

Once the video is viewed, the group members are encouraged to view the photographs of the exhibits or videos provided by the museum or posted by the members where their content is linked to our resources. Members have access to this via URL links to search results with the words "Portrait" (Figure 8.13, left) and "Devotion" (Figure 8.13, right).

Once the corresponding works are found, the group members are invited to provide their opinions in order to enable a comparative analysis between the Louvre exhibits and our video. They are also invited to use the URL links for these works and place them in

206   Digital Audiovisual Archives

the "Discussion" section at the bottom of the group homepage (Figure 8.14). This space also allows us to post resources in the form of documents. We therefore invite the group members to post documents about our resources for sharing them with other members of the group.

Results page for a search with the word "Portrait"   Results page for a search with the word "Devotion"

Figure 8.13. *Results of a search showing our videos on the Louvre Community platform*

Les messages les plus récents

Par Archives A | 31 mars 2011 | 18h26 |
Voir notre vidéo Portrait et dévotion et Rechercher les oeuvres du Louvre pour illustrer le discours de cette intervention!...

| Sujet de discussion | Démarré par | DISCUSSIONS | RESSOURCES | ADHÉRENTS |
		Réponses	Vues	Dernier message
Thème Portrait	Archives ADA	1	26	31 mars 2011	18h26

Figure 8.14. *Discussion space with the possibility of leaving comments on subjects and uploading related documents*

8.4. Conclusion

Our investigation has shown us the undeniable importance of social networks in valorizing audiovisual resources documenting the research in archeology and cultural and academic communication in general. The image of a "lack of seriousness" about Web 2.0 is no longer a subject of debate in cultural and academic institutions. However, the question still remains as to how to use it in the best way?

In fact, we did not have the opportunity to undertake a thorough and detailed evaluation of the performance of this investigation via different tools specific to social networks such as Twoolr[33], for statistics related to Twitter or WildFire[34] accounts, for measuring the speed of "Fan" progression on the Facebook account, and so on.

However, several basic indicators provided by different previously examined technologies are encouraging.

From a purely quantitative point of view[35], there are 866 "Friends" and 77 "Fans" on Facebook, and 460 subscribers (or *followers*) on Twitter. In addition, the number of views on YouTube is 2,062; 1,018 on Dailymotion, and 3,195 on Pearltrees. In May 2011 on the "fan" page of our Facebook, the number of active monthly users was 253 and the "likes" on our "fan" page varied between 50 and 160.

However, we have to go a long way to achieve total control over these technologies. For example, our policy of including the members of our different communities could be more active and the publication of our resources could be better programmed.

However, this investigation allows us to provide a more "dynamic" and less austere image of the academic world.

Our investigation relies on creating a new digital identity for this world, building social capital and a more open network. With its current and powerful functions, Web 2.0 also makes information more

---

33 http://twoolr.com/.
34 http://www.wildfireapp.com/.
35 Total correct as of 30th May 2011.

accessible to a wider public without language barriers which also responds to today's context of consumers' nomadic consumption style of content. This technology brings together popular and academic discourse. It also creates new ways of viewing academic work in different contexts as well as new means of narration, specifically based on the principle of combining different media.

Chapter 9

Tracing Video Usage:
The Potential of VDI

9.1. Introduction

Modern-day information society relies on increasing the number of digital resources. Music, films, software, and sensitive personal data (bank accounts, medical records, billing etc.) are stored and moved everywhere as digital files and broadcasted in their own formats. Designed to route information between computers, the Internet is rapidly evolving into an *Internet of Things*[1] where services, media, and *Real World Objects* (RWOs) (e.g. products, people and places[2]) and their corresponding data are uniquely identified. In the context of this new Internet, the main interest is no longer machines but content. At present, the content management solutions are proprietary, non-interoperable, and restricted to certain types of information. Hence, there is an increasing need for more effective means of managing and organizing information resources, ensuring their traceability and the ability to search and filter them, as well as to copy, protect, and synchronize them while guaranteeing their integrity and controlling access to them and their usage.

Chapter written by Francis LEMAITRE and Valérie LEGRAND-GALARZA.
1 http://en.wikipedia.org/wiki/Internet_of_Things.
2 See [GAL 11].

Convergence, a European 7th FP collaborative research project[3] aims to enhance the Internet using a publish-subscribe service model which is focused on the content and is based on a common container for all kinds of digital data, including people and RWOs. This common container, called *Versatile Digital Item* (VDI) is a structured package composed of digital data and meta-information with a unique identifier, such as a Website address, which includes the concept of *Digital Item*[4] in MPEG-21 format[5]. VDIs are designed to support all possible types of information, media, services, people, and physical objects independently of their structure or the geographic location of their content. The *Convergence* system therefore provides a work environment with:

– a unique architecture and shared mechanisms enabling the users to create, publish, subscribe to, name, search for, find, synchronize, and protect VDIs for both existing and new types of data;

– semantic capacities based on RDF[6], facilitating interoperability between VDIs provided from different sources and which are offered by a *Content Description Server* (*CDS*) storing domain and user ontologies;

– a logical distributed architecture for the storage, distribution, and manipulation of VDIs.

This new computing environment could pave the way for new ways of working with digital data which are still limited by current technologies and standards. The *Convergence* project should be able to respond to the needs of both professional and non-professional producers as well as consumers of all kinds of digital information, textual documents and RWOs through different media. Some of the new features offered by the Convergence project are the ability to automatically update distributed VDIs as well as certify their content, performing semantic searches, automatically removing

---

3 For more information, please consult the Convergence Web portal: http://www.ict-convergence.eu/.
4 See [BLE 09].
5 MPEG-21 is a description standard for multimedia content rights: http://mpeg.chiariglione.org/standards/mpeg-21/mpeg-21.htm.
6 Resource Description Framework, a metadata model: http://www.w3.org/RDF.

VDIs where they have passed an expiry date set by the user, as well as protecting the personal data, both for the producer and the consumer.

The *Convergence* project is a European Union *7th Framework Program*, which was initiated in June 2010 and will be terminated in February 2013, and is coordinated by the CNIT (*Consorzio Nazionale Interuniversitario per le Telecomunicazioni*) in Rome, Italy. The *Equipe Sémiotique Cognitive et Nouveaux Médias* (ESCoM) from the *Fondation Maison des Sciences de l'Homme* (FMSH) is participating in the project by defining and validating user scenarios for VDI technology as well as identifying specific needs for managing, describing, republishing, and retrieving digital media. More specifically, ESCoM plays a key role in developing and implementing a trial scenario using VDI technology, which is designed to respond to users' needs in the digitizing of intangible material and immaterial cultural heritage.

Therefore, the aim of this chapter is to describe this trial scenario entitled "Tracing video usages" which will be deployed and experimented with in 2012 by using an environment combining applications that are specifically designed for the project as well as the ASW Studio. The aim of this scenario is to demonstrate the power and advantages of VDI technology for collecting, processing, exchanging, sharing, and reusing audiovisual digital data and, more specifically, those produced by heterogeneous communities including both researchers and field professionals, as well as people or communities involved in the documentation process (artists, professionals, specialists, journalists, representatives, cultural organizations etc.).

9.2. Presentation of the scenario

9.2.1. *Principles and objectives*

The scenario of "Tracing video usage" is based on a concrete fieldwork as described in Chapter 4 which aims to collect, publish, disseminate, and use audiovisual data documenting the intangible cultural heritage of Andean populations in Peru and Bolivia. One of the main challenges of this project is to enable the sharing of collected, analyzed and disseminated content as well as the use and ethical exploitation of the contents in the context of academic research, cultural promotion, formal and traditional teaching, or even intercultural communication.

Valérie Legrand-Galarza participates in this project as part of her doctoral research in anthropology, focusing on the intangible cultural heritage of Hispanophone and Quechuaphone Andean populations. During her ethnographic fieldwork in Peru and Bolivia, she collects various types of data (video, photographic, and audio) documenting different parts of the cultural heritage (linguistic, artistic, religious etc.) of the communities in question that is, spoken language and oral traditions, music and performing arts, rituals and celebrations, arts and crafts, indigenous knowledge on nature and the universe, and so on. This collected data constitutes an open *field corpus* (see [STO 11a]) forming an essential documentary basis for this research.

In principle, the collected data can also be used for a variety of purposes by the socio-cultural communities concerned with, for example, programs for safeguarding and transmitting cultural traditions, intercultural education programs (e.g. raising awareness with young members of the community, teaching traditional knowledge and know-how), or even policies for valorizing the image of the community or the Quechua language[7]. The same data can also be a partially open material archive for the international community of researchers in social and human sciences or those who are involved in linguistic and cultural mediation, and defending cultural diversity or intercultural dialog (such as UNESCO). They can, of course, provide interesting material for formal teaching in schools and universities around the world. They can also be of interest for certain types of journalism and the media (traditional forms or on the Web).

However, for all these possible uses, explicit ethical conditions should be respected and the question of rights to images should be carefully examined from the point of view of the indigenous communities involved and a collective context. It is therefore essential to obtain an explicit consent from the creators or authors of this

---

7 For further information on this subject, see Chapter 4 regarding Quechuaphone communities.

collected data and from the population involved to use this material and respect the right of indigenous people to revoke or limit the use of their images. For example, specific parts of filmed material may not have permission to be reused in certain contexts or may not be publically accessible (where, for example, only members of the community have the right to view the whole material). In addition, the ethical question of returning the material is also considered, by returning raw or edited data to the communities involved.

Finally, this scenario demonstrates that VDI technology may represent a breakthrough for those who are working in safeguarding and valorizing intangible cultural heritage by contributing in:

– respecting human rights, that is in this concrete example of the rights of communities and holders of cultural heritage to take an active role in projects about their heritage;

– promoting cultural diversity by facilitating the circulation of knowledge on cultures around the world by responding to two fundamental expectations of the concerned persons: a) the dissemination of their cultural goods and b) the access to this heritage for future generations.

As an innovative tool, VDI technology could be used for "traditional" heritages. This also shows that these technological advances can constitute essential conditions for improving our knowledge about the world and traditional ways of living, if they are considered from the view point of several potential users (notably indigenous communities), if they take into account the expectations of these users and offer possibilities for training which are adapted to the use of these technologies by the persons involved.

9.2.2. Roles

There are four types of roles played by users in this scenario:

– *audiovisual producers* are those who have the rights to audiovisual corpora. Audiovisual producers create, publish, or remove *video VDIs*[8] (containing their encrypted audiovisual resources

---

8 See section 9.2.4.1.

associated with users' licenses) by informing the analysts when their videos are analyzed or posted online;

– analysts describe and interpret video content using thematic patterns, visual or acoustic patterns, linguistic and cultural adaptation of video sources for a specific audience. Analysts subscribe videos of an audiovisual producer, download and decrypt videos, create, publish or remove Analysis VDIs[9] (containing their analysis linked to specific users' licenses) and inform video channel owners. They are also informed when their analyses are posted online;

– video channel owners are responsible for thematic audiovisual Web channels. They create their channel VDIs[10], subscribe to analyses corresponding to specific thematic criteria, post or remove analyses from their channel and notify their subscribers. They are also notified when their analyses are posted online;

– subscribers subscribe to posts on channels corresponding to thematic criteria of their choice and consult these posts on audiovisual Web channels;

– *administrators* are in charge of users' subscriptions and maintain the ASW Studio's digital environment. They set up audiovisual channels, make videos available via streaming, and run the *Semioscape* database.

9.2.3. *Users*

People involved in this context are researchers and professionals working in audiovisual documentation of cultural heritage, university teachers and students, members of Andean population (Peru, Bolivia or Ecuador), archivists, journalists, documentary makers, and IT specialists. Some of them have played a particularly central role:

– Valérie, a PhD researcher working with Hispanophone and Quechuaphone population in Peru and Bolivia[11]. Valérie also runs the audiovisual channel "Andean Intangible Cultural Heritage Archive" (AICH) and plays the role of video channel owner

---

9 See section 9.2.4.1.
10 See section 9.2.4.1.
11 This work is examined in finer detail in Chapter 4.

– Violeta, specialist in Peruvian anthropology works with cultural institutions such as the INC (National Institution of Culture of Peru). She provides the audiovisual documentation on Andean intangible cultural heritage and has played the role of audiovisual producer.

– Elizabeth, specialist and teacher of intercultural communication, is responsible for the audiovisual channel "*Culture Crossroads Archive*" *(CCA)*. Elizabeth plays the role of video channel owner.

– Elizabeth's students in intercultural communication have been asked to analyze videos on subjects related to cultural diversity and intangible cultural heritage. They have consulted the *CCA* and *AICH* channels as both *analysts* and *subscribers*.

– Muriel and Jirasri, research engineers at ESCoM (a research lab as part of the *Fondation Maison des Sciences de l'Homme à Paris*). They have provided documentation on cultural heritage taken from the ARA corpus[12] from ESCoM-FMSH. They have also referred to the *CCA* and *AICH* channels and have the role of *audiovisual producers* and *subscribers*.

– Richard, an IT engineer from the *Fondation Maison des Sciences de l'Homme* in Paris. He provides users with the tools and technology required for their work in this digital environment. He plays the role of an *administrator*.

9.2.4. *The technical environment*

9.2.4.1. *VDIs*

For the technical scenario of "Tracing video usage", the following uses of VDIs have been identified:

1. *Video VDIs*: including encrypted audiovisual resources, metadata describing the video (title, date and location of recording, duration etc.) as well as licenses authorizing the users to watch, download, decrypt, analyze, or post the video (Table 9.1).

---

12 Audiovisual Research Archives: http://www.archivesaudiovisuelles.fr.

Semantic relationship	Component	Sub-component	Description
Is Identified by	Video Identifier		The video's unique identifier
Includes	Video Resource		Encrypted video resource
Is Described by	Video Metadata		
		Title	Title of the piece
		Subtitle	Subtitle
		Video Type	Genre
		Authors	Authors
		Producers	Producers
		Date	Date
		Location	Place
		Spoken Languages	Spoken Language(s)
		Short Description	Brief description
		Media Format	Format
		Media Duration	Duration
Includes	Licenses		
		Issuer	Audiovisual producer
		Principal	1. ESCoM 2. analyst 3. video channel owner 4. subscriber
		Rights	1. storing and broadcasting via streaming 2. decrypting, downloading and analyzing 3. posting 4. watching

Table 9.1. *Video VDIs*

Semantic relationship	Component	Sub-component	Description
		Conditions	Defined by the producer
		Encrypted Key	The video's encrypted key
Includes	Event Report Requests		
		Verbs	1. downloaded and/or decrypted video 2. analyzed video 3. posted video 4. analysis or post of the video removed
		Destination Addresses	The producer's address
Is Identified by	R-VDI identifier		The *video VDI*'s identifier
Is Signed by	R-VDI signature		The producer's certificate

Table 9.1. *(Continued) Video VDIs*

2. *Analysis VDI*: refers to a *video VDI* to which the metadata from the video analysis carried out in the ASW Description Workshop[13] is added along with the licenses that enable specific users to read or post the analysis (Table 9.2).

3. *Channel VDI*: relates to an audiovisual channel as well as analyses which are posted (in the form of references to corresponding *analysis VDIs*), as well as licenses enabling the users to post on the channel (Table 9.3).

---

13 See Chapter 3 in [STO 11a].

Semantic relationship	Component	Sub-component	Description
Is Identified by	Identifier Analysis		The analysis' unique identifier
Is Described by	Metadata Analysis		OWL metadata from the ASW Description Workshop
Includes	Licenses		
		Issuer	Analyst
		Principal	1. video channel owner 2. subscriber
		Rights	1. post 2. read
		Conditions	Defined by the analyst
Includes	Event Report Requests		
		Verbs	1. post analysis 2. post cancelled
		Destination Addresses	The analyst's address
Is Identified by	R-VDI identifier		The *analysis VDI's* identifier
Is Signed by	R-VDI signature		The analyst's signature

Table 9.2. *Analysis VDIs*

4. *Publication VDI*: relates to the dissemination to specific users of a new VDI storing on the network. This type of VDI is used to inform users about new videos (Table 9.4), analyses (Table 9.5), and posts on the network (Table 9.6).

Semantic relationship	Component	Sub-component	Description
Is Identified by	Channel Identifier		The channel's unique identifier
References	Analyses		
		Analysis Identifier	Identifier for an analysis posted on the channel
Is Described by	Channel Metadata		
		Title	Title
		Alias	Alias
		URL	Web address
		Short Description	Short Description
Includes	Licenses		
		Issuer	Channel owner
		Principal	1. ESCoM 2. subscriber
		Rights	1. storing 2. reading
		Conditions	Defined by the channel owner
Includes	Event Report Requests		
		Verbs	1. post analysis 2. post cancelled 3. new user's subscription
		Destination Addresses	Address of the channel owner
Is Identified by	R-VDI identifier		The *channel VDI*'s identifier
Is Signed by	R-VDI signature		The video channel owner's certificate

Table 9.3. *Channel VDI*

Semantic relationship	Component	Sub-component	Description
Is Identified by	Video Identifier		The video's unique identifier
Is Described by	Video Metadata		See *Table 9.1*
Includes	Licenses		
		Issuer	Audiovisual producer
		Principal	1. analyst
		Rights	1. reading
		Conditions	Defined by the producer
Includes	Event Report Requests		
		Verbs	1. publication read
		Destination Addresses	The producer's address
Is Identified by	P-VDI identifier		The *publication VDI's* identifier
Is Signed by	P-VDI signature		The producer's certificate

Table 9.4. *Publication VDI for a video*

Semantic relationship	Component	Sub-component	Description
Is Identified by	Analysis Identifier		The analysis' unique identifier
Is Described by	Analysis Metadata		See *Table 9.2*
Includes	Licenses		
		Issuer	Analyst
		Principal	1. video channel owner
		Rights	1. reading
		Conditions	Defined by the analyst
Includes	Event Report Requests		

Table 9.5. *Publication VDI for an analysis*

Semantic relationship	Component	Sub-component	Description
		Verbs	1. publication read
		Destination Addresses	The analyst's address
Is Identified by	P-VDI identifier		The *analysis publication VDI's* identifier
Is Signed by	P-VDI signature		The analyst's certificate

Table 9.5. *(Continued) Publication VDI for an analysis*

Semantic relationship	Component	Sub-component	Description
Is Identified by	Analysis Identifier		The analysis' unique identifier
Is Described by	Analysis Metadata		See *Table 9.2*
Is Described by	Channel Metadata		See *Table 9.3*
Includes	Licenses		
		Issuer	Channel owner
		Principal	1. subscriber
		Rights	1. reading
		Conditions	Defined by the channel owner
Includes	Event Report Requests		
		Verbs	1. publication read
		Destination Addresses	Address of the channel owner
Is Identified by	P-VDI identifier		The *publication VDIs* identifier
Is Signed by	P-VDI signature		The video channel owner's certificate

Table 9.6. *Publication VDI for a post*

5. *Subscription VDIs*: relates to a user's subscription who will then be notified when new VDIs on the network responding to their criteria are published. This type of VDI is used to tell the users about new videos (Table 9.7), analyses (Table 9.8), and posts on the network (Table 9.9).

Semantic relationship	Component	Sub-component	Description
Has Conditions	SPARL query		Conditions on metadata and/or the video's owner
Includes	Licenses		
		Issuer	Analyst
Includes	Event Report Requests		
		Verbs	1. new publication corresponding to subscription conditions
		Destination Addresses	The analyst's address
Is Identified by	S-VDI identifier		The *subscription VDI's* identifier
Is Signed by	S-VDI signature		The analyst's certificate

Table 9.7. *Subscription VDI for a video*

Semantic relationship	Component	Sub-component	Description
Has Conditions	SPARL query		Conditions on metadata and/or the author of an analysis
Includes	Licenses		
		Issuer	video channel owner
Includes	Event Report Requests		
		Verbs	1. new publication corresponding to subscription conditions
		Destination Addresses	The video channel owner's address
Is Identified by	S-VDI identifier		The *subscription VDI's* identifier
Is Signed by	S-VDI signature		The video channel owner's certificate

Table 9.8. *Subscription VDI for an analysis*

Semantic relationship	Component	Sub-component	Description
Has Conditions	SPARL query		Conditions on metadata of an analysis or a specific channel
Includes	Licenses		
		Issuer	Subscriber
Includes	Event Report Requests		
		Verbs	1. new publication corresponding to subscription conditions
		Destination Addresses	The subscriber's address
Is Identified by	S-VDI identifier		The *subscription VDI's* identifier
Is Signed by	S-VDI signature		The subscriber's certificate

Table 9.9. *Subscription VDI for a post*

9.2.4.2. *Tools and applications*

The technical environment used in this scenario offers a range of tools for each type of user. As demonstrated in Figure 9.1, there are five general applications, each incorporating a user authentication tool which is specific to the *Convergence* system.

1. The *Video Manager* offers a range of tools to audiovisual producers such as:

- *browse notifications*: this enables the producer to view event reports relating to his own videos (this is a default setting offered to the user),

- *encrypt video:* this enables the producer to restrict access to his/her audiovisual resources by encrypting them before posting them onto the network. Hence, users with a license as well as the necessary material (a smartcard and valid reader) can view these videos,

- create video: this enables the user to create and sign a *video VDI* including an audiovisual resource, metadata, licenses, and event report requests,

- post video: this enables the user to store a *video VDI* on the network after its compliance has been confirmed,

- publish video: this enables user to create and post a *publication VDI* referencing a video onto the network and notify analysts of this fact,

- unpublish video: this enables user to remove a *publication VDI* referencing a video and inform subscribed users,

- revoke video: enables user to remove a video VDI (as well as its incorporated video resource) from the network;

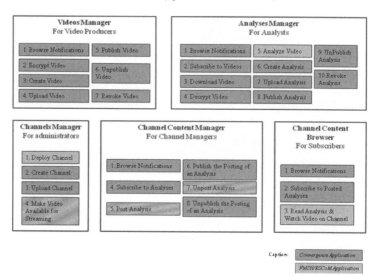

Figure 9.1. *Tools for the convergence scenario of "Tracing video usages"*

2. The Analyses Manager offers a range of tools to analysts:

- browse notifications: this enables the analyst to view event reports relating to video publications or relating to his analyses (this tool should be provided to the user by default),

- subscribe to videos: this enables the analyst to create and inject *subscription VDIs* in order to receive event reports when a video

responding to specific conditions (metadata, video owner) is posted to the network,

- download videos: this enables the analyst to download a video from the network if allowed by their license,

- decrypt video: this enables the analyst to decrypt a previously downloaded video in order to view or analyze it,

- analyze video: this enables the analyst to carry out semiotic descriptions of videos using the Segmentation Workshop[14] in the ASW Description workshop[15],

- *create analysis*: this enables user to create and sign an *Analysis VDI* incorporating an analysis in the form of metadata interacting with the CDS server[16], licenses and event report requests,

- post analysis: this enables user to store an analysis VDI on the network after its compliance and user rights have been confirmed.

- publish analysis: this enables user to create and include a publication VDI referencing analyses on the network and as such notify video channel owners about them,

- unpublish analysis publications: this enables user to remove a publication VDI referencing an analysis and inform subscribed users,

- *revoke analysis: this enables user to remove an analysis VDI (as well as its metadata) from the network*;

3. The *Channels Manager* offers a range of tools to administrators:

- deploy channel: this enables the administrator to create an audiovisual channel Web portal using Semiosphere technology[17],

- create channel: this enables user to create and sign a *channel VDI* incorporating metadata, licenses, and event report requests,

- post channel: this enables user to store a *channel VDI* on the network after its compliance and user rights are confirmed,

14 See Chapter 2 in [STO 11a].
15 See Chapters 3, 4, 5, and 6 of [STO 11a].
16 See section 9.1.
17 See Chapter 9 in [STO 11a] and section 9.3.13.

- *make video available for streaming*: this enables user to *download* and *decrypt videos* (in the same way as in the *Analyses Manager*), and then post it by FTP onto streaming servers;

4. The *Channel Content Manager* offers a range of tools to the video channel owner for:

- browse notifications: this enables the video channel owner to view the event reports related with the publications of analyses or posts (this should be automatically available to the user),

- subscribe to analyses: this enables the video channel owner to create and post *subscription VDIs* to receive event reports when an analysis responding to specific conditions (metadata interacting with the CDS server, author of the analysis) is published on the network,

- post analysis: this enables the video channel owner to post an analysis on the channel using the ASW Publication Workshop[18],

- *publish the posting of an analysis*: this enables user to update a *channel VDI* and then to create and post a *publication VDI* referring to an analysis and channel. Subscribers are therefore notified about the posting of this analysis to the channel,

- Unpublish the posting of an analysis: this enables user to update a channel VDI and then remove a publication VDI referring to a post and inform subscribed users,

- Unpost analysis: this enables user to remove an Analysis from a channel using the ASW Publication Workshop;

5. The *Channel Content Browser* provides a range of tools to subscribers:

- *browse notifications*: this enables the subscriber to view the event reports related with the posts of analyses (this tool is automatically provided to users),

- *subscribe to posted analyses:* this enables the subscriber to create and post *subscription VDIs* in order to receive event reports when

---

18 See Chapters 7 and 10 in [STO 11a].

an analysis matching specific conditions (metadata interacting with the CDS server, a specific audiovisual channel) is posted onto a channel,

- *read analysis and watch video on channel*: this enables the subscriber to view information about an analysis posted on a channel and then view this post on the Web portal of the corresponding audiovisual channel.

9.3. Walkthrough

The scenario of "Tracing video usages" is composed of a series of stages referring to tools using both VDI technology and the ASW studio. These tools enable user to treat, analyze, and post audiovisual resources in an environment offering powerful features for interactions between users and for controlling their usage.

The following sections detail the actions carried out by the user and the system for each type of activity identified in this scenario:

1. user registration and authentication;

2. creating and publishing videos;

3. subscribing to videos;

4. removing videos;

5. downloading videos;

6. creating and publishing analyses;

7. subscribing to analyses;

8. removing analyses;

9. creating a channel;

10. posting an analysis onto a channel;

11. subscribing to posted analyses;

12. removing posts;

13. viewing analyses posted on channels.

9.3.1. *User registration and authentication*

Each user receives a smart card configured with a 4 digit PIN and his personal identifier. In addition, each card has a personal and group certificate confirming the user's identity and membership when the VDIs are signed.

For authentication, each user must have a card reader and a valid smart card and must type the correct PIN code. During authentication, there is a mutual authentication between the reader and the card (Figure 9.2).

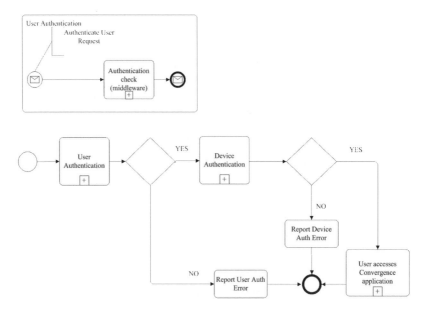

Figure 9.2. *Authentication*

The use of a smart card, PIN code, and certificates ensures optimum security of the environment, reducing the risks of identity theft (because both the card and PIN code would have to be stolen to do so), or illegal copying of the system (only card readers certified by the producer can carry out tasks).

9.3.2. *Creating and publishing videos*

This task is carried out by the audiovisual producers such as Violeta, Muriel or Jirasri with the *Video manager* application. Their aim is to make videos available to analysts and ESCoM on the network (Figure 9.3) and inform them (Figure 9.4) while keeping this restricted to permitted users alone.

The producers confirm their identity (with the smart card and reader as described in section 9.3.1), open the *Video encryption* tool and then:

1. select a video file to encrypt;

2. identify the new file's location and begin encryption;

3. generate an encrypted (new) video file in the specified location. The encryption key is incorporated into the new file;

4. incorporate the encryption key into the smart card, which can only be used by authorized users.

The producer then opens the *Create Video* tool and:

1. Fills a form to describe the following components of the video: title, sub-title, genre, author(s), producer(s), date of recording, language(s), and description;

2. indicates the file location for the previously encrypted video;

3. creates video licenses for:

   - ESCoM, to broadcast the video via streaming,

   - analysts to decrypt, download and/or analyze the video,

   - video channel owners to post the video,

   - subscribers to view the video;

4. creates notification requests which inform user when:

   - the video is downloaded or decrypted,

   - the video is analyzed,

   - the video is posted,

   - any analysis or post of the video is removed;

5. a *video VDI* is created, incorporating the encrypted video resource as well as its description in the form of metadata, licenses, and notification requests;

6. VDI is signed with the user's signature.

The producer has to then open the *Video post* tool and:

1. send the *video VDI* which was previously created on the network;

2. check the video VDI for compliance that is:

- signature of the VDI is confirmed,

- integrity of the data is verified.

3. if successful, the VDI is stored on the *Convergence* network.

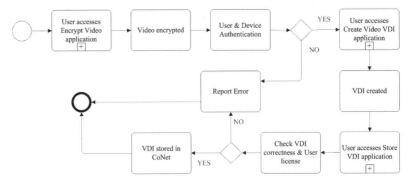

Figure 9.3. *Creating a video*

The producer has to then open the *Video publisher* tool and:

1. creates a *publication VDI* referencing the *video VDI* which has been previously uploaded on the network and containing licenses allowing analysts and ESCoM to view the VDI;

2. injects the *Publication VDI* into the network;

3. the analysts and ESCoM who have subscribed to this type of video are notified of this new publication (subscribing to videos is described in the following section).

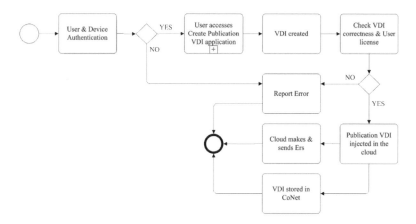

Figure 9.4. *Publishing a VDI*

9.3.3. *Subscribing to videos*

Subscribing to videos is a task carried out by, for example, Elizabeth's students using the *Analysis manager*. This means that they will be informed when new videos of potential interest to them are published (Figure 9.5).

The analyst confirms his identity and then launches the *Subscribe to videos* tool and:

1. completes a form describing their subscription criteria:

- title, sub-title, genre, author(s), producer(s), date and place of recording, language(s), and/or a description of the video,

- owner of the video;

2. creates a *subscription VDI* containing these subscription conditions;

3. injects the *subscription VDI* into the network;

4. notifies the users, when a *publication VDI* corresponding to the subscription conditions defined in the *subscription VDI* is injected into the network.

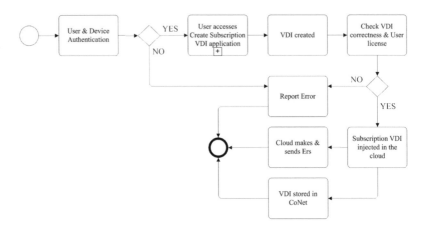

Figure 9.5. *Subscribing to VDIs*

9.3.4 *Removing videos*

This activity is carried out by audiovisual producers such as Violeta, Muriel or Jirasri using the *Video manager* application. The aim of this is to remove a video uploaded on the network (Figure 9.7), and also cancel its publication (Figure 9.6).

The producer confirms his identity and then opens the *Remove a video publication* tool and:

1. is presented the list of publications (*publication VDIs*) injected by the producer;

2. selects a publication and removes it:

   - the user's license allowing him/her to remove the *publication VDI* is verified,

   - a request to remove the VDI is sent to the network,

   - the VDI is removed from the network;

3. sends a notification of its removal to the users involved, including:

   - the subscribers to this publication VDI,

- the analysts having analyzed the related video,

- the video channel owners having posted the video to the channel.

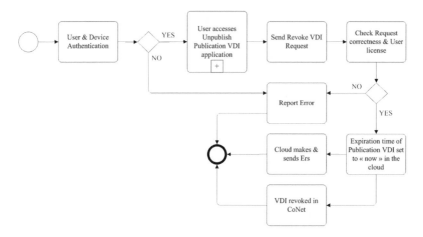

Figure 9.6. *Removing a publication*

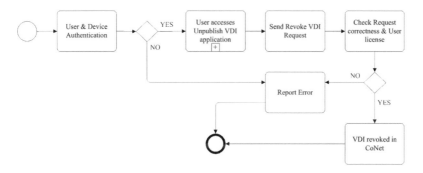

Figure 9.7. *Removing a VDI*

The producer then opens the *Remove a video* tool and:

1. is presented the list of videos (*video VDIs*) uploaded by the producer;

2. selects a video and removes it:

- the user's license enabling him/her to remove the *video VDI* is verified,

- a request to remove the VDI is sent to the network,

- the VDI and video resource are removed from the network.

9.3.5. *Downloading videos*

This is carried out by analysts such as Elizabeth's students using the *Analysis manager* application. After having received a notification that a new video has been published, their aim is to download the video resource in order to analyze it (Figure 9.8). Administrators such as Richard also undertake this task with the aim of making this video resource broadcastable on streaming channels.

The analyst must first confirm his identity and open the *View notifications* application and:

1. is presented the list of videos (*video VDI*) to which the analyst has subscribed;

2. selects a video to download.

The analyst then opens the *Download a video* tool:

1. the analyst identifies the file location for the download;

2. the user's license enabling him/her to download this *video VDI* is verified;

3. the VDI, including the encrypted video file is downloaded to the selected file location.

Finally, the analyst opens the *Decrypt a video* tool:

1. the user's license enabling him/her to decrypt the *video VDI* is verified;

2. the video resource is decrypted using the decryption key incorporated into the user's smart card;

3. the produced video file can be read by any type of media reader including that found in the Segmentation Workshop[19].

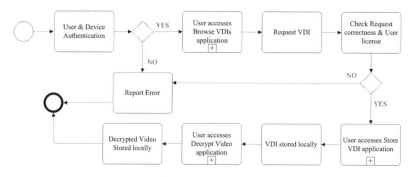

Figure 9.8. *Downloading a video*

9.3.6. *Creating and publishing analyses*

This task is carried out by analysts such as Elizabeth's students using the *Analysis manager* application. The aim of this is to semiotically describe a video, make it available to the video channel owners on the network (Figure 9.9) and inform them of the fact (Figure 9.4).

The analysts initially confirm their identity and download the video (as described in section 9.3.5 of this chapter).

The analysts then use the ASW Segmentation Workshop and the ASW Description Workshop[20] to analyze the video. This process of analysis is saved locally in the form of OWL format metadata[21] while referencing the CDS server ontologies[22].

The analyst then opens the *Record an analysis* tool and:

1. selects the previously created file containing OWL metadata;

---

19 See Chapter 2 of [STO 11a].
20 See Chapters 3, 4, 5, and 6 of [STO 11a].
21 Ontology Web Language, description language for ontologies:http://www.w3.org/TR/owl-ref.
22 See section 9.1.

2. selects the *video VDI* corresponding to the analyzed video;

3. creates licenses for the analysis to:

   - the video channel owners to post the analysis,

   - the subscribers to read the analysis;

4. create notification requests which allow the analysts to be informed when:

   - the analysis is posted,

   - a posted analysis is removed;

5. an *analysis VDI* is therefore created incorporating OWL metadata as well as licenses, notification requests, and a reference to the analyzed *video VDI*;

6. the *VDI* is signed with the user's certificate.

The analyst then opens the *Post an analysis* tool and:

1. sends the *Analysis VDI* which was previously analyzed on the network;

2. the VDIs compliance is verified:

   - the user's license allowing him/her to analyze the referenced video is also verified,

   - the VDI should be signed,

   - the integrity of the data is also verified;

3. if successful, the VDI is stored on the *Convergence* network.

The analyst then opens the *Publish an analysis* tool and:

1. creates a *publication VDI* referencing the previously uploaded *analysis VDI* and also containing licenses allowing the video channel owners to view the VDI;

2. injects the *publication VDI* to the network;

3. notifies the video channel owners about this new publication, who have subscribed to this type of analysis (subscribing to analyses is described in the following section).

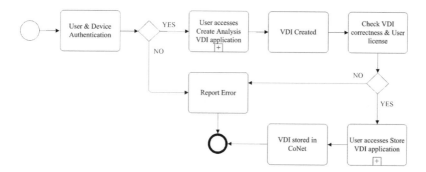

Figure 9.9. *Creating an analysis*

9.3.7. *Subscribing to analyses*

This task is carried out by the video channel owners such as Valérie and Elizabeth using the *channel content manager* application. The aim of this task is that they are informed when new analyses of their interest (i.e. whose subjects correspond to their channel's theme) are published (Figure 9.5).

The video channel owners confirm their identity and then open the *Subscribe to analyses* tool and:

1. Fill in a form to describe his/her subscription criteria such as:

- analyses' owner,

- semantic conditions, that is conditions to which the analyses' metadata must correspond and be applied,

- free texts of specific parts of metadata (for example, *analyses where the title contains the term "Quechua"),*

- conceptual terms ranging from a thesaurus from a domain ontology (e.g. places *or regions in the Andes – Huancavelica, Acomayo, Lambayeque, etc. Andean musical instruments - Charango, Bombo, etc. Andean festivals and rites – Corpus Christi, Chukcha rutukuy, Todos santos, Wasichakuy, etc.*); to the categories of a thesaurus from a domain ontology (e.g. subjects such as *"indigenous languages of the Andes", "oral traditions in the Andes", "Living artistic traditions in the Andes", "musical traditions of the Andes", etc.*);

2. a *subscription VDI* containing these subscription conditions is created;

3. the *subscription VDI* is injected to the network;

4. when a *publication VDI* corresponding to the subscription conditions defined in the *subscription VDI* is injected to the network, the user receives a notification.

9.3.8. *Removing analyses*

This is carried out by analysts such as Elizabeth's students using the *Analysis manager* application. The aim of this is to remove an analysis uploaded on the network (Figure 9.7) and also to remove its publication (Figure 9.6).

The analyst initially authenticate, opens the *Remove an analysis* tool and:

1. is presented the list of publications (*VDI publications*) recorded by the analyst;

2. selects a publication and removes it:

- the user's license allowing him/her to remove the *publication VDI* is verified,

- a request to remove the VDI is sent to the network,

- the VDI is removed from the network;

3. sends a notification of its removal to the users concerned, including:

- subscribers to this publication VDI,

- the video channel owners who have posted the analysis on their channel.

The analyst then opens the *Remove an analysis* tool and:

1. is presented the list of analyses (*analysis VDIs*) recorded by the analyst;

2. selects an analysis and removes it:

- the user's license allowing him/her to remove the *analysis VDI* is verified,

- a request to remove the VDI is sent to the network,

- the VDI and its metadata are removed from the network.

9.3.9. *Creating a channel*

This task is carried out by the administrators such as Richard by using the *Channel manager* application. This involves creating an audiovisual channel streaming different videos which are accompanied by analyses relating to a specific theme.

The administrator has to initially launch an audiovisual channel in the form of a Web portal using the *Semiosphere* technology[23].

The administrator therefore opens the *Register a channel* tool and:

1. Fills a form that describes the following components of the channel: title, alias, URL, and description;

2. creates licenses for the channel by applying to:

- ESCoM to host the channel,

- video channel owners to update the channel,

- subscribers to browse the channel;

3. creates notification requests which allow him/her to be informed when:

- an analysis is posted on the channel,

- a post is cancelled,

- a user subscribes to the channel;

4. creates a *channel VDI* incorporating its description in the form of metadata, its licenses, and notification requests;

5. signs the VDI with the user's certificate.

___

23 See Chapter 9 of [STO 11a] and section 9.3.13.

The administrator then opens the *Post a channel* tool and:

1. sends the *channel VDI* which was previously created on the network;

2. the VDI's compliance is verified:

- the VDI's signature is confirmed,

- data integrity is verified.

3. if successful, the VDI is stored on the *Convergence* network.

9.3.10. *Posting an analysis onto a channel*

Posting analyses is carried out by the video channel owners such as Valérie or Elizabeth by using the *Channel content manager* application. After having received a notification about a new post of an analysis of their theme, their aim is to post this analysis and its corresponding video on their channel and to inform interested subscribers (Figure 9.10).

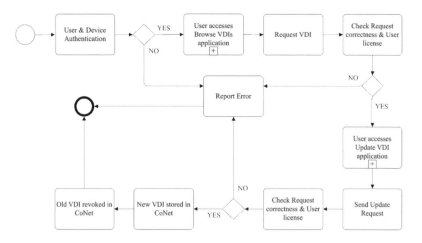

Figure 9.10. *Posting an analysis on the channel*

The video channel owner initially opens the ASW Publication Workshop[24] and posts the analysis on the channel.

The video channel owner confirms his/her identity and then opens the *View notifications* tool and:

1. is presented the list of analyses (*analysis VDIs*) to which the video channel owner is subscriber;

2. selects the analysis to post.

The video channel owner then opens the *Publish an posted analysis* tool and:

1. indicates the selected *analysis VDI*;

2. creates a new *channel VDI* where the selected *analysis VDI* is referenced;

3. the VDI is signed with the user's certificate;

4. the new channel VDI is sent to the network;

5. the VDI's compliance is verified, this involves confirming that:

- the user's license allowing them to remove the old *channel VDI* is verified,

- the user's licenses allowing him/her to post the analysis as well as the corresponding video are verified,

- the VDI's signature is confirmed,

- the integrity of the data is verified.

6. if successful, the VDI is stored on the *Convergence* network;

7. a *publication VDI* is created referencing the *analysis VDI* and the new *channel VDI* containing the licenses enabling subscribers to view this VDI;

8. the *publication VDI* is injected to the network;

---

24 See Chapters 7 and 10 of [STO 11a].

9. users who have subscribed to this type of analysis and this channel receive a notification of this new post (subscription to posts is described in the following section).

9.3.11. *Subscribing to posted analyses*

This task is carried out by subscribers such as Elizabeth, Muriel or Jirasri's students by using the *Channel content browser*. This means that they will be informed when new analyses which may be of interest to them are posted on a channel (i.e. whose identified subjects correspond to one or more themes of their choice) (Figure 9.5).

The subscriber initially authenticates, opens the *Subscribe to posted analyses* tool and then:

1. fills a form to describe his/her subscription criteria, including:

- audiovisual channel(s),

- and/or semantic conditions, that is conditions to which metadata of posted analyses must and could be applied,

- free texts from specific parts of metadata (e.g. *analyses where the title contains the term "Quechua"*),

- conceptual terms ranging from those from a domain ontology thesaurus (e.g. *places or regions in the Andes – Huancavelica, Acomayo, Lambayeque, etc. musical instruments - Charango, Bombo, etc. Andean festivals and rites – Corpus Christi, Chukcha rutukuy, Todos santos, Wasichakuy, etc.*); to categories of a thesaurus from a domain ontology (e.g. *subjects such as "indigenous languages of the Andes", "oral traditions in the Andes", "Living artistic traditions in the Andes", "musical traditions of the Andes", etc.*);

3. the *subscription VDI* is injected to the network;

4. the user is notified when a *publication VDI* corresponding to the subscription conditions defined in the *subscription VDI* is injected onto the network.

9.3.12. *Removing posts*

This task is carried out by the video channel owners such as Valérie or Elizabeth using the *Channel content manager*. The aim of this is to remove a post of an analysis from a channel (Figure 9.10), and to inform subscribers (Figure 9.6).

The video channel owner has to open the ASW Publication Workshop[25] and remove the analysis from the channel.

The video channel owner initially authenticates and opens the *Remove an posted analysis* tool and:

1. indicates the *analysis VDI* to be removed from those referenced on the channel;

2. creates a new *channel VDI* where the selected *analysis VDI* is no longer referenced;

3. the VDI is signed with the user's certificate;

4. the new *channel VDI* is sent to the network;

5. the VDI's compliance is verified:

  - the user's license allowing him/her to remove the old *channel VDI* is verified,

  - the VDI's signature is confirmed,

  - the data's integrity is verified.

6. if successful, the VDI is stored on the *Convergence* network;

7. the *Publication VDI* referencing this post is removed from the network;

8. users who subscribed to this type of analysis and this channel receive a notification of its removal.

9.3.13. *Viewing analyses posted on channels*

This task is carried out by Elizabeth, Muriel and Jirasri's students by using the *Channel content browser* application. After having

---

25 See Chapters 7 and 10 of [STO 11a].

received a notification of a new post of an interesting analysis, their aim is to read this analysis and view the corresponding video (Figure 9.11).

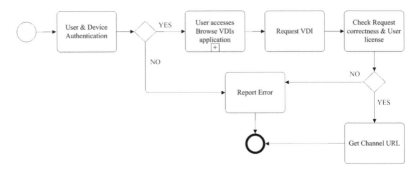

Figure 9.11. *Browsing a post*

The subscriber authenticates and then opens *browse notifications* tool and:

1. is presented the list of posts to which the user has subscribed;

2. selects a post;

3. is presented the information relating to this post including:

    - principal metadata from the analysis (title, date, author(s), description, etc.),

    - metadata from the channel to which the analysis is posted, title, alias, URL, and description;

4. the subscriber is redirected to the post's URL on the Web portal of the corresponding audiovisual channel.

9.4. Conclusion

Apart from the technical challenges involved, one of the main intellectual objectives of this chapter is to demonstrate how a revolutionary technology can reinforce the production, exploitation, and sharing of cultural and academic heritage by highly diverse users while maintaining an ethical approach to audiovisual recordings documenting sensitive areas of expertise and respecting intellectual property and the different rights affecting this knowledge. The Convergence project has shown that the use of VDI technology could represent a genuine advance for people working in the field of preserving and valorizing intangible cultural heritage by enabling them to easily trace different uses of digital resources.

As we have previously mentioned, it can also be shown that the VDI technology contributes:

1) to respect human rights, that is the rights of communities and custodians of cultural heritage to remain as final deciders over any use of their heritage;

2) to promote cultural diversity and intercultural dialog facilitating the circulation of knowledge about world cultures and responding to two fundamental expectations of those involved: a) the dissemination of their cultural goods and b) access to this heritage for future generations;

3) to the creation of a next generation tool which can be of service to "traditional" heritages, which shows that technological advances can constitute fundamental contributions to our knowledge of the traditional world on the condition that they are examined in a respectful way for the people involved and that they are thought of in relation to various expectations from different kinds of end-users. These advances also enable the people involved to be trained in the use of these technologies.

Apart from the very specific case of Andean population and researchers working in this context, we can also hope that this scenario will evoke and increase interest among various custodians of cultural heritage around the world (such as those representing communities and social groups) and figures working in the field of cultural heritage. In the context of the current digitalization of culture in the form of textual, photographic, and audiovisual data, VDI technology represents real progress for the "circulation" of digitalized content and use by multiple users, with a diverse range of profiles, interests, and expectations.

Finally, this test scenario is also designed to explore the various possible uses for new social media and Web 2.0 in the context of producing, disseminating, and using this content (educational, professional, scientific use etc.), specifically those with a strong academic value or which are culturally sensitive, where intellectual property, ownership, and use must be respected according to a specific ethical approach concerning digital resources. In general, VDI technology enables each digital resource and audiovisual resource (in particular) to be located, identified, and "traced" on the Web. This is therefore an excellent guarantee for owners of this type of resource. It has also been shown that thanks to this technology, even the most minor comment about an audiovisual resource on the Web or various social media sites can be communicated to the author or the "moral owner" of the resource. These different socio-technological advances are a real intellectual breakthrough promoting social dialog and the exchange of knowledge in an ethical framework which guarantees that the rights of cultural goods are respected.

Glossary of Specialized Terms

NOTE: Expressions in bold and followed by an asterisk (e.g. "**ASW-HSS project***") appear in the glossary.

A

Analysis (of an audiovisual corpus)

1) A term denoting one of the two main categories of tasks and activities of work on an audiovisual corpus. The other category is **processing*** of an audiovisual corpus.

2) The work of analysis involves explicitizing the *potential* **value*** of an audiovisual text for a given audience (the **analyst*** could be this audience). A potential **value*** may be new information provided about a particular topic, missing or unpublished images, explanations which facilitate better understanding of a fact, etc.).

3) In the context of the ASW-HSS project, we distinguish between six main types of analysis of an audiovisual corpus: a) locating a potential value (analysis which consists of identifying the *relevant* segments or passages in an audiovisual text, and segmenting it); b) **paratextual analysis*** (a task which involves producing so-called identifying information on an audiovisual text and/or one of its segments); c) **audiovisual description*** (a task which consists of carrying out a description/interpretation of the visual and audio shots

---

Glossary written by Peter STOCKINGER.

of an audiovisual text); d) **thematic description*** (a task which consists of analyzing the content of an audiovisual text or one of its segments, i.e. the topics they deal with); e) **pragmatic analysis*** in the broader sense (a task which consists of explicitly stating the possible uses/users of an audiovisual text and increasing its interest and usefulness for the audience or for a specific use, in the form e.g. of user instructions, linguistic or cultural translation/adaptation, etc.).

Analyst (Role of)

1) This term refers to the intellectual work devoted to an audiovisual (or, more usually, textual) corpus: a) *identifying* a corpus of work (or **analysis corpus***); b) *locating* the relevant passages or "moments"(as regards a given objective) and *segmenting* (i.e. "extracting" the relevant passages and moments); c) *controlled** or *free* description** of the passages and *indexing per se*, d) and finally – if applicable – *translation-adaptation* of the previously described passages.

2) The role of the analyst is one of several which characterize work in the context of digital archives (or libraries). Other important roles which were problematized as part of the **ESCoM*** research are: the **role of the publisher*** and the **role of the knowledge engineer*** (or the "concept designer").

3) The role of analyst takes a number of rather different forms: simple "day-to-day" activity of classifying personal archives; the work of the librarian/archivist, classifying and indexing a collection according to predefined criteria; or the work of a specialist (an "expert") in the field documented by an audiovisual collection.

4) The role of the analyst requires a number of skills (i.e. knowledge and knowhow), of which the following three must be highlighted: a) *textual analysis skills* (i.e. the ability to produce a so-called semiotic expert assessment); b) *analytical skill* (i.e. the ability to produce a so-called referential expert assessment); and c) knowledge and know-how of the *technologies and tools* needed to carry out and disseminate an analysis (i.e. always being abreast of technological developments, identifying the techniques and tools which are appropriate to the analysis and making effective use of these techniques and tools to carry out and disseminate the analysis).

5) Given the increasingly obvious importance of identifying, describing, publishing, disseminating and appropriating relevant information in the context of a society which is largely conditioned by a knowledge-based economy, the role of the analyst is now rapidly evolving to include new fields and professions.

C

Concept (see: Conceptual term)

Collection (audiovisual -)

1) The term "audiovisual collection" denotes the entire set of audiovisual data which are available in an audiovisual archive and which (at least in part) "feed" the functionally distinct types of **audiovisual corpora*** that we may encounter in the working process of audiovisual production-publication.

Corpus (audiovisual)

1) A set of visual, sound, filmic etc. texts of any type/genre, size, editorial readiness ... which has a particular function according to the phase of the **working process*** (of audiovisual production-publishing) in which it is developed and used.

2) In the context of the ASW-HSS project, we distinguish between the **field corpus***, the **processing corpus*** and the **processed corpus***, the **analysis corpus*** and the **analyzed corpus***, the **publication corpus***and the **published corpus***.

3) The procedures to be followed when compiling an audiovisual corpus should be as explicit as possible and defined in the form of guides making up the technical documentation accompanying the **working process*** (of audiovisual production-publishing). Indeed, depending on its place and its function in the working process of audiovisual production-publishing, an audiovisual corpus must fulfill a series of expectations and needs and may therefore be appraised in relation to criteria such as empirical scope, internal consistency/ weighting, epistemic quality, etc.

Analysis corpus

1) The analysis corpus brings together all the audiovisual data that the analyst has selected for analysis, i.e. a set of activities aimed at explicitizing the potential **value*** of the corpus (or a given part of the corpus) for a given audience. This work constitutes one of the main stages of the **working process*** in the context of the **ARA program*** and is carried out using the **ASW Description Workshop***.

2) The analysis corpus may be made up of data taken from different sources: i) data from a single **field corpus*** (most commonplace) or from a number of field corpora (created by the same person/team or by different actors); ii) data from one or more (physically) **processed corpora***; iii) data from other sources (i.e. other **audiovisual collections*** ...); iv) **audiovisual documents*** forming part of one or more already-**published corpora*** online (on a site such as that of the ARA) and which will be subject to new analyses, re-descriptions, re-interpretations, etc.

3) The analysis corpus, which forms the input of the **analysis*** stage of the working process of audiovisual production-publishing, must be functionally distinguished from the **analyzed corpus,** which results from an analysis (description, indexing, etc.).

4) It is also helpful to distinguish the analysis corpus from the **processing corpus***, i.e. the corpus of audiovisual data chosen to be subjected to *technical* or authorial changes to the "appearance" and the linearity of an audiovisual database.

Analyzed corpus

1) All the audiovisual data analyzed (described, indexed, commented upon, translated/adapted ...) documenting one or more **fields*** (an event, a display, a piece of heritage ...).

2) The analyzed corpus results from the analysis of audiovisual data, which is one of the main phases of the **working process*** in the context of the **ARA program*** and is carried out using the **ASW Description Workshop***.

Field corpus

1) All the data collected or produced from a **field*** dedicated to gathering information to document a scientific or cultural manifestation or "field" research *per se* (e.g. an archeological excavation, a sociological survey, an anthology of oral expressions as part of an ethno-literary research project, etc.).

2) In the context of the ARA program, the collection of the audiovisual data and the constitution of a field corpus are governed by a set of principles which are expounded in an online document entitled "Collection and preservation of audiovisual data". This document is available for consultation on the ARA Website: http://www. archivesaudiovisuelles.fr/EN/about4.asp.

Processing corpus

1) All the data which have been chosen to be processed by a technician or the author. *Technical processing* encompasses the activities of "trimming", physically cleaning the files containing the data collected in the field corpus, improving the visual or sound quality of the files, etc. *Authorial processing* is mainly concerned with editing the audiovisual data (according to a montage scenario), creating transitions and special effects, postsynchronizing the sound and image tracks, adding voiceover comments, and so on.

2) The data forming part of a corpus of processing may belong to one or (or more, this is the most recurring case) **field corpora*** but they may also come from other **audiovisual collections***, or even already processed and/or published data.

3) The corpus of processing constitutes one of the two main inputs of the processing/analysis stage of the **working process*** of audiovisual production-publishing (the other input is formed by the **analysis corpus***).

Processed corpus

1) All the audiovisual data derived from the (technical or authorial) processing stage of the **working process*** of audiovisual production-

publishing – audiovisual data documenting one or more **fields*** (an event, a display, a piece of heritage …).

Publication corpus

1) All the audiovisual data making up the input of the actual publishing phase (one of the main phases of the **working process*** in the ARA program) and carried out using the **ASW Description Workshop***.

2) The relevance of the publication corpus must be evaluated in relation to the objectives of a given publication. In any case, it may be made up of data of a different nature and taken from different sources: i) from only one **analyzed corpus*** (this is the most common situation in the context of the "normal" activities of the ARA program*); ii) from several analyzed corpora*; iii) from one or more **corpora** of **processed*** (but not necessarily analyzed) data; iv) from one or more **field corpora*** (neither necessarily processed nor analyzed); v) from already **published corpora***, etc.

Published corpus

1) All the audiovisual data which are available to a general or specific audience in the form of a chosen **genre of publication*** (in the ARA program in the form of, e.g. an event site, a themed folder, an interactive video-book, a bilingual folder, etc.).

2) A functional distinction must be drawn between the **publication corpus** and the published corpus. The publication corpus brings together all the audiovisual data used as input for the process of publication via the ASW Publishing Workshop. However, the publisher/author is free to choose, within the audiovisual publication corpus, a given element that he/she really wants to publish, to the detriment of other items which are publishable but are not chosen by the publisher/author. (However, in another publishing process, the same publisher/author or another person taking on this role may come back to the unpublished publishable items to create a new publication with them …). The published corpus encompasses only those elements which are in fact published online in the form of a given **publishing genre***.

D

Document (audiovisual) – (audiovisual text)

1) A term denoting an audiovisual object which has in principle been *processed, analyzed and published*, i.e. an audiovisual object which, by way of a set of activities forming part of the **working process*** of audiovisual production-publishing, is given the *status* and *function* – quite rightly, and at least in its authors' eyes – of *documenting something*, reporting, providing information, knowledge, satisfying curiosity, etc.

2) An audiovisual document/text is only available to us in the form of a specific **publishing genre***. As part of the activities of publishing of the **ARA program***, it is available to us, e.g., in the form of an **interactive* video-book**, a documentary, a report, a **themed folder***, an **educational folder*** etc.

3) The audiovisual document is one of the "tangible", "visible" results of the **published corpus*** (published online in the context of the ARA program).

4) The digital audiovisual document is not necessarily a static, set, definitive audiovisual text. On the contrary, particularly by way of republication*, the audiovisual document may evolve over time and be enriched, change form, etc.

Domain of knowledge/expertise

1) The domain of knowledge is the referential universe which is covered by the **metalanguage of description*** and, more particularly, the library of **models of description*** of a given **audiovisual collection***.

2) The expression "domain of knowledge/expertise" highlights that we must distinguish between the domain as it is cognitively represented by the **knowledge engineer*** (= *domain of knowledge in the sense of a fairly reliable expert assessment, more-or-less universally accepted* ...) and the *real domain* which is supposed to correspond to the domain of knowledge in the form of an expert assessment.

3) In the ASW-HSS project, several domains of knowledge have been defined and explained in the form of specific metalanguages of description (also called **domain ontologies***) i.e. the domains of knowledge covered by the main experimental workshops of the ASW-HSS project – CCA*, ArkWork*, LHE*, AICH* – and FMSH-ARA.

Description

Audiovisual description (type of –)

1) Audiovisual description is a specific type of description of an audiovisual corpus which is mainly concerned with the visual, audio and audiovisual shots in the videos being analyzed. For example, it might look at the different camera angles of a profilmic event, the different framing and camera movements; it might also focus on the sound effects, the "soundscapes" typical of a given type of scene (e.g. of given places or accompanying a certain social practice, etc.).

2) A systematic audiovisual description leads to what could be called a library of *visual* and/or *acoustic* and/or *audiovisual motifs*, i.e. of sorts of recurring stereotypes which characterize the writing of an audiovisual corpus.

3) Like any other descriptive activity, audiovisual description is carried out by way of interactive forms at the disposition of the analyst in the ASW **Description Workshop***.

Controlled description (procedure of –)

1) Unlike the **procedure of free description***, controlled description is a procedure which relies exclusively on a **thesaurus*** of predefined terms (or "descriptors") to denote the **domain of knowledge*** that is addressed in a video, an audiovisual text.

2) The procedure of controlled description is based on several activities of description (each activity being defined in the **hierarchical meta-lexicon of conceptual terms*** of semiotic analysis – a meta-lexicon which constitutes one of the main **ASW metalinguistic resources*** required for elaborating **models of description***). In this procedure, the only compulsory activity is to select at least one

predefined term in the list of such terms in order to identify and possibly classify, the object of the description. Like any other activity of description, this is also carried out by way of interactive forms available to the analyst in the ASW **Description Workshop***.

Free description (procedure of –)

1) The procedure of free description is one of the most important procedures of description and along with the **controlled description*** (by way of a **thesaurus***) it constitutes the most central procedure in the **ASW-HSS project***.

2) "Free description" means that the analyst provides the appropriate value so that a **conceptual term*** can adequately represent a thematized domain of knowledge in the form of a **topic*** in an audiovisual corpus. In **controlled description***, these values are predefined in the form of terms or descriptors making up a **thesaurus***.

3) The procedure of free description is based on several activities of description (each activity being defined in the **hierarchical meta-lexicon of conceptual terms*** of semiotic analysis – a meta-lexicon which constitutes one of the **ASW metalinguistic resources*** required for elaborating **models of description***). In this procedure, the only compulsory activity is to enter a minimal (linguistic) expression in order to appropriately designate/denominate the domain of knowledge which is dealt with in a video, an audiovisual text. Like any other activity of description, this is also carried out by way of interactive forms available to the analyst in the ASW **Description Workshop***.

Paratextual description (type of –)

1) Paratextual description is a specific type of description which clarifies the formal identity of an object being analyzed (a video, a segment of video, an image …), i.e. its title, its author(s), its genre, possibly the date and place of publication, etc. It also clarifies issues of rights (copyright, usage rights …) and if need be, the "main topic" to which the analyzed object belongs (leaving the explicitation (*per se*) of the topic to the thematic description).

2) Paratextual description offers an identification/presentation of an audiovisual object which corresponds to the 15 criteria of description defining the Dublin Core standard.

3) Like any other activity of description, this is also carried out by way of interactive forms available to the analyst in the ASW **Description Workshop***.

Pragmatic description (type of –)

1) Pragmatic description is a specific type of description which is concerned with explicitly stating the potential uses of the audiovisual text it is dealing with and adapting it, wherever possible (and without **processing*** (*per se*) of the "material" object), to the profile and expectations of a given audience. The adaptation may take the form of a translation (literal, summarizing, free …) and/or an intellectual/ cultural "reworking" (as is the case, e.g. as part of the popularization of a particularly specialized content so as to make it understandable to a broader audience).

2) Like any other activity, this one is also carried out via interactive forms at the disposition of the analyst in the **ASW Description Workshop***.

Thematic description (type of –)

1) The thematic description is a specific type of description which spells out the **topics***, i.e. the content or message of an audiovisual text, i.e. of an audiovisual text or corpus of audiovisual texts.

2) The thematic description is carried out using a library of **models of description*** of the content of the audiovisual objects which are supposed to document a given aspect of the domain of knowledge covered by a video-library, a portal, or more often an audiovisual production-publishing program.

3) Obviously, thematic description varies the most between the different domains of knowledge, as opposed to other types of description (**paratextual***, **audiovisual***, **pragmatic***, peritextual …) which are relatively independent from the referential specificities of a given domain. Hence, implementing a systematic thematic

description is an immense task in terms of modeling the domain of knowledge to be dealt with, and then defining and implementing a metalanguage of description appropriate to the peculiarities of the domain in question.

4) Like any other activity, this is also carried out by way of interactive forms at the analyst's disposal in the **ASW Description Workshop***.

F

Field

1) The term "field" designates the phase in the **working process*** (of audiovisual production-publication) which is dedicated to the collection of audiovisual data documenting either a scientific event (conference, research seminar …), a cultural event (concert, exhibition …) or another type of event (e.g. political, social …), or even a piece of "field" research *per se* (dedicated, for example, to documenting a cultural patrimony, a social practice, etc.). The "tangible" result of this stage is the field corpus.

2) As part of a program of production-distribution of knowledge heritage (such as the **ARA program***), the stage which takes place in the field constitutes one of the crucial moments (a "milestone") in the working process (of audiovisual production-publication).

Folder

Bi/multilingual folder

1) The bi/multilingual folder is a publishing genre which is specified and developed to expressly account for the problems of distributing a monolingual audiovisual recording in a knowledge market which is intrinsically multilingual.

2) The bi/multilingual folder offers different versions (reasonably faithful or, on the contrary, abridged, approximate, adapted, simpli-fied …) of an audiovisual recording (created in a given language) in one or more target language(s).

3) This publishing genre was tested by **ESCoM*** for the **ARA program*** as part of several French and European R&D projects (in particular see **SAPHIR*** and **LOGOS***. There is now a whole series of bilingual folders (French/Spanish; French/English; French/Russian; French/Arabic; etc.) which can be consulted either on the **ARA portal*** site or on thematically delimited portals such as **PCM (Peoples and Cultures of the World)***, **DLC (Linguistic and Cultural Diversity)*** or **SCC (Semiotics, Culture, Communication)***.

Educational folder

1) The educational folder is a specific genre of publication which uses/reuses audiovisual recordings (processed or not, analyzed or not) to create educational resources (*per se*) for either formal or informal education.

2) As a general rule, the educational folder is organized around a series of chapters where each chapter is supposed to represent a phase in the acquisition and appropriation of a certain type of knowledge or know-how. Each chapter contains audiovisual material and a collection of additional information which is useful to the learner or the teacher. The folder itself comprises guides aimed at the teacher and the learner as well as suggestions of tests and validating knowledge.

3) This genre of publication was tested by **ESCoM*** for the **ARA program*** as part of the European project **LOGOS***. Today, there is a whole collection of educational folders covering a variety of topics and which may be consulted either on the **ARA portal*** site, or on thematically delimited portals such as **DLC***, **PCM*** or **SCC***.

Thematic folder

1) The thematic folder, as its name suggests, brings together different audiovisual contributions on a theme or topic. Depending on the explicit objectives of communication, the thematic folder may take different forms: a folder which recaps a question, a folder which sparks a debate, a folder about a controversial issue, an awareness-raising folder, etc.

2) This genre of publication was tested by **ESCoM*** for the **ARA program*** as part of the European project **LOGOS***. Today, there is a whole collection of educational folders covering a variety of topics and which may be consulted either on the **ARA portal*** site, or on thematically delimited portals such as **DLC***, **PCM*** or **SCC**.

Form (interactive working)

1) The interactive form is the **analyst***'s (or, according to the case, of the **writer/author***'s) working interface enabling him to use the different models making up the **metalanguage*** (of description, of publication …) in his work of **analysis*** (or publishing), dealing with the **domain of knowledge/expertise*** of a given audiovisual archive.

2) Hence, the **Description Workshop*** is made up of a series of interactive forms enabling an **analyst*** to carry out a **meta-description***, an **audiovisual description***, a **thematic description***, etc. The **Publishing Workshop***, is also made up of interactive forms enabling a **writer/author*** to "upload" audiovisual data, choose publishing models, import analyzed corpora in order to publish them, adapt them to a publishing model, etc.

G

Genre of publication

1) A genre of publication is a *culturally and historically situated model* which lends a text a certain form, a certain "gestalt" which is recognizable by those who have an appropriate skill (reading, comprehension). Generally speaking, a genre of publication may be identified by the simultaneous recourse to a series of criteria such as the content, the narrative (but also formal and physical) organization, the audiovisual *mise-en-scène*, etc.

2) The ARA program uses several genres of publication – in particular the **interactive video-book***, the **thematic folder***, the bilingual folder, the video-lexicon. Each genre of publication is explicitly described. It is converted into a model which the editor-analyst, by way of an interactive form, may envisage **publishing*** or **republishing*** a given audiovisual corpus.

M

Metalanguage of description

1) A structured set of models of description i.e. **interactive forms*** in the ASW **Description Workshop*** which are used by the analyst when working on an audiovisual corpus, an individual audiovisual text, or a specific passage (segment) from an audiovisual text.

2) The semiotic theory of the audiovisual text constitutes the frame of reference for elaborating the ASW **metalanguage of description***. Hence, in accordance with this theoretical framework, the **metalanguage of description*** distinguishes between several functional types of models of description among which: (i) a class of models of description reserved for *producing the meta-description* itself (clarifying the content, the objectives, the authors, the target audience, etc. of a particular analysis); (ii) a category of models of description reserved for clarifying the *paratextual data* of the audiovisual objects being analyzed: title of the object, author(s), genre, language, intellectual property, etc.; (iii) a significant category of models dedicated to the analysis of the *content* itself conveyed by an audiovisual corpus; (iv) a category of models more particularly dedicated to the *audiovisual mise-en-scène of the content* conveyed by an audiovisual corpus (models which serve for analyzing the visual and acoustic shots); (v) a category of models dedicated to the *contextual* and *linguistic adaptation* of an audiovisual corpus. In other words, the ASW metalanguage of description is a **generic ontology***, called **ASW ontology***.

3) As part of the ASW-HSS project and its different experimental fields, metalanguages of description have been created for six domains of knowledge/expertise. These correspond to the main **experimental workshops*** of the project: the **CCA Program***, **LHE Program***, **ArkWork Program***, **AICH***, **PACA*** and **ARA/FMSH***. These six domains share all the models of description of type (i), type (ii), type (iv) and type (v). Only type (iii) models of description systematically vary between the three workshops CCA, ArkWork and LHE – thus each of these workshops has its own models for describing audiovisual content which is adapted to their domain of knowledge/expertise. On the other hand, the AICH and PACA workshops reuse a subset of type (iii) models of description dedicated

to analyzing audiovisual content from the domain of expertise of the CCA workshop by adapting them to the referential specificities of their respective domains. Finally, the **ARA/FMSH*** workshop, which has a domain of expertise that is somehow "transversal" to those of the other workshops, borrows (from each of these domains) the models that it "needs" in order to process its own audiovisual corpora. These metalanguages are what we call **domain ontologies*** derived from a **generic ontology*** which is the **ASW ontology***.

Meta-description (ASW –)

1) The ASW meta-description forms part of the activity of analysis of an audiovisual object. It enables the analyst to specify the content, objective, audience etc. … of his analysis.

2) The meta-description of an analysis is carried out via **interactive forms*** intended for this specific task in the ASW **Description Workshop***.

Model of description

1) A model of description is a hypothesis of the "best way" to describe a concrete object. It is part of the **metalanguage of description*** of a domain of knowledge/expertise.

2) A model of description is composed of a set of metalinguistic resources notably including **conceptual terms*** which are organized into **schemas*** and **sequences***.

3) In the context of the ASW-HSS project, several libraries of models of description have been elaborated and tested. A library of models corresponds to a domain of knowledge/expertise.

4) Besides libraries of models of description which are specific to the **domain of knowledge*** (such as the **LHE Workshop***), a *common library* of models of description which *does not depend* on the domain of knowledge, has been identified, defined and realized. It may be used to analyze any audiovisual corpus. These models of description guide **paratextual description*** of an audiovisual text, its **audiovisual description*** *stricto sensu*, and its **pragmatic description***.

Model (publishing-)

1) A publishing model expresses a specific **genre of publication***
with the aid of which a **publication corpus*** may be published and
distributed online. Examples of specific genres of publication are, the
interactive video-book*, the **thematic folder***, the **bilingual folder***,
etc.

2) Similarly to the models of description, the publishing models are
part of the ASW metalanguage of description where they form a
separate library.

3) In the context of the ASW-HSS project, we focused more on
developing models of description and less on developing publishing
models. Consequently, the current publishing models seem rather
rudimentary and frozen.

Knowledge engineer (role of–; also: "Concept designer")

1) Along with the roles of the **analyst*** and the **writer/author***,
this is one of the three main roles which have been identified as part of
the **ASW-HSS project***.

2) The knowledge engineer (also called "concept designer") is the
role which brings with it the delicate – and very difficult – task of
defining and creating the **models of description*** of audiovisual
corpora documenting a **domain of knowledge/expertise***. If necessary
for the development of new **models of description*,** his work
(sometimes) requires making changes to the ASW **metalinguistic
resources*** in the form of local additions or the creation of **"user"
resources*** (as opposed to the **common resources***).

3) The knowledge engineer is supposed to be perfectly conversant
with the metalinguistic resources without which there could be no
model of description* or **publishing model***, no **interactive form***
in the **Description Workshop*** and **Publishing Workshop***.

4) However the knowledge engineer is also supposed to be familiar
with the techniques of conceptual analysis, description/modeling of
knowledge as well as approaches and disciplines such as cognitive
sciences, artificial intelligence, semiotics and linguistics in the broader
sense. Finally he must be able to liaise, on the one hand, with the

people and teams responsible for the technical development of the models of description and the publishing models, and on the other hand with all the participants of a project of analysis and publishing of audiovisual corpora.

O

Object (of analysis)

1) The object of analysis is the object, the entity to which an **analysis*** (a description, a commentary, an interpretation etc. ...) refers.

2) As part of the ASW-HSS project, we distinguish between different categories of objects of analysis: i) objects of analysis which are composed of the referents to a **domain of knowledge/expertise*** which is peculiar to a video-library/a portal; ii) objects which serve for the spatial and temporal localization of the referents; iii) objects of a discursive and enunciative nature serving to give a specific vision to the thematized referents in an audiovisual text; iv) objects for the *mise-en-scène* or the audiovisual expression of the thematized referents; and v) objects which serve to carry out a metadiscourse (a comment, an opinion ...) either on the act of analysis or on the object of the analysis (the audiovisual text).

Object (audiovisual-) (see: Audiovisual Text)

Ontologies (ASW domain–)

1) An ASW domain ontology is a metalanguage of description which was developed in order to analyze audiovisual corpora documenting a specific domain of knowledge/expertise.

2) A domain ontology relies on the generic ASW ontology, borrowing some of its relevant conceptual terms, models of description and some parts of the common thesaurus (in addition to its own metalinguistic resources, if necessary). The metalinguistic additions which are specific to a domain form part of a special branch in the meta-lexicon of the ASW conceptual terms, in the ASW models of description and in the ASW common thesaurus.

2) As part of the ASW-HSS project, domain ontologies were defined for the CCA, ArkWork, LHE, AICH and FMSH/ARA workshops.

Ontology (ASW generic–) (see: ASW metalanguage)

P

Procedure of analysis

1) A procedure of analysis is a task composed of one or more activities of description (each of these is defined in the **metalanguage***, the ASW **generic ontology***).

2) In the context of the ASW-HSS project, two basic procedures of analysis (of description) were defined, namely **controlled description*** and **free description***. A third procedure is the composite procedure relying on both the basic ones.

Process (working – of audiovisual production-publication)

1) As part of the **ARA program***, the working process facilitating the constitution, publication and distribution of scientific or cultural heritage can be broken down into five main stages: i) preliminary activities prior to a field work *lato sensu* taking place; ii) field activities (*lato sensu*) recording and collecting all the data documenting that field; iii) processing and analysis of the audiovisual corpus; iv) audiovisual publication; v) activities which put the finishing touches to the working process.

2) Each phase is composed of a set of specific tasks or activities which are instrumented and described in the technical documentation which accompanies the working process.

Processing (of an audiovisual corpus)

1) One of the two main categories of tasks and activities forming part of an audiovisual corpus, the other being the **analysis**.

R

Relation (conceptual–)

1) A conceptual relation represents a specific type of link which can be established between objects (of analysis)* and represented by **conceptual terms*** or **concepts***.

2) The conceptual relations form part of the **ASW metalanguage*** which distinguishes different types of conceptual relations. The most important distinction is made between i) relations which define the *links between the objects of a domain of knowledge/expertise* and ii) relations which define *the links between **objects of analysis*** and **procedures of analysis***.

3) A conceptual relation serves to define the configurations between **conceptual terms*** forming the **ASW metalanguage*** – configurations in the form of **schemas***, **sequences*** or **models***.

Resource (audiovisual-)

1) A term denoting any audiovisual text which holds a cognitive and practical **value*** for a given audience. An example of such a **value*** would be to satisfy one's curiosity, need for information, etc.

Resources (metalinguistic)

1) Term design any element belonging to the ASW **metalanguage*** and which helps the model maker in implementing a **domain ontology***, i.e. **models of description*** which are appropriate to a **domain of knowledge/expertise***.

S

Schema (conceptual–)

1) The conceptual schema is a *micro-configuration* of **conceptual terms*** (composed of at least one conceptual term) which, along with other conceptual schemas, constitutes a **sequence*** of a model of description. The conceptual schema enables us to create **relations***

between two or more **conceptual terms***. It forms part of the ASW metalanguage of description.

2) The ASW **metalanguage of description*** notably distinguishes between two complementary types of conceptual schemas: the category of schemas which represent a given *part of the referential domain* **of the domain of expertise*** (for example, schemas which represent, in the AICH domain of knowledge, the *rituals* and *celebrations*, the *languages* and *families of languages*, the *localities* and the *periods*, etc.); the category of schemas which represent a given activity of description forming part of the ASW **procedures of analysis***.

Schema of indexing

1) The schema of indexing specifies what the analyst must do when choosing a particular activity which is part of a **procedure of analysis***. An activity and, *a fortiori*, a procedure of analysis may be made up of several schemas of indexing. It is presented as an **interactive form*** composed of fields, tables and other elements that the analyst has to fill in.

2) The schemas of indexing are part of the **ASW metalanguage*** where they constitute a library which differentiates between the *linguistic, textual, audiovisual, with the aid of a thesaurus, in reference to a standard* (such as LOMFR or Dublin Core …), etc. schemas of indexing.

Schema (referential–)

1) The referential schema is a specific type of **conceptual schema*** which sets the referential value of a **conceptual term*** beforehand. For example, if the referential domain of knowledge is limited to French literature of the Middle Ages (this is a case forming part of the **LHE*** domain), the conceptual term [PERIOD] is *a priori* set by the expression "Middle Ages" and is then interpreted by appropriate numerical values to represent the temporal boundaries of that time. In other words, the **conceptual term*** [PERIOD] cannot be used in order to designate other temporal referents such as, e.g. the temporal referent "18th Century".

Sequence

1) A **model of description*** is composed of several sequences. Each sequence serves to describe/analyze a given object.

2) As part of the ASW-HSS project, we distinguish between four main types of sequences: (i) sequences which serve to describe the thematization in an audiovisual corpus; (ii) sequences which serve to describe the *mise-en-scène* of a thematized domain in an corpus (audiovisual *mise-en-scène* either in the form of a held discourse or in the form of a specific visual or sound *mise-en-scène**); (iii) sequences serving to contextualize (spatial, temporal frame …) a thematized domain; (iv) sequences serving to better explain the analyst's point of view, the content and the objectives of the analysis.

3) A sequence is derived from the following two components: (i) the "**object of analysis***" component (i.e. the object in the sequence which is subjected to the analysis) and the "**procedure of analysis***" component (i.e. the methods according to which a given object is analyzed).

T

Term (conceptual)

1) A conceptual term (sometimes also simply called "concept") is a metalinguistic expression that designates a given type of **objects*** (in the ASW-HSS project, we distinguish 5 specific types of objects).

2) The conceptual terms are part of the ASW **metalanguage of description*** where they are organized in the form of a hierarchy of concepts. This hierarchy of concepts notably distinguishes between i) conceptual terms representing the **objects of analysis*** of the ASW domain of expertise and ii) conceptual terms representing the ASW activities and **procedures of analysis***.

3) The conceptual terms representing the objects of analysis (= first class of conceptual terms) form the "domain of analysis" part of the **model of description***, and the conceptual terms representing the procedures of analysis (= second class of conceptual terms) form the analytical part (*per se*) of the **models of description***.

Thesaurus

1) The thesaurus is one of the main resources for **controlled description***, as part of a work of **analysis*** of an **audiovisual corpus***.

2) As part of the implementation of the different **experimental workshops*** of the **ASW-HSS project***, first a restricted and very simple thesaurus (countries of the world, temporal periods, languages of the world, authors of French literature, French regions and districts, etc.) was created. Gradually, this original/simple thesaurus was complemented by new *facets:* a facet corresponds to a **conceptual term*** (or a **schema*** of conceptual terms) and is interpreted by a hierarchical list of predefined terms (of "descriptors").

3) The ASW thesaurus is part of the resources of the ASW **metalanguage of description*** (in the same way as the indexation generated by the analysts by way of the procedure of **free description***). In particular, we can distinguish between *common thesauruses* (i.e. common to all domains of knowledge/all groups of users of ASW metalinguistic resources) and *particular thesauruses* which are specific to a given domain of knowledge/expertise (for example, the **AICH*** domain possesses, as well as the **ACH*** domain, its own thesaurus facets).

V

Value (of an audiovisual text)

1) A term denoting the capacity of an audiovisual text to fill a gap (satisfy a need, a desire …) of information or knowledge among an audience.

2) The **analysis** of an audiovisual text consists of explicitly stating this (so-called potential) value of the text for a given audience (the analyst may himself be that audience). If need be, with or without appropriate **processing**, the analyst may conform, i.e. adapt the profile, the authorial identity of the audiovisual text, to the expectations and the needs (desires, sheer curiosity …) of a target audience.

Video-book (interactive)

1) The interactive video-book is a specific genre of publication of an audiovisual audiovisual corpus. Its structure shows similarities to a "book" in the conventional sense of the word. In particular, it is made up of chapters offering the interested reader the opportunity to navigate through an audiovisual record (which may last several hours) by "leafing through" (i.e. as if the reader were leafing through a book …).

2) The interactive video-book is one of the "standard" models of publication of the **ARA program***.

Video-lexicon

1) The video-lexicon is a specific genre of publication of an audiovisual corpus which looks very similar to a traditional thematic dictionary: the thematically delimited chapters of such a dictionary include – in alphabetical order – a list of leading terms or expressions which are defined and exemplified in dedicated articles. A video-lexicon is composed of several thematically delimited "chapters"; each chapter contains a set of leading terms and each leading term feature is dealt with by small audiovisual segments dedicated to it.

2) This genre of publication was tested by **ESCoM*** for the **ARA program*** as part of several French and European research projects (in particular see **SAPHIR*** and **LOGOS***). Today there are prototypes of video-lexicons on world languages and world cultures, which are distributed on the **DLC*** and **PCW*** Websites.

W

Writer/author (role of–)

1) Besides the roles of the **analyst*** and the **knowledge engineer***, the writer/author represents a third role which has been identified, problematized and orchestrated as part of the **ASW-HSS project***.

2) The writer/author intervenes during the publishing stage (as part of the **working process*** of audiovisual production-publishing. The analyst and the writer/author may be the same person or the same

group, but obviously this is not always the case. Similarly, the role of writer/author may be played by a single person at a given moment, but it may also be played by a group, by the same person or by different people who are distant in time and space.

3) In concrete terms, the writer/author uses the **Publishing Workshop*** in **ASW Studio*** in order to: i) constitute his publishing corpus; ii) select and, within the current technical limitations of the ASW **Publishing Workshop***, adapt the genre of publication to his needs; iii) prepare his corpus prior to its publication (select the elements to be published, check the metadata, add "new pages" ...) and; iv) publish his corpus.

Glossary of Acronyms and Names

NOTE: Expressions in bold and followed by an asterisk (e.g. "**ASW-HSS project***") appear in the glossary.

A

ACH portal

1) ACH is the acronym for "Azerbaijani Cultural Heritage" which is a portal serving as a field of experimentation to the **ASW-HSS project***.

AICH portal

1) AICH is the acronym for "Andean Intangible Cultural Heritage" which is a portal serving as an experimental field to the **ASW-HSS project* and the Convergence* project**.

AmSud (portal)

1) Abbreviation for "Mediateca Latinoamericana", a portal and online video-library of the ARA Program* which collects and broadcasts audiovisual corpora documenting the historical, cultural and social world of Latin America.

Glossary written by Peter STOCKINGER.

2) AmSud was developed in 2007 as part of three research projects: **Divas***, **Logos*** and **Saphir***.

3) The audiovisual collection of the AmSud video-library is composed of around 440 hours of recorded interviews, conferences, cultural events (concerts, exhibitions etc.), field research (on German immigration into Chile, French immigration into Mexico, the Chilean coup d'état in 1973, the Argentinean dictatorship etc.) as well as documentaries and reports (e.g. on the life and culture of the indigenous people). Most of the audiovisual recordings available on the AmSud portal are in French or Spanish.

4) The official URL of AmSud is: http://www.amsud.fr/ES/.

ARA© Program

1) The ARA Program is a R&D project of **ESCoM***, which was set up in 2001 as part of the **OPALES*** project on semantic indexing of audiovisual resources.

2) The ARA program is dedicated to digital audiovisual libraries and their uses especially in research and (formal or informal) educational contexts as well as the promotion of scientific and cultural heritage.

3) The ARA program in particular develops resources and tools necessary for the processing (description, indexing etc.) and online publication of audiovisual corpora.

4) The ARA program (insofar as its resources permit) also carries out audiovisual production for the FMSH as well as different (French, bilateral, European etc.) R&D projects in which ESCoM is involved.

5) The ARA program manages a variety of video-libraries: the **ARA video-library*** itself; the **ARA-FMSH*** video-library (from late 2011); the **AmSud video-library***; the **PCW video-library***, the **DLC video-library***; the **Averroès video-library***; the **MDD video-library***; the **SCC video-library***; the **ArkWork video-library***; the **LHE video-library***; the **CCA video-library***; the **AICH video-library***; the **ACH video-library*** and the **Azéri Buta video-library***.

6) Very detailed documentation on the ARA Program may be consulted online on the ARA Website: http://www.archives audiovisuelles.fr/FR/about4.asp (documentation last updated in late 2009).

ARA© video-library

1) Acronym for "Audiovisual Research Archives"

2) The ARA is the general video-library of the ARA Program. This video-library broadcasts around 5,500 hours of (online) videos in about fifteen languages. The authors and directors of this collection form an "international community" of around 2,500 researchers, teachers, intellectuals, artists, politicians, journalists, professionals … working in 85 countries around the world.

3) The ARA documents the main parts of research in human and social sciences. It also encompasses recordings of cultural and educational performances (exhibitions, concerts, lectures …), audiovisual documentations of field research (on European emigration, the victims of the Latin American dictatorships, traditional food preparation, etc.) as well as reports and documentary films.

4) The audiovisual collection is composed on the one hand of productions created by ESCoM, 2001–2009 (and, at a much slower rate, from 2009 up to the present day) and on the other, audiovisual contributions belonging to other French and foreign institutions and/or to particular active researchers.

5) The URL of the official site of the ARA video library – available in eight languages – is: http://www.archivesaudiovisuelles.fr/FR/.

ArkWork portal

1) Abbreviation for the *"Arkeonauts' Workshop"*.

2) ArkWork is the online video-library of the **ArkWork program*** which is one of the main domains of application and experimentation of the **ASW-HSS project***.

3) ArkWork has an audiovisual collection of around 135 hours of videos entirely dedicated to research on archeology in France and the rest of the world.

4) The URL of the ArkWork portal site is: http://semioweb.msh-paris.fr/corpus/ada/1789/accueil.asp.

ArkWork Program

1) Abbreviation for the "Arkeonauts' Workshop".

2) The ArkWork Program constitutes one of the **experimental workshops*** of the **ASW-HSS project*** dedicated to the constitution of an audiovisual corpus documenting research on archeology, the implementation of a **metalanguage of description*** for this domain of knowledge, the analysis of the corpus using the **ASW Studio*** and the publication of the analyzed corpus – also using the **ASW Studio*** – in the form of a Web portal offering many forms of access to the corpus in question: access by **topics of knowledge***, access by **thesaurus***, access by **collections of filmic documents***, etc.

3) A particularly important point which was addressed in the context of the ArkWork program is experimentation with new logics of diffusion and promotion of cultural and scientific heritage via the social networks and Web 2.

4) The ArkWork program is evolving through a series of concrete achievements: a Web portal comprising the ArkWork video-library composed of a corpus of around 135 hours of audiovisual texts on archeology; experimental video channels on YouTube, DailyMotion and Vimeo; Twitter and Facebook networks; "aggregations of contents via applications such as Scoop.it, Pearltrees or Netvibes; etc.

5) The URL of the ArkWork Website is: http://semioweb.msh-paris.fr/corpus/ada/1789/accueil.asp.

ASW Description Workshop©

1) The Description Workshop of an audiovisual text (or, shorter, the *ASW Description Workshop*) is the working environment enabling the analyst to proceed to an analysis of an audiovisual text in its entirety or one of its parts. It is part of the **ASW Studio***.

2) The Description Workshop is composed of three main functional parts: i) a first part reserved for the ***meta-description*** * itself (i.e. the presentation of the analysis and its objectives); ii) a part reserved for the *description of the audiovisual object in its globality*; iii) a part reserved for the *description of the specific **segments** * of the audiovisual text* previously identified by the analyst.

3) Parts (ii) and (iii) of the analysis of the audiovisual text in its entirety and a given specific segment from an audiovisual text are again broken down into a series of more functional parts enabling the analyst to carry out a systematic description of his object.

4) The work of analysis of an audiovisual text is carried out as a series of **interactive forms***. Each interactive form represents a **model of description***. A model of description is formed from the **ASW metalinguistic resources***. Hence, we distinguish a library of interactive forms dedicated to the meta-description (i.e. the explanation of an analysis, its content, its objectives …), a library of interactive forms dedicated to the analysis of a video, an audiovisual text in its entirety and a library of interactive forms dedicated to the analysis of a specific segment forming part of an audiovisual text.

5) The interactive forms may be adapted to the specific needs of a given analyst, or a given group of analysts since each form represents a **model of description*** which was created from the **ASW metalinguistic resources***. However, the adaptation of an interactive form sometimes requires a greater effort as regards adaptation and even re-definition of the **models of description*** or the **ASW metalinguistic*** resources which are necessary in order to elaborate a **model of description***. This work of adaptation or re-definition of models of description is carried out using the **ASW Modeling Workshop***.

ASW Experimental Workshop

1) An ASW Experimental Workshop is used as part of the ASW-HSS project in order to test and validate its R&D results. In particular it serves to test the models of description which have been created for this project and therefore, the interactive forming part of the **ASW Description workshop*** but also the ASW Publishing Workshop.

2) Conceptually speaking, an experimental workshop encompasses: i) a limited domain of knowledge/expertise, ii) actors from the domain (specialists, experts, stakeholders …), iii) intellectual resources (academic literature, thesauruses, ontologies, terminologies …), iv) corpora of work (audiovisual recordings documenting the chosen domain), v) shots and experimental objectives, vi) achievements and (temporary and/or definitive) results documenting the experiments.

3) As part of the ASW-HSS project, three experimental workshops were defined and set up according to the conceptual framework defined in (2) from the beginning of the project: the CCA, ArkWork and LHE programs.

4) Once these three workshops reached a certain level of maturity (of "reliability"), two other "experimental workshops" were designed and put in place: the **AICH*** and **ACH*** programs, whose main objective is to reuse the results obtained from the first three workshops and apply them to different domains of knowledge/expertise.

5) Finally, two more experimental workshops will continue to exploit the results of the ASW-HSS project after it has ended. These are the **ARA-FMSH*** and the **CCA-Intercultural*** works.

ASW-HSS project

1) ASW-HSS is the acronym for "Audiovisual Semiotic Workshop for the description of audiovisual corpora on human and social sciences".

2) ASW-HSS is a research project of the ESCoM/FMSH financed by the ANR (National Research Agency) in France (reference #: ANR-08-BLAN-0102-01). ASW-HSS was started in January 2009 and will officially end in late December 2011. However, the results from this project will be used in new research projects.

3) The main objective of the ASW-HSS project is to develop **metalinguistic resources*** (i.e. a **metalanguage***) for describing audiovisual corpora in order to transform them into resources *per se*, i.e. "tools", "instruments" of knowledge in specific contexts and uses (particularly in research itself, education, promotion of cultural and scientific heritage, etc.).

4) The elaboration of metalinguistic resources for describing audiovisual corpora relies on the semiotics of the audiovisual text [STO 03] as well as on discourse analysis. The **ASW metalinguistic resources*** are notably comprised of 1) *meta-lexicons of conceptual terms* (or concepts) that are necessary for describing an audiovisual text, 2) specialized *models of description* on analyzing a given structural aspect of an audiovisual text e.g. the visual or acoustic shot, the thematic or discourse level, etc. 3) an extensive *thesaurus* of predefined terms or "descriptors".

5) The ASW metalinguistic resources are used in a sophisticated working environment called **ASW Studio*** composed of a workshop for segmenting audiovisual corpora, a workshop for describing audiovisual corpora, a workshop for publishing the described audiovisual corpora and a workshop for managing the metalinguistic resources themselves.

6) The ASW metalinguistic resources themselves as well as the ASA Studio were developed, tested and validated in several **experimental workshops***, consisting of intensive works of description, publishing and promotion of audiovisual corpora. All these experimental workshops may be consulted on the ASW-HSS portal: http://semiolive.ext.msh-paris.fr/asa-shs/.

7) All the activities and all the results of the ASW-HSS project are publicly available for consultation on its official site: http://www.asa-shs.fr/.

ASW Modeling Workshop©

1) The ASW Modeling Workshop is one of the four workshops making up the ASW Studio.

2) It is used by the knowledge engineer or "concept designer" to define, develop, test and validate the models of description used in the **Description Workshop***, as interactive forms, to analyze audiovisual corpora.

3) Currently, the Modeling Workshop takes the form of a piece of software which was developed by **ESCoM*** named **OntoEditor*** and which enables the software engineer to: i) develop and/or manage the metalinguistic resources needed in order to create models of

description; and ii) create the models of description themselves by using the available metalinguistic resources. It also includes tools which were co-developed with INA-Research and which serve to convert the **ASW metalinguistic resources*** and the **models of description*** and **publication*** into **OWL*** (Ontology Web Language) standard and vice versa.

ASW Publishing Workshop©

1) The ASW Publishing Workshop is part of the ASW Studio. As its name suggests, it serves for publishing audiovisual corpora which have been processed and described beforehand in the ASW Description Workshop.

2) The Publishing Workshop enables us to publish audiovisual corpora in the form of a portal site (similar in type to **ArkWork***, **LHE*** or **CCA***) but also in the form of specialized folders (**thematic folders***, **bilingual folders***, **educational folders*** ...) or **video-lexicons***, **narrative paths***, etc.

3) As part of a program of *uploading of audiovisual corpora* – in accordance with a pre-established publishing policy – the publishing process is automatically respected. This is the case, e.g. of the **ARA portal*** site but also experimental portal sites as part of the **ASW-HSS project***.

4) However, the ASW Publishing Workshop opens the way for customized publishing, or even **republishing*** of already-published audiovisual corpora on the basis of **publication models***, again represented by **interactive forms***. It offers the **writer/author*** the possibility of reusing either already-published audiovisual corpora (for example in the form of a **thematic*** or **bilingual folder***) or described and indexed corpora (in the **Description Workshop***) to "create" (publish or republish) digital audiovisual resources according to his own needs or interests, taking account of his audience and their expectations. This option has been tested in the **LOGOS*** and **SAPHIR*** projects (to see concrete results, see the **DLC*** and **PCW*** Websites.). On the contrary, it does not constitute an object of research for the **ASW-HSS*** project. The ASW Publishing Workshop, in its current version, has only the most basic functions for customized

publishing/republishing of previously-described and indexed or published audiovisual corpora.

5) The ASW Publishing Workshop is currently presented as a **working environment*** which is made up of a set of Web services developed by ESCoM and encompassed by the appellation **Semiosphere***.

ASW Segmentation Workshop©

1) The ASW Segmentation Workshop is a specialized working environment for cutting an audiovisual text into segments ("passages" or "sequences") of interest to the **analyst***. It is part of the **ASW Studio***.

2) The ASW Segmentation Workshop now comprises of a tool enabling us to cut an audiovisual text: the Interview tool which was originally developed by INA and then adapted to the technical needs of cutting audiovisual texts as part of the **ARA Program***. In the coming months, the *Interview* tool may be replaced by better-performing tools facilitating "multilayered" cutting as well and the segmentation of static images. The Segmentation Workshop environment has a set of technical and explanatory documents available to any person or institution wishing to use it.

ASW© Studio

1) The ASW Studio is a working environment which facilitates the segmentation, analysis (description, annotation, indexing, linguistic adaptation ...), the online publication of audiovisual corpora as well as the management (definition, adaptation ...) of the **ASW metalinguistic resources***.

2) The ASW studio comprises **four** main parts called "**Workshops**": i) the **segmentation workshop*** for audiovisual texts (videos, for now); ii) the **description workshop*** for an audiovisual text and/or some parts (segments) of it; iii) the **publishing workshop*** for an audiovisual text or corpus of audiovisual texts; iv) the **modeling workshop*** for metalinguistic resources (concepts, configurations of concepts, thesauruses ...).

3) Each workshop takes the form of i) a *specialized **working environment*** and ii) one of *technical documentation, help files, concrete examples*, etc. Hence, the ASW Studio comprises a working environment for the segmentation of a video, a working environment for the description/analysis *per se* of a video, a working environment for the publication of a video or corpus of videos and, finally, a working environment for scenario specification i.e. definition and development of the metalanguage that is needed to analyze and publish audiovisual corpora.

4) The existing working environments are not equally developed: the most elaborate environment is the one for analyzing audiovisual corpora. However, all the environments are operational. Similarly, the technical documentation which has to accompany each environment is often written in a rudimentary way.

5) In turn, each working environment possesses one or more software suites, computer applications etc. **Interview*** from the INA (Institut National de l'Audiovisuel) is the software which is currently used in the **Segmentation Workshop***; **Semiosphere*** is a set of applications developed by ESCoM and which serves as a "technological building block" for the **Publishing Workshop***; the working environment of the **Description Workshop*** is composed of a set of applications for managing libraries of information input forms ("models") and the data generated by the analyst; finally, the **Modeling Workshop*** currently uses an xml editor called **OntoEditor*** (also developed by ESCoM) for defining **metalinguistic resources***.

6) The ASW Studio was developed by ESCoM as part of the **ASW-HSS project*** (2009–2011) funded by the ANR (Agence National de la Recherche) as part of the "Programme Blanc 2008" ("2008 White Program").

Averroès video-library

1) Averroès is the name of a video-library and portal dedicated to the France-Mahgreb cultural space.

2) Averroès was set up in 2009 with tools belonging to the ARA program and with European and French funding (as part of the

SAPHIR and LOGOS projects). To date, it has a small audiovisual collection of some 50 hours of videos.

3) The URL of the Averroès portal is: http://www.france-maghreb.fr/FR/.

Azeri Buta video-library

1) Azeri Buta is the name of a video-library and portal dedicated to Azerbaijani culture, which was put in place in 2009–2010 using tools from the ARA Program.

2) Azeri Buta has a small audiovisual collection of around 35–40 hours of online videos.

3) The URL of the Azeri Buta portal is: http://semioweb.msh-paris.fr/corpus/azeributa/FR/.

C

CCA-Intercultural Program

1) Acronym for a special branch of the CCA program consisting of its use as part of a course in intercultural communication that is the *Communication and Intercultural Department* at the *National Institute of Oriental Languages and Civilizations* (INALCO). This course – four or possibly 5 years in duration – starts at the beginning of the second year of the Bachelors degree course, through the third year and then leads to a Masters in intercultural communication which is a two-year-long complementary course, with the possibility of a gap year between the first and the second year of the Masters degree.

2) The function of the CCA-Intercultural Program as part of this course at INALCO is *threefold*: i) to serve as an audiovisual basis for image-based teaching, in the form of educational folders, thematic folders, video-lexicons, etc.; ii) to serve as a experimental field for students who are producing new audiovisual objects (for example, "small multimedia objects", Web-documentaries …) or analyzing corpora forming part of CCA-Intercultural; iii) to serve as a point of distribution, sharing and promotion of the works created as part of this course.

3) CCA-Intercultural officially began in October 2011.

4) For more information about the intercultural course: http://www.inalco-interculturel.fr/.

5) For more information about the audiovisual programs as part of this course: http://webculturecommunication.wordpress.com/.

CCA portal

1) Acronym for "Culture Crossroads Archives".

2) The LHE is the online video-library of the **LHE program*** which is one of the main domains of application and experimentation of the **ASW-HSS project***.

3) The URL of the ArkWork portal site is: http://semioweb.msh-paris.fr/corpus/arc/FR/.

CCA Program

1) Acronym for "Culture Crossroads Archives".

2) The CCA Program constitutes one of the **experimental workshops*** of the **ASW-HSS project***, dedicated to compiling an audiovisual corpus documenting cultural diversity and intercultural communication, putting in place a **metalanguage of description*** for this domain of knowledge, analyzing the corpus using **ASW Studio*** and publishing the analyzed corpus – also via the **ASW Studio*** – in the form of a portal offering various forms of access to the corpus in question: access by **topics of knowledge***, access by **thesaurus***, access by **collections of filmic documents***, etc.

3) A particularly important point which is addressed as part of the CCA program is the exploitation of audiovisual archives in the context of university education and the promotion of university heritage (produced and created by researchers, teachers and students). CCA will serve as a working environment and the audiovisual portal to the *Communication and Intercultural Department* of the INALCO (*National Institute of Oriental Languages and Civilizations*) and to courses in intercultural communication at undergraduate level (B2 and B3) and masters level (M1 and M2). Use will be made of these archives

in five main ways: i) lessons using appropriate audiovisual resources that are available on the CCA portal; ii) lessons on the analysis of audiovisual texts; iii) lessons on the creation and publication of audiovisual texts; iv) lessons using new social media to collect, analyze, distribute and promote audiovisual content; v) projects to create thematic audiovisual pieces of heritage that stem from languages and civilizations taught at the INALCO (example: African literary heritage; Andean heritage in relation to the **AICH program***, etc.).

4) The ARC program evolves through a series of concrete achievements: a Web portal comprising the CCA video-library which is composed of a corpus of around 140 hours of audiovisual texts; Twitter and Facebook networks; "aggregation of content from Netvibes, Scoop.it …" etc.

5) The URL of the CCA portal site is: http://semioweb.msh-paris.fr/ corpus/arc/FR/.

CONVERGENCE project

1) Convergence is a European R&D project which started in June 2010 and will last until February 2013. It is coordinated by the CNIT (Consorzio Interuniversitario per le Telecomunicazioni) in Rome and financed as part of the 7th Framework Program; No: FP7-257123). The aim of the CONVERGENCE project is to enrich the Internet with a new model of *publishing-subscription* service, focused on the *content* and based on a common container for any type of digital data, including individuals and real world objects (RWOs). This common container, called *Versatile Digital Item* (VDI), is a structured packet of digital content and meta-information, identified in a unique way (as a Website URL could be) which extends the concept of *Digital Item* defined by the MPEG-21.

2) The interest of ESCoM and the ARA program in this project is related to the fact that any use of an online video may be tracked via VDI technology. This opens the way to a circulation of digital content and an appropriation of the latter which respects the rights of their authors and owners. The chosen field of experimentation is the production, diffusion and sharing of culturally sensitive contents forming part of the intangible cultural heritage of the Quechua-speaking Andean communities (see the **AICH program***).

3) The URL of the official site of the Convergence project is: http://www.ict-convergence.eu/.

D

DIVAS project

1) DIVAS is the acronym for *"Direct Video & Audio Content Search Engine"*, a European R&D project financed as part of the 6th Framework Program. It started in early January 2007 and ended in February 2009. Led by Greek firm Archétypon, **ESCoM***/FMSH was a member of the consortium composed of research laboratories and German, Austrian, Israeli, Russian and Belgian firms.

2) The DIVAS project dealt mainly with the possibilities of automatic indexing of audiovisual resources both at the visual shot level and at the acoustic (musical and speech) level.

3) One of **ESCoM***'s main tasks as part of the DIVAS project was to select and re-index an audiovisual corpus from the **ARA Program*** (and documenting topics deriving from the domain of linguistic and cultural diversity) as accurately as possible. A few concrete results of this work are published on the **DLC*** portal developed by **ESCoM*** for the DIVAS project: http://www.languescultures.fr/FR/.

DLC portal

1) DLC is the acronym for the French "Diversité Linguistique et Culturelle" (Linguistic and Cultural Diversity) portal, developed in 2007–2008 as part of the **SAPHIR project***.

2) The URL of the DLC portal is: http://www.languescultures.fr/.

E

ESCoM©

1) ESCoM (Cognitive Semiotic and New Media Team) is a research program of the FMSH in Paris. Created in 1991, ESCoM specializes in the domains of text and discourse semiotics applied to

issues of production, analysis and publishing-distribution of digital knowledge heritage. A second axis of ESCoM's research is cultural analysis and the intercultural communication (developed in cooperation with Filière Communication et Formation Interculturelles (CFI – Intercultural Communication and Learning Stream) of the National Institute of the Oriental Languages and Civilizations (INALCO) in Paris).

2) In 2001, as part of the French R&D project **OPALES***, the ESCoM created the **ARA program*** which constitutes, its most important experimental work.

3) Since 1994, the ESCoM has been regularly involved in French and European R&D projects. Of these, the **ASW-HSS project*** is one of the most important as it has enabled the team to carry out more than 10 years of R&D research dedicated to the description, indexing and publication of audiovisual corpora in a digital context.

4) The URL of ESCoM's official Website is: http://www.semionet.fr/FR/default.htm.

ESCoM Suite 2011©

1) ESCoM Suite 2011 is already the third edition of a set of tools and software mainly developed by the ESCoM and serving to produce, publish and manage data and audiovisual archives.

2) The ESCoM Suite 2011 is composed of the following tools: *OntoEditor* (an XML editor for creating and managing the metalinguistic resources which are necessary for describing audiovisual corpora); *Interview* (software for the segmenting and analyzing videos, co-developed with NAI Research); AVAM ("AudioVisual Archive Manager", a tool for publishing and managing audiovisual publications), *ESCoM Playlist Maker* (a tool enabling us to create playlists based on a description/indexation carried out in *Interview* and with the objective of publishing that description/index), *ESCoM ffCoder* (a tool for encoding video files intended to be published in "streaming" format).

3) The tools which make up the ESCoM Suite are integrated into different workshops belonging to the **ASW Studio* (Segmentation Workshop*, Description Workshop*, Modeling Workshop*,**

Publishing Workshop* etc.). The ESCoM Suite will replace the ASW Studio.

F

FMSH-AAR (FMSH-ARA) video-library

1) Acronym for the French "Fondation Maison des Sciences de l'Homme – Archives Audiovisuelles de la Recherche" Web portal.

2) FMSH-ARA is the video-library of the **ARA Program*** which contains and distributed the audiovisual recordings of the scientific events of the FMSH and/or funded, sponsored … by the FMSH.

3) In particular, the FMSH-ARA video-library contains the audiovisual collections of the following programs: PIEA, IEA, Programme Chine, Programme Inde, Programme CEI, Programme Japon, Programme Amérique Latine, Programme Proche et Moyen Orient, F2DS, Editions FMSH, Entre Sciences, ESCoM, "Café Scientifique", TIC-Migration.

4) Currently under development, FMSH-ARA benefits from the **ASW metalinguistic resources*** and from the **ESCoM-ASW technological environment*** developed as part of the **ASW-HSS project***. ARA-FMSH constitutes one of the **experimental workshops*** of the **ASW-HSS project***.

5) The first version of the FMSH-ARA library will be publicly available from late 2011.

I

Interview

1) Interview is a software package for virtually cutting editing a digital video, originally developed by the INA. In the context of a convention between the INA and the FMSH in 2005, the Interview software was incorporated into the digital working environment of the **ARA program*** and still serves today for segmenting videos with a view to publishing them on the **ARA portal*** as well as on all the other portals forming part of the **ARA program***.

2) An updated version of this software currently serves as the segmentation tool of the **Segmentation Workshop*** of the **ASW Studio***.

3) In the context of the French project **SAPHIR*** (2006–2009), coordinated by the INA and involving ESCoM as a partner in the consortium, a new segmentation tool was developed by the INA. This tool – *Studio Saphir* – is more powerful and richer than Interview (in addition to a far more refined and sophisticated work of segmentation, it also facilitates the segmentation of images into zones or regions defined by the analyst). The replacement of Interview by Studio Saphir and its integration into the **Segmentation Workshop** of the **ASW Studio** is envisaged for 2012.

K

KNOSOS project

1) KNOSOS (2003–2005) is an R&D project, financed by the European Leonardo da Vinci program and coordinated by the University Of Technology MUSIC laboratory – Laboratory of Distributed Multimedia Systems) in Chania, Greece. The project aimed at running courses in the field of digital audiovisual technology and multimedia.

2) ESCoM was able, in 2004–2005, to create a series of about twenty lessons dedicated to teaching oneself about the working process of production, analysis and publication of audiovisual corpora.

3) The URL of the site for accessing the online lessons dedicated to audiovisual production/publishing created by ESCoM is: http://semioweb.msh-paris.fr/knosos/.

L

LHE portal

1) Acronym for "Literature from Here and Elsewhere".

2) LHE is the online video-library of the **LHE program*** which is one of the main domains of application and experimentation of the **ASW-HSS project***.

3) The URL of the LHE portal site is: http://semioweb.msh-paris.fr/corpus/ALIA/FR/.

LHE Program

1) Acronym for "Literature from Here and Elsewhere".

2) The LHE Program constitutes one of the **experimental workshops*** of the **ASW-HSS project*** dedicated to compiling an audiovisual corpus about French and World literature, analyzing its using the **ASW Studio*** and publishing the analyzed corpus – also via the **ASW Studio*** – in the form of a Website offering various forms of access to the aforementioned corpus: access by **topics of knowledge***, access by **thesaurus***, access by **collections of filmic texts***, etc.

3) A particularly important point which is addressed as part of the LHE program is the work of the **analyst*** of the corpus. Far from reducing this task to a "simple" archivistic indexation, the analyst is here considered a specialist in the literary domain who is responsible for the highly complex task of explaining, and "showing" through his work, the added value (the interest, the relevance, the usefulness …) of an audiovisual text or a part of an audiovisual text for a given audience.

3) The LHE program takes the form of a Web portal and an online video-library comprising around 150 hours of videos, most of which are minutely analyzed and indexed, as well as a series of specialized publications which are adapted to specific educational uses.

4) The URL of the LHE portal site is: http://semioweb.msh-paris.fr/corpus/ALIA/FR/.

LOGOS project

1) LOGOS is the acronym for *"Knowledge on demand for ubiquitous learning"*, a European R&D project financed as part of the 6th Framework Program. It started in January 2006 and ended in February 2009. Coordinated by Antenna Hungárica in Budapest, **ESCoM***/FMSH was a member of the consortium of research laboratories and firms from France, Bulgaria, Greece, Slovakia, UK,

Hungary and Finland. The aim of the LOGOS project was to develop and test an environment for analysis and publishing of multimedia objects for distance learning.

2) Based on the **ARA program***, **ESCoM*** designed and developed the "People and Cultures of the World" (PCW) site, for which a metalanguage of description and publishing had to be defined and created with the aid of the tools which were designed by the LOGOS consortium.

3) The URL of the (experimental) portal site **PCW*** is: http://www.culturalheritage.fr/FR/.

M

MDD portal

1) MDD is the acronym for the French "Mondialisation et Développement Durable" Web portal (Globalization and Sustainable Development), developed in 2008/2009 as part of the **LOGOS project***.

2) The URL of the MDD portal is: http://www.evolutiondurable.fr/FR/.

O

OntoEditor

1) OntoEditor is an XML editor, developed by **ESCoM*** for the creation and management of the **metalinguistic resources*** (hierarchy of conceptual terms, schemas and models of description …) that are needed for analyzing audiovisual corpora.

P

PCW portal

1) PCW is the acronym for "People and Cultures of the World", a portal which was developed in 2007–2008 as part of the **LOGOS project***.

2) The URL of the PCW portal is: http://www.culturalheritage.fr/FR/.

S

SAPHIR project

1) SAPHIR ("System of Assistance to Hypermedia Publishing") is a French research project financed by the INA (Institut National de l'Audiovisuel) and coordinated by INA Research which started in 2006 and ended in late 2010.

2) As part of close co-operation with INA Research, **ESCoM*** focused its efforts on the semiotic analysis of audiovisual corpora, the definition of a **metalanguage of description*** adapted to the processing of corpora belonging to the **ARA program*** as well as a *metalanguage of publication* which favors the video-lexicon (genre). ESCoM also developed, as part of this project, an improved version of **Interview***, a tool for segmentation and "basic" description of videos, and integrated it into the **working process*** of the **ARA program***.

3) The results of the SAPHIR project formed the main input for the R&D activities of the **ASW-HSS*** project.

SCC project

1) SCC is the acronym for (in Italian) "Semiotica, Cultura, Comunicazione" which is a portal which was developed in 2007–2008 as part of the **SAPHIR project*** in the form of a partnership with the Facoltà di Scienze della Comunicazione della Sapienza Università di Roma.

2) The URL of the PCW portal is: http://www.archiviosemiotica.eu/IT/.

Bibliography

[AUB 04] AUBERT L., "Question de mémoire: les nouvelles voies de la tradition", *Internationale de l'Imaginaire: Le patrimoine culturel immatériel (les enjeux, les problématiques, les pratiques)*, vol. 17, p. 113-123, Babel, 2004.

[BAU 06] BAUDE O. (ed.), *Corpus oraux, Guide des bonnes pratiques*, Presses universitaires d'Orléans – CNRS Editions, Paris, 2006.

[BNF 09] BIBLIOTHÈQUE NATIONALE DE FRANCE, Ecrire un cahier des charges de numérisation de collections sonores, audiovisuelles et filmiques, Ministère de la Culture et de la Communication, Comité de pilotage numérisation, Mission de la Recherche et de la Technologie, Paris, August, 2009.

[BEL 11] BELISLE C., "Internet et la lecture", *Canal U*, 1 June 2011, [online] available at: http://www.canal-u.tv/canalu/content/view/full/ 94994 (Registration accessed 8 June 2011).

[BLE 09] BLEFARI MELAZZI N., "CONVERGENCE: extending the media concept to include representations of real world objects", in *20th Tyrrhenian International Workshop on Digital Communications*, *The Internet of Things*, Pula, Italy, 2009.

[BOR 08] BORTOLOTTO C., "Les enjeux de l'institution du PCI", *Culture et Recherche*, vol. 116-117, spring-summer, p. 32-34, Département de la recherche, de l'enseignement supérieur et de la technologie du ministère de la Culture et de la Communication, 2008.

[CAR 08] CARDO D., "Le design de la visibilité: un essai de typologie du web 2.0", *InternetACTU.net*, 28 April 2008, [online] available at: http://www.internetactu.net/2008/02/01/le-design-de-la-visibilite-un-essai-de-typologie-du-web-20/ (Accessed 2 May 2011).

[CHA 10] CHA M., HADDADI H., BENEVENUTO F., GUMMADI K.P., "Measuring user influence in twitter: the million follower fallacy", in *Fourth International AAAI Conference on Weblogs and Social Media*, May 2010, [online] available at: http://twitter.mpi-sws.org/icwsm2010_fallacy.pdf (Accessed 8 June 2011).

[COR 03] CORNU M., *Droits des biens culturels et des archives*, CECOJI, Paris, 2003.

[DEL 09] DELENGAIGNE X., GONTIER F., *Les outils multimédias du web: équipements, services et savoir-faire pour communiquer sur Internet*, CFPJ Editions, Paris, 2009.

[DES 09] DESSAUX C., ZILLHARDT S., TABBANE S. (eds), "Numérisation du patrimoine culturel", *Culture et recherche*, vol. 118, Département de la recherche, de l'enseignement supérieur et de la technologie du ministère de la Culture et de la Communication, 2008-2009.

[DUV 04] DUVIGNAUD J., "Le langage perdu", *Internationale de l'Imaginaire: Le patrimoine culturel immatériel (les enjeux, les problématiques, les pratiques)*, vol. 17, p. 11-14, Babael, 2004.

[FAY 08] FAYON D., *Web 2.0 et au-delà – Nouveaux internautes: du surfeur à l'acteur*, Economica, Paris, 2008.

[GAL 11] GALLUCCIO L., MORABITO G., PALAZZO S., "On the potentials of object group localization in the internet of things", in *IEEE International Symposium on a World of Wireless Mobile and Multimedia Networks*, Lecce, Italy, 2011.

[GAR 08] GARCIA G., "Deux études sur le patrimoine immatériel", *Culture et Recherche*, vol. 116-117, spring-summer, p. 29-31, Département de la recherche, de l'enseignement supérieur et de la technologie du ministère de la Culture et de la Communication, 2008.

[GER 06] GERVAIS J.-F., *Web 2.0 les internautes au pouvoir: Blogs, Réseaux sociaux, Partages de vidéos, Mashups*, Dunod, Paris, 2006.

[GRE 66] GREIMAS A.J., *Sémantique Structurale*, Larousse, Paris, 1966.

[GRE 08] GRENET S., PIERRE J., "Kate Moss et les bars de Cayenne: ethno-chic et actifs immatériels", *Culture et recherche*, vol. 116-117, spring-summer, p. 23-25, Département de la recherche, de l'enseignement supérieur et de la technologie du ministère de la Culture et de la Communication, 2008.

[HOT 08] Hottin C., "Une nouvelle perception du patrimoine", *Culture et Recherche*, vol. 116-117, spring-summer, p. 15-17, Département de la recherche, de l'enseignement supérieur et de la technologie du ministère de la Culture et de la Communication, 2008.

[KAP 11] Kaplan M., Haenlein M., "Les médias sociaux", in *Recherche et application en marketing*, 15 September 2010, [online] available at: http://www.afm-marketing.org/rubriques/numerospecial_ram.php (Accessed 30 May 2011).

[KHA 04] Khaznadar C., "Patrimoine culturel immatériel: les problématiques", *Internationale de l'Imaginaire: Le patrimoine culturel immatériel (les enjeux, les problématiques, les pratiques)*, vol. 17, p. 51-58, Babel, 2004.

[LAS 48] Lasswell H.D., "The structure and function of communication in society", in Bryson L. (ed.), *The Communication of Idea*, p. 37, Harper and Brothers, New York, 1948.

[LEB 10] Le Bechec, M., Territoire et communication politique sur le web régional breton, PhD thesis, University of Rennes 2, 2010.

[LES 04] Le Scouarnec F.-P., "Quelques enjeux liés au patrimoine culturel immatériel", *Internationale de l'Imaginaire: Le patrimoine culturel immatériel (les enjeux, les problématiques, les pratiques)*, vol. 17, p. 26-40, Babel, 2004.

[NAI 04] Nair Venu G., "La sauvegarde du théâtre dans le Kerala: quelques expériences", *Internationale de l'Imaginaire: Le patrimoine culturel immatériel (les enjeux, les problématiques, les pratiques)*, vol. 17, p. 188-194, Babel, 2004.

[PAI 04] Pais de Brito J., "Le patrimoine immatériel: entre les pratiques et la recherche", *Internationale de l'Imaginaire: Le patrimoine culturel immatériel (les enjeux, les problématiques, les pratiques)*, vol. 17, p. 151-160, Babel, 2004.

[PRI 10] Pringuay V., "Le Musée du Louvre lance la Communauté Louvre", WebTribulation, 15 December 2010, [online] available at: http://webtribulation.com/2010/12/15/le-musee-du-louvre-lance-la-communaute-louvre/ (Accessed 21 April 2011).

[RAY 10] Raymond J.-L., "Paper.li, créez votre journal quotidien en ligne à partir d'un compte Twitter", NetPublic, 6 September 2010, [online] available at: http://www.netpublic.fr/2010/09/paper-li-creez-votre-journal-quotidien-en-ligne-a-partir-d-un-compte-twitter/ (Accessed 1 January 2011).

[ROB 09] ROBERT C., "Un portail de veille partagée sous Netvibes", *BBF*, vol. 4, p. 61-64, [online] available at: http://bbf.enssib.fr/consulter/bbf-2009-04-0061-011 (Accessed 16 June 2011), 2009.

[ROW 11] ROWE M., "Forecasting audience increase on YouTube", in *Proceedings of the International Workshop on User Profile Data on the Social Semantic Web (UWeb)*, co-located with 8th Extended Semantic Web Conference, 30 May 2011, Heraklion, Crete, Greece, [online] available at: http://www.wis.ewi.tudelft.nl/uweb2011/uweb2011-main-proceedings.pdf.

[SME 04] SMEETS R., "Réflexions autour d'un projet de convention internationale pour la sauvegarde du patrimoine culturel immatériel", *Internationale de l'Imaginaire: Le patrimoine culturel immatériel (les enjeux, les problématiques, les pratiques)*, vol. 17, p. 197-206, Babel, 2004.

[SMY 11a] SMYRNAIOS N., "Twitter: un réseau d'information social" in Inaglobal, 1 February 2011, [online] available at: http://www.inaglobal.fr/numerique/article/twitter-un-reseau-d-information-social (Accessed 1 June 2011).

[SMY 11b] SMYRNAIOS N., "Les réseaux sociaux: reflet des différences culturelles?", Inaglobal, 24 February 2011, [online] available at: http://www.inaglobal.fr/numerique/article/les-reseaux-sociaux-reflet-des-differences-culturelles (Accessed 2 May 2011).

[STO 02] STOCKINGER P., Auteur, textualité électronique et édition multi-support, Support en ligne d'une conférence donnée dans le cadre de la Journée d'études consacrée à la problématique de l'auteur face aux logiques de l'édition multi-support à l'Université de Paris XIII – Villetaneuse, le 20 June 2002 (document online: available at: http://www.semionet.fr/ressources_enligne/conferences/2002/Paris_XIII/Charts_Communication.pdf).

[STO 03] STOCKINGER P., *Le document audiovisuel*, Description et exploitations pratiques, Hermès-Lavoisier, Paris, 2003.

[STO 05a] STOCKINGER P., *Les sites web*, *Procédures de description, d'évaluation et de conception*, Hermès-Lavoisier, Paris, 2005.

[STO 05b] STOCKINGER P. (ed.), Le programme "Archives Audiovisuelles de la Recherche", 2005, [online] available at: http://www.semionet.fr/ressources_enligne/doc_escom/2005/aar.pdf.

[STO 07] STOCKINGER P., "La place de l'hypertextualité dans le traitement de corpus audiovisuels et/ou multimédias numériques", to consult at the following address: available at: http://www.semionet.fr/ressources_enligne/Enseignement/06_07/tim/fascicule_1.pdf.

[STO 11] STOCKINGER P. (ed.), *Les archives audiovisuelles*, Hermès-Lavoisier, Paris, 2011.

[UNE 01] UNESCO, Déclaration de l'UNESCO sur la diversité culturelle, UNESCO, available at: http://unesdoc.unesco.org/images/0012/001271/127160m.pdf, 2001.

[UNE 03] UNESCO, Convention pour la sauvegarde du patrimoine culturel immatériel, UNESCO, available at: http://unesdoc.unesco.org/images/0013/001325/132540f.pdf, 2003.

Internet Sites

Archives Audiovisuelles de la Recherche (AAR):
www.archivesaudiovisuelles.fr/FR/about6.asp

Bibliothèque nationale de France, Gallica:
http://gallica.bnf.fr

Culture azerbaidjanaise:
http://www.azerbaijan.az/portal/Culture/General/general_a.html

Equipe Sémiotique Cognitive et Nouveaux Médias (ESCoM):
http://www.semionet.fr/ressources_enligne/doc_escom/2005/aar.pdf

Europeana:
http://europeana.eu

Ministère de la Culture et de la Communication, Patrimoine numérique:
http://www.numerique.culture.fr/mpf/pub-fr/a_propos.html

UNESCO, Safegarding of intengible cultural heritage:
http://www.unesco.org/culture/ich/index.php?lg=EN&pg=home

UNESCO, Azerbaijan's UNESCO World Heritage Sites:
http://www.unescoworldheritagesites.com/azerbaijan-unesco-world-heritage-sites.htm

UNESCO, Azerbaijan – Information related to Intangible Cultural Heritage:
http://www.unesco.org/culture/ich/index.php ?pg=00311&cp=AZ

UNESCO, Qu'est-ce que le patrimoine culturel immatériel:
http://www.unesco.org/culture/ich/index.php ?lg=fr&pg=00002

UNESCO, Bibliothèque numérique mondiale (BNM):
http://www.wdl.org

Site du Pôle Images-Sons:
http://www.imageson.org

Portail du CLIO (Centre de Littérature Orale):
http://www.clio.org/

Portail de Décryptimages:
http://www.decryptimages.net/index.php

Site de l'association "Structures sonores Baschet et pédagogie":
http://www.baschet.org/

List of Authors

Muriel CHEMOUNY
Equipe Sémiotique Cognitive et Nouveaux Médias (ESCoM)
Fondation Maison des Sciences de l'Homme (FMSH)
Paris
France

Jirasri DESLIS
Equipe Sémiotique Cognitive et Nouveaux Médias (ESCoM)
Fondation Maison des Sciences de l'Homme (FMSH)
Paris
France

Aygun EYYUBOVA
Equipe Sémiotique Cognitive et Nouveaux Médias (ESCoM)
Fondation Maison des Sciences de l'Homme (FMSH)
Paris
France

Valérie LEGRAND-GALARZA
Centre d'Etude et de Recherche sur les Littératures et les Oralités du
Monde (CERLOM)
Institut National des Langues et Civilisations Orientales (INALCO)
Equipe Sémiotique Cognitive et Nouveaux Médias (ESCoM)
Fondation Maison des Sciences de l'Homme (FMSH)
Paris
France

Francis LEMAITRE
Equipe Sémiotique Cognitive et Nouveaux Médias (ESCoM)
Fondation Maison des Sciences de l'Homme (FMSH)
Paris
France

Elisabeth de PABLO
Equipe Sémiotique Cognitive et Nouveaux Médias (ESCoM)
Fondation Maison des Sciences de l'Homme (FMSH)
Paris
France

Peter STOCKINGER
Filière Communication et Formation Interculturelles (CFI)
Institut National des Langues et Civilisations Orientales (INALCO)
Equipe Sémiotique Cognitive et Nouveaux Médias (ESCoM)
Fondation Maison des Sciences de l'Homme (FMSH)
Paris
France

Index

A

Ali Ben Bekar, 17
analysis, 5-8, 16, 18-20, 22, 24-27, 31, 36-
   38, 41-43, 83, 97-99, 102, 116, 118, 122,
   125, 127-129, 136, 143-145, 205, 214,
   217-223, 225-227, 229, 231, 234-244,
   247-251, 254, 255, 259-268, 274, 275,
   277, 279, 280, 283, 285, 287, 289, 290
   of a segmented video, 8
   semiotic image analysis, 7, 19
Andean, 63-65, 70, 76-78, 82-84, 89, 90,
   92, 97, 99-103, 114, 117, 211, 212,
   214, 215, 237, 242, 245, 271, 283
anthropology, 21, 45, 63, 99, 134, 212, 215
Apture, 179, 180
arts and crafts, 77, 80, 82-85, 102, 121,
   122, 124, 131, 212
ArkWork portal, 142, 143, 146, 147, 149,
   150, 152, 154, 155, 159-162, 164, 167,
   189, 191, 200, 273, 274, 282
ASW environment, 89, 96, 118, 132, 136
ASW-HSS project, 3, 5, 19, 21, 41, 64,
   74, 83, 89, 95, 96, 103, 105, 110, 111,
   113, 114, 116-118, 138, 141-143, 196,
   197, 247, 249, 254, 255, 260-264, 267-
   269, 271, 273-278, 280, 282, 285-288
ASW segmentation environment, 235
ASW Studio, 3, 6, 18, 73, 127, 131, 132,
   135, 136, 138, 141, 211, 214, 227, 270,
   274, 277-280, 282, 285, 287, 288

ASW workshop, 273-280, 285-287
   description, 274-280, 282, 285, 289, 290
   publication, 70, 115, 207, 218, 220-
      226, 230-233, 236, 238, 241-243
   segmentation, 225, 235
A Thousand and One Nights, 5-11, 13-19,
   21, 123
audiovisual text, 7, 8, 15, 18, 24, 41-46,
   49, 51, 55, 56, 89, 131-133, 247, 248,
   253-256, 260, 261, 263, 265, 268, 274,
   275, 277, 279, 288
authorial function. See author consent
   forms, 113, 114

B

Barboff, Mouette, 24, 26-29
Baumgarten, Jean, 4
bilingual education, 99-101
Bolivia, 64, 76, 82, 84, 93, 100, 211, 212,
   214
Bruno, 7, 15, 16

C

central utterance, 25
Chraïbi, Aboubakr, 7-9
classical Arabic literature, 7, 8, 10
community, 6, 18, 45, 51, 55, 66, 67, 72-74,
   78, 81, 82, 92, 94, 100, 103, 142, 153,
   156, 196, 198-204, 206, 212, 213, 273
   rural, 67, 72, 74

conceptual term, 29, 249, 255, 265-268
content curation platform, 196
context, 6, 11, 14, 18, 22, 24, 32, 36, 45-
    49, 57, 106, 135-138, 208, 209, 212,
    214, 245, 246, 274, 282, 285-287
    educational, 136, 137, 246, 273
    of use, 8, 18, 20, 35, 36, 44, 47, 49
contextualization, 28
Convergence (project), 64, 70, 74, 103,
    210, 211, 223, 224, 230, 236, 240, 241,
    243, 245
co-operation, 290
cultural center, 24, 74, 75, 101, 102
corpora, 6, 18, 22, 42, 44, 56, 60, 113-115,
    117, 118, 213, 249-252, 259, 261-263,
    271, 272, 276-281, 285, 287, 289, 290
    analysis, 141, 214, 217, 225-227, 229,
        231, 234-244
    field, 142, 143, 160
    published, 42, 43, 45, 47, 50, 51, 54
    processed and analyzed, 42
Correia Carvalho Sousa, 26
Cransac, 5
Cuzco, 63, 64, 74, 78, 92, 101

D

Dailymotion, 45, 142, 165, 166, 185, 192,
    198, 207, 274
dance, 81, 82, 84, 97, 120, 121, 123
Décryptimages (web portal), 5, 19, 71,
    75, 109
description model, 75, 83, 84, 87, 88, 96,
    97, 110
discursive contextualization, 12

E, F

educational/valorizing themes, 22
electronic writing, 20
ethics, 67, 71, 103, 117
event site, 252
Facebook, 141, 142, 145-148, 150-154,
    156-158, 166-168, 191, 195, 198, 207,
    274, 283
    likes, 207, 153
    Wall, 147, 150, 154

pages
    personalized home page, 154, 155
    professional, 150, 152-156, 167,
        199, 210, 246
    profile, 146, 152, 153, 199, 200,
        256, 268
folder, 43, 46, 53-58, 136, 252, 253,
    257-259, 262, 278
    bilingual, 44, 47, 252, 258, 259, 262, 278
    communication, 11, 12, 18, 44, 45, 47,
        56, 191, 193, 194, 198, 203, 207,
        212, 215, 258, 281, 282, 285
    educational, 5-7, 21-24, 35, 41, 43, 44,
        46, 56-58, 191, 196, 253, 258, 259,
        272, 278, 281, 288
    thematic, 43, 44, 46, 53-56
    valorization, 22, 37, 44
five, 11, 49

G, H, I

geographic location, 30, 32, 143, 210
Gervereau, Laurent (historian), 5, 19
Google, 177, 189, 190, 192, 195
    Earth, 177
    Maps, 177
Greiner, Frank, 4
heritage, 3, 22, 25, 36, 41, 56, 63-66, 70,
    71, 73-80, 83, 85, 86, 89, 90-94, 100,
    101, 105-123, 125, 131, 132, 136-138,
    146, 150-153, 156, 158, 164, 191, 193,
    195-197, 211-215, 244, 245, 271
    online literary heritage, 3
    living, 63, 64, 75, 89-92, 98, 118, 213,
        237, 242
hypertextuality, 18
identity, 45, 107, 119, 120, 122, 153, 207,
    228, 229, 231, 232, 234, 235, 237, 241-
    244
ImageSon, 20
indexing, 10, 11, 18, 22, 31, 34, 41, 110,
    111, 113, 115, 131-133, 272, 279, 284,
    285
    detailed, 6, 8, 13, 26-29, 32, 33, 152, 273
    general, 11, 20, 23, 25, 26, 37, 41, 44,
        46, 60, 154, 164, 192, 197, 207,
        223, 246, 273

indigenous languages, 93, 237, 242
informed consent, 66, 96
Intangible Cultural Heritage, 22, 63, 64,
    65, 71, 75, 76, 78, 81, 82, 84, 89, 95,
    102, 103, 112, 119, 211-215, 245
interactive, 33, 46, 50-52, 64, 65, 89-91,
    93, 102, 226, 275, 277, 278
interactive video book, 46, 50
intercultural context, 45
intertextual relation, 45
inventory, 69, 78, 100, 101, 119
iPad, 186
iPhone, 186
iPod
    touch, 186
iTunes, 184, 186

K

key words, 194, 195, 199, 204
know-how, 25
knowledge, 3, 6, 20, 24, 32, 37, 43, 45,
    54-56, 58, 59, 72, 73, 75-85, 88, 93-95,
    99-102, 105, 107-110, 116, 118, 120,
    122, 137, 138, 145, 212, 213, 245, 246,
    274, 276, 277, 282, 285, 288

L

Lacouture, 4
Library, 11, 28, 29, 35, 39
    Gallica digital library, 195
    scenarios, 22, 25
    subjects, 26, 28, 30, 34
linguistics, 99, 134
linked segments, 26
literary material, 14, 15
Louvre community discussion group
    competition, 203
    profiles, 203, 245

M

Mahou, Jacques, 24, 26, 33
Masson, Jean-Yves, 4, 5, 51
media, 3, 18, 19, 65, 75, 89, 92, 94, 99,
    108, 138, 141, 142, 152, 156, 195, 197,
    198, 208-212, 235, 246, 283

decrypting, 216
encrypting, 223
memory, 68, 80, 93
meta-description, 26, 27, 58, 133
mobile communication
    BlackBerry, 187
    Nokia, 184-186
    RSS feed, 191
Moulins Bourgeois, 24
MPEG-4, 70
multimedia archives, 91
music, 7, 15, 17, 77, 80, 82-84, 97, 99,
    102, 209, 212, 287

N, O, P, Q

narrative, 8, 9, 13-16, 25, 46, 51, 59, 60,
    80, 82, 278
    axis, 7, 10, 25-27, 29, 32, 37
    path, 59
Netvibes, 189-192, 196, 198, 274, 283
new technologies, 64, 66, 90, 91, 93, 94,
    98, 102, 106-108, 110, 138
orality, 64, 100
OWL, 235
paper.li, 165-167
patterns, 11, 214
    discursive, 14, 32
    thematic, 21, 23, 32, 35
    visual, 108, 121, 123, 124, 131, 214,
        277, 284
picking out, 48
pivot axis, 26, 37
    online literary heritage, 3
    living, 19, 53
pearltrees, 167, 196-198, 207, 274
    curator, 164, 196
performing arts, 80, 81, 84, 85, 121, 123,
    131, 134, 136
Peru, 64, 72-75, 82, 84, 93, 100, 211,
    212, 214, 215
potential resource, 41, 56, 136
publication genres, 50
publication, 6, 7, 18, 20, 35, 39, 42-50,
    53-60, 66-68, 70, 72, 74, 89, 113, 115,
    120, 121, 123, 148, 165, 272, 274, 278-
    280, 283, 285, 287, 290

Quechua, 45, 63, 66, 67, 70, 73, 75, 80, 82, 89, 93, 96-100, 102, 212, 237, 242, 283

R

RDF, 210
Rencontres d'Aubrac, 5
reproduction, 65
republication, 22, 39, 42-44, 48, 53, 55, 56
    model, 25, 27, 28, 39, 47-49, 51, 52, 54-56, 58, 59
research-action, 75
revalorization, 93
revitalization, 64, 94, 95, 100
rich-media, 179
rights, 66, 71, 72, 96, 101, 102, 112, 114, 115, 210, 212, 213, 225, 245, 246, 283
rights of peoples and communities, 71

S

Sadan, Joseph, 7, 10, 11
safeguarding, 63, 71, 75, 77, 80, 89, 90, 94, 95, 98, 112, 160, 212, 213
segmentation, 8-10, 24, 26-28, 38, 97, 127, 128, 131, 149, 159, 279, 280, 285, 287
    partial, 26
    total, 47, 207
S.M.Os (small multimedia objects), 44
structure of audiovisual texts, 24
Semantic web, 216-223
sharing, 45, 49
Semiosphere, 35, 225, 239
Shams al Naar, 17
Slideshare, 193, 194
social networks, 145, 153, 155, 166, 194, 195, 198, 207, 274
speech, 26, 35, 70, 80, 93, 100, 284
synthetic translation, 145, 149, 150

T

tampoura (instrument), 128

thematic
    access, 43
    sequences, 23
thesaurus, 32, 33, 43, 125, 126, 130, 134, 143, 237, 242, 274, 277, 282, 288
topic, 25, 29, 30, 31
tradition, 14, 22, 63, 72, 75-78, 91, 93, 94, 100
transmission, 29, 84, 86, 87, 90, 94, 109
Twitpic, 142, 185
Twitter, 141, 142, 157-159, 161, 162, 164-168, 185, 191, 194, 195, 198, 207, 274, 283

U, V, W, Y

UNESCO, 22, 63, 64, 66, 71, 74-77, 79, 80, 84, 85, 107, 108, 112, 118-120, 126, 152-154, 156, 158, 198, 212
UNESCO Convention for the Safeguarding of the Intangible Cultural Heritage, 71, 112
user, 20, 44, 46, 127, 129-132, 142, 156-158, 165, 166, 190, 197, 198, 223
    administrator, 163, 215, 225, 239, 240
    analyst, 25, 28, 42, 216, 218, 220-222, 224, 225, 231, 234-236, 238
    audiovisual producer, 215, 216, 220
    authentication, 227, 228
    role, 6, 7, 38, 71, 107, 138, 143, 151, 211, 213-215
    subscriber, 216, 218, 219, 221, 223, 226, 227, 242, 244
valorizing, 22, 37, 41
VDI. Verdatile Digital Item, 210, 211, 213, 215, 217-227, 230-234, 236, 238-243, 245, 246
video, 26-28, 32, 33, 37, 38
Vimeo, 164, 166, 192, 198
    MPEG-4, 186
YouTube, 45, 92, 108, 109, 142, 155, 156, 164-166, 190, 192, 195, 198, 207
    interactive transcription, 175